Eddie O'Sullivan
Never Die Wondering

Eddie O'Sullivan
Never Die Wondering
The Autobiography

Eddie O'Sullivan

with Vincent Hogan

Century · London

Donation 14.10.2010

Published by Century 2009

4 6 8 10 9 7 5 3

First published in Great Britain in 2009 by
Century
Random House, 20 Vauxhall Bridge Road,
London SW1V 2SA

www.randomhouse.co.uk

Addresses for companies within The Random House Group Limited can be found at:
www.randomhouse.co.uk

The Random House Group Limited Reg. No. 954009

A CIP catalogue record for this book
is available from the British Library

ISBN 9781846053993

The Random House Group Limited supports The Forest Stewardship
Council (FSC), the leading international forest certification organisation. All our
titles that are printed on Greenpeace approved FSC certified paper carry the FSC logo.
Our paper procurement policy can be found at www.rbooks.co.uk/environment

Mixed Sources
Product group from well-managed
forests and other controlled sources
www.fsc.org Cert no. TT-COC-2139
© 1996 Forest Stewardship Council
FSC

Picture credits:
Images 4, 5, 6, 8, 10, 11, 13, 14 and 16 © INPHO/Billy Stickland;
images 9 and 15 © INPHO/Dan Sheridan; image 12 © INPHO/Cathal Noonan.

Printed and bound in Great Britain by Clays Ltd, St Ives plc

To Noreen, Katie and Barry

ACKNOWLEDGEMENTS

Celebrity is an odd condition. In a small country like Ireland, it bestows certain privileges that can feed even the flimsiest ego. It might be a concert back-stage pass or an un-requested hotel-room upgrade, little kindnesses that elude the majority of paying customers.

But it has its flip side. Sometimes, under the glare of public scrutiny, it can feel as if your story becomes a movie about someone else's life. As Irish rugby coach, I was routinely depicted as dour and power-hungry. My reputation became a kind of caricature, family and friends often remarking that they could not reconcile it with the Eddie O'Sullivan they knew.

This was a relief because I didn't recognise the man being depicted either.

If I had one, over-riding motivation to write this book, that was it. To let people see behind that image and come to their own conclusions about me. To that end, I would like to offer my sincere thanks to Vincent Hogan for his help in gathering the threads of my story and weaving them into such coherent pattern.

I would like to thank Noreen, Katie and Barry – the three

most important people in my life – for their endless love and support.

I would like to thank all those who helped Vincent put together the different strands of my story, particularly those who contributed their thoughts to the back of the book – Jack Clark, Brian O'Brien, Niall O'Donovan, Keith Wood, Brian O'Driscoll and Patrick 'Rala' O'Reilly.

It's hard to articulate adequately the respect I feel for all the people I've shared dressing-room space with across the years, be they players or staff. To list them all individually here would require a chapter in itself. Suffice to say, I've been lucky in the calibre of people I've worked with.

I'd like to thank John Baker for his solid guidance and judgement through rough and smooth.

And, finally, I'd like to thank editor, Tim Andrews, for his assistance in putting the finishing touches to *Never Die Wondering*.

I hope you enjoy the read. It tells the story of a man, not a caricature.

Eddie O'Sullivan, July 2009.

CONTENTS

1

RUMOUR FACTORY

Its not easy to appreciate the comedy in a routine that identifies you as its punchline.

So I wasn't exactly slapping my sides the morning after our elimination from RWC 2007 when our final press conference in Paris pretty much became a stand-up's prop. Risteard Cooper's impersonation of RTE TV journalist Colm Murray drew a few guffaws from the floor. Good luck to him.

Maybe some find laughter therapeutic when their world has just caved in. And it's certainly all too easy to lose perspective in sport. We'd just had a shocking World Cup, but nobody died. Whatever wounds any of us were carrying to 'Charles de Gaulle' that day, the only real casualties were reputations.

In this instance, mine especially. I understood that. We'd been touted before the tournament as potential winners and, frankly, didn't run around frantically trying to douse that optimism. We knew what we had and what, potentially, we could achieve. If our game returned to the kind of choreography that had flattened England in the Six Nations, why not dare to dream?

It didn't though and, at my lowest ebb, the criticism now

turned to open mockery in a Paris hotel. I thought it a little pathetic.

Much had been made of the IRFU's decision to give me a new contract *before* the tournament and now, of course, this fed an absolute frenzy of criticism. All that had gone before counted for nothing. I wore the dunce's hat. A comedian posing as a journalist led the ridicule.

Our non-performance in France would feed a level of inquiry almost in keeping with the pursuit of corrupt planners and crooked bankers that has, in recent times, so fixated the Irish public. A Genesis report was commissioned, just as in 2002 when Roy Keane's departure from Saipan effectively split the country.

Everyone assumed there was a hidden story and I couldn't honestly blame them. Our time in France had been spent in such a blizzard of rumour and innuendo that the impression of major discord within the squad became inescapable. The rumours arrived in daily bulletins and, as best we could, we tried to make light of them.

Travelling to training, one of the resident court jesters (usually Frankie Sheahan or Brian Carney) would step to the front of the bus and call the 'protagonists' together. 'Drico, you are accused of punching Peter Stringer in the dressing room after the Georgia game. Gentlemen, come up here to kiss and make up . . .'

Within hours of naming the team to play France, we were having dinner when the phone of Karl Richardson, our Media Liaison Officer, rang. I had left Geordan Murphy out of the match 22 and certain journalists seemed fixated on that decision. Karl was sitting beside me now, Geordan just across the table.

The reporter on the line said he'd heard that Geordan had stormed out of camp and gone back to Leicester. 'I don't think so,' said Karl.

'He hasn't left the camp then?'

'Well, he's sitting across from me having his dinner as we

speak.' Karl then said in a pointedly loud voice, 'Geordan, there's a rumour that you've stormed out and gone back to Leicester!'

'Well, obviously, I haven't,' replied Geordan.

Other stories from the front line? Denis Leamy's form had suffered because I wouldn't allow him take his medication for diabetes! The Munster and Leinster players were at each other's throats.

Bear in mind, too, this was the week that *L'Equipe* did their contemptible hatchet job on Ronan O'Gara. I confronted the French journalist responsible after a press conference and told him he was a disgrace to his profession. His sole defence was that he had used the word 'rumour' in the allegations about ROG's private life. Incredibly, he took that as a licence to print lies.

We were aware of where he had sourced his information too, an Irish journalist who seemed especially sensitive to being seen anywhere close to our French 'friend' at that same press conference.

That Saturday, *L'Equipe* turned the gun on me. A real character assassination job. Pretty much no one noticed, though, because the game now dominated the newsprint. And it struck me that, whatever quibbles I might have had with the Irish media, I'd still happily choose most of them ahead of their French counterparts.

The night before our elimination by Argentina, a former international – Trevor Brennan – appeared on Irish television to plug his autobiography. Speaking on *Tubridy Tonight*, Trevor painted a pretty wretched picture of conditions within the Irish camp and he based that depiction on a conversation he said he'd had with Alan Quinlan. Now the story ran that after hearing about that interview I had stormed up to Quinny's room, hauled him out of bed and demanded an explanation.

The reality? Niall O'Donovan, the assistant coach, got a text from home about 11.15 p.m. saying Trevor had been on TV, quoting Quinlan about how bad things were in the Irish camp. Apparently, he'd considered 'doing a Roy Keane' out of France but reckoned nobody would even notice if he had gone. So Niallo texted Quinny, something along the lines of, 'Trevor's hung you out to dry on RTE.'

Quinny was just off the lobby, checking his emails. He immediately texted back. Niallo had coached him since he was seventeen. The two were close. 'Can I see you in the lobby?' he said.

Quinny was absolutely disgusted with Trevor. He felt he'd been used opportunistically to create a stir. Me? I never even discussed the issue. Quite apart from not having hauled him out of bed, I didn't even bring it up in conversation. Twenty-four hours before a do-or-die World Cup game, it was pretty low down on my list of priorities.

I will admit to being pretty disappointed with Trevor, though. In 2002, I could have done with him for the summer tour to New Zealand. We were coming off a Six Nations hammering in Paris and he was just the kind of hard-nosed, uncompromising back-row forward I felt I'd need in the so-called 'House of Pain'.

But he had a shoulder problem that required minor surgery and, having just signed a contract to join Toulouse, I knew that coming to New Zealand would mean him missing pre-season in France. Toulouse was a massive opportunity for Trevor. We discussed it on the phone and he said he was happy to travel if I needed him.

'Look Trevor,' I said, 'get the operation out of the way and start your career with Toulouse on the right foot.' He was married with a kid and I was looking at the bigger picture. Trevor had his operation and never looked back. Five years later, I thought he could have shown more class.

But this was the kind of trivia fizzing all around us, sometimes at the expense of far more serious matters. One of the saddest aspects to our tournament would be the story of Simon Best falling ill with a problem that, effectively, ended his career as a professional rugby player. Simon took ill on a 'down day' in Bordeaux returning to the hotel feeling disorientated and having difficulties with his speech. He was immediately transferred to the local hospital where an irregular heartbeat was identified as the problem. The realisation that his career was over shocked us all to the core.

But this, it seemed, wasn't interesting enough to get more than the most rudimentary of coverage against the more salacious works of fiction. I'm not pretending our World Cup base was Utopia. It wasn't. The hotel in Bordeaux left a bit to be desired and the food was certainly abysmal. Finding a suitable base had been hugely problematic. The hotels offered to us were uniformly mediocre and I'd had a huge row with two World Cup officials on this issue the day before we played France in the 2006 Six Nations.

They came to my room and were pushing for us to choose from the list, accusing me even of trying to undermine them by taking a reconnaissance trip of my own. This, I denied. 'You did and we have proof,' they said.

I stood up and announced 'Well this meeting has just ended. I'm not going to be called a liar . . .'

Suddenly, they were aghast. They panicked and started to back-pedal. 'No, no, that's not what we're saying . . .' I'd had enough though. I told them that, if they didn't get us a hotel that was up to scratch in Bordeaux, I would base the team in Paris for the duration of the tournament. This would have been calamitous for them. Bordeaux had paid the French Federation to get the Irish team down there. Us staying in Paris would, essentially, have seen the Federation break a contract. But most of the hotels we had been offered were appalling. They were two- or, at best, three-star by Irish standards. We sent a stiff letter to RWC to complain.

In the end, we settled on Sofitel, Le Lec. It wasn't great. Just a big, modern hotel in the middle of nowhere, plopped down beside a man-made lake. The plus points were that we had our own private gym, a massive team room, a swimming pool and access to a perfect training pitch just ten minutes down the road.

The negatives? Well, let me tell you about the food.

We brought our own nutritionist, Ruth Wood Martin, to Bordeaux with us and the hotel chefs tried to work with her. But it just never seemed to click come meal time. There were maybe four typically French restaurants dotted around the hotel and the food in all four seemed to arrive either overcooked or undercooked. Ideally we would have used our own chef, but the hotel would not allow it.

In time I think everything about the place began to chafe. We were playing terrible rugby and, as a little uncertainty set in, the problems with our base seemed to amplify in the mind. I will say that the only complaints I heard from the players were to do with the food. One night a week, they'd take themselves to a nearby greasy-spoon style cafe, just to break the monotony. This wasn't ideal, to put it mildly.

Also, there was a sense of siege developing. When the players returned from training, most of them would head for a cooling dip in the pool. One day photographs appeared in a newspaper at home showing them poolside under the heading 'How do you expect to win matches when you're sunning yourselves by the pool?'

Another day, a group of them travelled to a nearby village for lunch and, when they didn't all leave together, it was depicted as some kind of collapse of team discipline. It was as if they'd been caught on the piss when, in fact, their behaviour was exemplary.

Over time, I've no doubt they came to hate the hotel in Bordeaux and everything about it. I know Ronan O'Gara wrote in his book that the original plan had been to stay in a brand-new Radisson, but 'it wasn't finished in time'. This wasn't the case.

The Radisson was never going to be ready in time and, even if it had been, the French Federation would never have signed off on a five-star hotel.

So the Sofitel, Le Lec kind of became our prison. Between the swirl of rumour, the mediocre food and the general sense of disconnect that grew from being based, essentially, in an industrial estate, we couldn't wait to get out of the place.

And did I mention the rugby?

The build-up to RWC 07 was like a slow skydive into the mouth of a volcano. We lost two summer Tests in Argentina that were, essentially, 'A' internationals. I used them to give guys on the periphery a chance, the exact same plan we'd used prior to the 2003 World Cup, with one key difference. That tournament had started in October but, because the French now wanted a longer season for their own Championship, this one would begin the first week in September.

The scheduling cut out a month of pre-season, so we took a twin-track approach. Our best players would skip the tour and concentrate on that pre-season work. It was logical. The media, subsequently, dubbed the guys left behind as 'the untouchables', but I had outlined the plan at our winter camp in Portugal after the 2006 autumn series. Everybody knew (including the IRFU), and, generally, agreed.

We were supposed to then have three warm-up games, against South Africa, Scotland and Italy. The Springboks pulled out. Why? It was rumoured that they were miffed over New Zealand winning the vote to stage RWC 2011. Who's to say? They ended up, bizarrely, playing a game against Connacht in the Sportsground. We didn't replace the fixture.

I had a clear dilemma for the Scotland and Italy games. Did I field my best fifteen or wrap them up in cotton wool? The Six Nations had confirmed my oft-stated view that we didn't have the depth to be able to afford the loss of key players. Brian O'Driscoll and Peter Stringer missed the game with France at Croke Park and I will always believe that cost us a Grand Slam.

So I chose the cotton wool approach, my priority being to keep guys healthy.

The Scotland defeat (21–31) at Murrayfield would be our only loss to them during my tenure as Ireland coach. I used the game to blood people like Tommy Bowe, Brian Carney and Rob Kearney. Shane Horgan twisted his knee in the warm-up and almost missed the World Cup as a result.

The alarm bells had begun to ring.

I could see that the Scots were ahead of us in terms of match practice. They looked much sharper, a team further down the road than us. We flew to a warm-weather camp in the south of France after and, sensing we needed more game time, I accepted an invitation to play the local side, Bayonne.

This was a mistake. With one of their key players, former French international Richard Dourthe, setting the tone through some pre-match verbals, they proved absolutely filthy. There was a point in the game where I remember thinking to myself, 'This is fucking lunacy!' I couldn't wait for it to end.

At half-time, I'd had words with referee, Wayne Barnes. In an extremely hostile environment, I felt he hadn't been giving us any protection. Barnes was furious with me. 'You can't come to me like this,' he said. However I was more preoccupied with player safety than with etiquette.

I told him that I'd take the team off the field if he didn't get control of the game. It had turned ugly once we got a couple of scores up and nothing was being done to rein it in. In the closing minutes, their New Zealand-born lock, Makaera Tewhata, threw a punch off the ball and an expression I'd last heard on the 2005 Lions tour now made my blood run cold.

'Drico's down . . .'

That evening was spent in the hotel lobby, waiting for the results of an MRI on our captain's cheek. His face was swollen like a pumpkin. Eventually our doc, Gary O'Driscoll, arrived in with the news that Drico's sinus was fractured and he was touch-and – go for our opening game in the World Cup.

The Bayonne coach apologised afterwards and, at an official RWC function in Paris just before the tournament began, the French manager and captain – Joe Maso and Rafael Ibanez – both made a point of declaring the incident 'a disgrace'.

As France were in our World Cup group, maybe a few of the Bayonne people thought they were fulfilling some kind of patriotic deed. This notion, I was assured by Maso, would have been utterly repugnant to the French management. Drico was actually supposed to be at that function in Paris, but I wouldn't hear of it. We were flying out of Dublin the following day to our camp in Bordeaux and he had still to have his cheek formally cleared for the tournament.

He would make it in the end, but Tewhata's punch had been, literally, millimetres away from putting him out of the World Cup.

By now, of course, I had a real sense of foreboding. Our final warm-up game had produced a larcenous 23–20 defeat of Italy at Ravenhill. We were shocking, a late, disputed try by ROG giving us what I can categorically describe as the least enjoyable Test win of my time in charge of Ireland.

Even the build-up had been fraught. Huge pressure came on us from certain quarters to have 'God Save the Queen' played beforehand. In fairness to the Ulster Branch, it wasn't coming from them. There was a strong non-rugby element pressing hard. Then a few of our own people started pushing for 'Amrann na bhFiann'. It descended into tit-for-tat patriotism.

The flatness of our play was now a real cause for concern. I'd pretty much put out the full Test team, bar our captain, but there was no confidence in their play. I spoke to Niallo. He shared every single one of my worries. The players looked like they hadn't played enough rugby. In an ideal world, I'd immediately have rewound three months.

But this wasn't an ideal world. We were headed into the mouth of the volcano.

One of the sayings I've been known to use in rugby is: 'You can't un-ring a bell!'

And that was our essential difficulty in France now. We arrived at the tournament undercooked. My call, my mistake, I accept that. Suddenly, the team was in dire need of rugby and we'd run out of time to give it to them. Wrapping the players in cotton wool had backfired.

In Belfast I had seen them almost shy away from physical contact against the Italians. We had a crisis now and that crisis meant a rewriting of my original World Cup plan. I had intended selecting two very different teams for the openers against Namibia and Georgia. But, after struggling to beat the Namibians 32–17, I knew I had to put the Test side out again.

The Georgia game was nightmarish. I have an abiding memory of the Georgians camped on our line with ten minutes left and we couldn't get the ball off them. If they had scored, they'd probably have won the match and going out of the World Cup to Georgia would have been utter humiliation. We fell over the line 14–10 in the end and, afterwards, I had the senior players up to my room. We were shell-shocked, but there was no panic. Nobody was tossing the toys out of the pram, saying, Fuck this! We still believed that, if things came right, we could beat France in Paris.

But the mood at home had curdled now. I remember seeing a so-called 'fan' interviewed on RTE after the Georgia game declare himself 'ashamed to be Irish'. And all I could think was, 'Fuck, I'm glad I'm not in the trenches with you, mate'.

I then heard that the Union's Director of Fitness, Liam Hennessy, was on his way to Bordeaux. The fire-fighting had begun. Liam and I go back a long way, almost thirty years in fact to our days together in Thomond College. He had been fundamental to our planning for RWC 2007 and the four-year bulking up of players we considered so essential after our tired elimination from the 2003 tournament.

Liam fully endorsed the 'cotton wool' approach, believing – like me – that our priority should be to arrive in France with a group of fit, healthy players. Now I couldn't help wonder what his intention was coming to Bordeaux.

I invited him up to my room the moment he arrived.

He immediately started questioning me about our training sessions and suggested that, perhaps, he might have 'a chat' with the players. I wouldn't hear of it. Our training was unchanged from what we'd always done. Training wasn't the problem. Lack of rugby was.

Basically, I told Liam to stay out of the way. The last thing I needed was him having little *tête-à-têtes* with players in the background. Bottom line, there was nothing being done in training that hadn't been agreed upon in advance. I felt he had arrived, essentially, to be seen to be hands-on.

'Liam, I don't want you around here,' I said. 'You've no business here. You're not going to be coaching the team, training the team or having meetings with the team. This is a war zone, things aren't going well. It's up to me to sort it out. The best thing you can do is go!' And he did.

In a sense, we continued this conversation the week before we played Italy in the following year's Six Nations. I felt that he had hung me out to dry in the Genesis Report, claiming that I'd 'overpractised' the team. If I have a problem with someone, I'm not one for tiptoeing around it.

It was the Tuesday morning in Killiney and I asked for him to come to my room. He arrived up with Eddie Wigglesworth, the IRFU's Director of Rugby, and stood his ground. Said he had the paperwork to prove that the team was 'overpractised'. Then he came up with this term called 'the forty-eight-hour rule'.

'What's that?' I asked.

'You shouldn't train them in the forty-eight hours immediately after a game.'

'But we've always trained within forty-eight hours of playing.'

'No we haven't.'

'So if we play England in Croke Park on a Saturday evening and the game ends at 7.30 p.m., you're telling me we don't train before 7.30 that Monday night?'

I felt he was bullshitting. Based on the information I had recieved from the Genesis people, he had been the only one making any accusations against me and none of those accusations were backed up with any evidence. Not one of the players had complained of being pushed too hard.

I had been offered the opportunity to apportion blame myself and didn't take it. Any of the fitness advice we'd been given beforehand – be it our use of the cryotherapy facility in Spala, whatever – I agreed with. I wasn't now going to go and start throwing stones. Yet the word coming back from Genesis was that Liam said I'd basically burnt out the team.

I'd had enough. I admit I told Liam to 'fuck off' out of the room and that was the last time we spoke.

I'm not quite sure what people expected of me in the immediate aftermath.

Within minutes of our 15–30 loss to Argentina in the Parc des Princes, I was asked by a TV reporter pitchside if I intended to resign. The question didn't surprise me, but I did think it was unfair. I hadn't even had a chance to speak to the players and she seemed to expect me to make some immediate announcement. To me, it wasn't a question looking for an answer. It was a question looking for a reaction.

I was very angry. It embodied the tone of the whole media coverage. 'Kick them when they're down' type of thing. We were on our knees emotionally and the general instinct seemed to be to give us a good kicking now. You could detect a palpable sense of delight in some quarters that things had gone so badly wrong.

I couldn't get away, of course, from the fact that we'd played abysmally in the tournament. Our play reminded me of pre-qualifying for the previous World Cup, when we'd gone to Russia and, basically, been a bundle of nerves. Confidence is a brittle thing and, right now, ours was in small pieces on the floor.

Right up to the French game, I think we genuinely believed we could pull things round. But referee Chris White blew us off the park that night and the defeat left us needing to score a minimum of four tries against the Pumas for a bonus point win. I have to hand it to the players, they never gave up. But we needed absolutely everything to go right for us, while Argentina just had to wait for our mistakes.

No question, they took great pleasure in knocking us out. If Argentina could have picked a team they wanted to piss off more than any other in the World Cup, I've no doubt they'd have chosen us. There was definite bad blood between the teams and that was reflected in the amount of on-field 'sledging'. Felipe Contepomi said something disparaging in the press about me afterwards. For a guy who got his medical degree in Ireland, I found that pretty ungracious.

In the dressing room after the game I sincerely thanked the players for their efforts. 'Nobody can point a finger at any of ye,' I said. 'Ye never once stopped trying. Ye never gave up.'

We had a sense of the kicking that now loomed, but we

weren't alone. Wales were heading home as well. Australia would soon follow. New Zealand too. In fact, in my darkest moments after the World Cup, I used think of Graham Henry and the 24-hour *Talk Rugby* stations in New Zealand. Many of the All Blacks fans had decided to time their arrival in France for the semi-finals. They were flying in just as their team flew home.

Coming back, I was in a very dark place. I felt absolutely gutted and my biggest concern now was for the family. Some of the media commentary had become so lacking in insight or balance, all sense of perspective seemed lost.

I didn't consider quitting. To me, there was a logical reason for our non-performance. The Genesis report would say exactly what I expected, that (a) there was no trouble in the camp and (b) we just hadn't played enough rugby in the build-up. There was absolutely no suggestion of me losing the confidence of the players and, as such, I didn't feel there was any reason to walk away.

I'd missed our 25th wedding anniversary while at the World Cup, so Noreen and I now flew down to Nice for a couple of days while the tournament was still in progress. It felt strange watching France and Argentina get to the semi-finals. Essentially, the two teams that got out of our group finished third and fourth in the world.

To me, that just confirmed the opportunity that had slipped through our fingers. Had we brought our Six Nations form to France, we'd have been in with a real shout.

Instead, we were now facing into a hostile winter. And, if I didn't turn things around, the blood in the water would be mine.

2

ENDGAME

The night before the Lions squad was announced for this summer's tour to South Africa, I sat in a tiny apartment in Boulder, Colorado, surfing the Net for speculation on Ian McGeechan's intentions.

It was about 11 p.m. locally and I will admit to a wistful thought that it could have been me striding into that Heathrow hotel the following morning to announce my selection to challenge the Springboks. Instead, I faced the more mundane business of haggling over the price of a rucking net and seeing if, perhaps, I could book a meeting room in Charleston free of charge.

Heading into the 2007 World Cup, I was considered a front-runner to coach the 2009 Lions. I'd have loved the job. Having seen at close quarters the mistakes made during the 2005 tour of New Zealand, I had very definite ideas on how the trip to South Africa should have been managed.

But my share value plummeted at the key moment, Ireland enduring that miserable World Cup and following it up with just two victories out of five in the 2008 Six Nations, my worst return in seven seasons as national coach. In a matter of months, then, I went from front-runner to – essentially – slipping off the radar.

I can't deny that this was hard to take. I think I'd have been a pretty decent Lions coach, had I got the opportunity.

Ireland's form didn't exactly reflect a meltdown. Two of our defeats (against France and Wales) were by a single score, yet the loss in Paris alerted me to the pretty toxic attitude that now informed the work of certain journalists. The week after that game I took a call from one sportswriter wishing to 'disassociate' himself from the behaviour of two of his colleagues in the press box after one of the French tries.

Apparently, these two Irish journalists jumped up and cheered the score, almost involuntarily betraying their desire to see the back of me. Hearing that was one of my lowest moments as a coach. I felt sickened.

My last official engagement as Ireland coach had brought one unexpectedly pleasant surprise. We'd lost our final game in the Six Nations, thumped 10–33 by a Danny Cipriani-inspired England at Twickenham. Though I hadn't yet actually decided to resign, I realised I'd certainly have to consider my position.

In the dressing room afterwards, I stayed non-committal. There was a deathly silence in the place and I just thanked everyone for the effort put in. 'What happens next, I don't know,' I said. My words may have borne a tone of resignation, but I was genuinely undecided.

I then headed out to do the customary RTE television interview. On the way, I passed a young English journalist I felt I'd been quite helpful to over the previous few years. He didn't look up, but as I moved through a door, I could hear him murmur to a colleague, 'Dead man walking.'

To some degree I was lost in private thoughts at the post-game banquet as England captain Phil Vickery got up to speak. I didn't know Vickery and was a little startled to hear him mention my name. But he began to talk really touchingly of the contribution I had made to Irish rugby. He said he understood the pressure I was coming under now but that he hoped 'sense would prevail' and I'd be allowed to continue my work as coach.

I thought it was a wonderfully magnanimous thing for him to do at a time when my predicament had to be a long way down any list of English priorities. Before I left the function, I went to his table and thanked him.

Our journey home from London the following day had a comical dimension. We'd flown into a private airfield on the Thursday and been taken straight to our base at Penny Hill Park. But high winds now closed the airfield, so we were re-routed to Gatwick. The place was like a zoo and, by the time we got airborne, four hours had been lost.

I went to Killiney to collect my car and had a quick cup of tea with my agent, John Baker, before heading home to Moylough. 'Have you thought about what you want to do?' John asked.

'I have,' I said. 'I just want a night to sleep on it.'

The IRFU, in fairness, had given me the Six Nations to fix things and, for whatever reason, I hadn't got them fixed. Our defeat in Paris had been a mirror image of previous near misses, the French building a lead only for us to almost catch them on the home straight; we'd lost to a single line-break against Wales and, then, we'd gone to Twickenham without our midfield, both Brian O'Driscoll and Gordon D'Arcy being out injured.

We certainly hadn't been conspicuously lucky but I sensed too that media negativity had begun to undermine confidence within the team. Now that same media was agitating for news. By the time I got home, I felt exhausted and went to bed. But before I did, I made the decision to resign. My reasoning has always been to sleep on a decision before making any announcements. If you wake contented, then you know it's the right decision. If not, it's time for a rethink.

I woke the following morning feeling a calm sense of achievement. Nobody from the Union had put the remotest pressure on me to go, but – on reflection – it was a 'no-brainer'. Much as I, personally, might have been tempted to stay on, would it have been the right decision for the team, for my family, for the IRFU?

The answer to all three, I had to admit, was almost certainly, 'NO!'

We decided to delay releasing the news until 9 p.m. the following day in the hope that it might fall somewhere between late bulletins and breakfast TV and, essentially, be 'old hat' within 24 hours. I didn't want a media circus.

On the Tuesday, I came to Dublin to put things in order and was sitting alone in a bedroom in the Citywest Hotel that evening as 'BREAKING NEWS' began to flash across the TV screen. I felt perfectly serene watching the announcement of my resignation.

Early the following morning, a photographer materialised outside the house, forcing Noreen to close the blinds. Her brother, Martin, who lives locally, informed the local garda sergeant.

The photographer's car was parked badly and the sergeant gently told him that it might be a wise thing to move it from the main road. Soon after, it started to rain heavily and, by the time I arrived down from Dublin, the photographer had departed.

Paul O'Connell had phoned me the moment the story broke. Brian O'Driscoll, Shane Horgan and Donnacha O'Callaghan subsequently wrote letters. Over time, I would get to communicate with most of the players I'd worked with so closely for the previous six and half years and I can say – hand on heart – I departed on good terms with them all.

It's funny how the media gets a view on a coach's relationship with certain players. The impression was always given that I didn't like Geordan Murphy, that we were endlessly at loggerheads.

That wasn't the case. True, I often preferred Girvan Dempsey as my fullback, but this was a rugby decision, nothing more.

Geordan, after all, had six caps to his name when I became Irish coach. By the time I finished, he had almost sixty. I must have seen something in him.

Geordan is a guy I have a lot of time for. Of course, he was upset with me at times. What top player wouldn't be if he thinks he's been wrongly omitted from a team? But it was never vindictive, never personal. Maybe seven months after leaving the Ireland job, I was in London to coach an international fifteen in the 'Help for Heroes' fund-raising game for injured veterans of the wars in Afghanistan and Iraq. I bumped into Geordan at one of the functions and we had a really enjoyable chat.

Actually, we had a good laugh about speculation that had been linking me with the coaching job at Leicester, where Geordan is such a coveted player.

'Lucky for you I didn't get it,' I said, grinning.

'Jesus yeah, I'd have been ruined,' he said laughing.

That event was a real eye-opener. I met some extraordinary people there, guys whose lives had been turned upside down in seconds. It was an incredible dose of reality. We get sucked into sport and, sometimes, losing a big game can feel like the end of the world.

When we talk about rugby, we talk about courage and putting your body on the line. And we mean it. But the truth is we don't know what real courage is. The guy running 'Help for Heroes' put it to us in pretty stark terms. He said, 'You're at one end of the pitch and one of your buddies needs help at the other. What do you do? To a man you're ready to help him, right? Just one thing before you go. Unfortunately fifteen per cent of you won't make it back and another twenty per cent will come back badly injured. OK?

'Now off you go and rescue your buddy!'

It was a crash course in perspective that reminded me of a trip to Auschwitz with the Irish team in 2001. We were spending three weeks in Spala and, to break the tedium, decided to bring the players to Krakow for the weekend. En route, we took a detour to the scene of Nazi mass murder.

And on this glorious, sun-splashed Friday, we slipped through the gates of Auschwitz for a two-hour tour that proved incredibly harrowing. Maybe the most disturbing sight was a long room with this huge glass case running the length of it, filled with victims' shoes. Another was full of suitcases. Another of spectacles.

And it hit us right between the eyes that these items belonged to real people, real victims about to be sent to the gas chambers. We were told the putrid history of the place, saw the hatches through which cyanide pills were tossed and couldn't but notice the bullet marks in the walls.

Coming away that day, I will always remember the absolute silence on the bus, the palpable sense of incredulity at man's inhumanity to man. The following day, driving back to Spala, we were watching the movie *Stand By Me*. When the credits came on at the end and the theme song began to play, 45 voices on the bus spontaneously sang it out in unison.

And I couldn't help think that, somehow, Auschwitz was still in people's heads.

To begin with, my time out of work was strange. I'd been a part of the Ireland coaching set-up for eight and half years and, so, the June day they played New Zealand in Wellington, I felt completely at sea, sitting at home in County Galway, almost aching for involvement in a game being played at the far end of the planet.

I did go to America for a while, two personal friends inviting me across to give clinics at Brown University in Rhode Island and Notre Dame. They put the word around and, suddenly, a ten-day visit had swollen to five weeks. Eventually, I had to turn down invitations to Utah, Dallas and Philadelphia.

And I loved that simple energy of being back on a training pitch with players. It kind of reasserted my love for the game and an absolute desire to get back on the horse.

When the chance then arose to be Eagles coach, I jumped at it. It's a different world to Ireland, no question. Budgets are tight, logistics hugely difficult. But I wasn't new to US Rugby. I'd served a large part of my coaching apprenticeship in America and I always loved the energy there, the hunger for information.

The standard may not be what I became accustomed to with Ireland, but the work ethic certainly is. You have to respect what these people do. I had the coaches in for a staff meeting on Easter Sunday and it went on for ten hours because we simply had to get everything covered in a single day. I'd forgotten how big the country is. I went on a road trip to have a look at our summer facilities and it took me four full days to see three venues.

A lot of the US players have put their careers on hold to play for the Eagles. And that's a dangerous thing to do in the current economic climate. Yet they do it unquestioningly. Some of these guys are desperate to get America to the next World Cup despite the fact they themselves will probably be gone by the time it comes round.

It strikes me that America hasn't changed since I was last here. Ireland has. I was home in April and the general sense of morbidity and depression over the ailing economy was overwhelming. The blame game was in full flow. In America, they were looking for answers. In Ireland, culprits.

I could recognise that because, to some extent, I'd been through it. When things went wrong for Ireland at the 2007 World Cup, someone had to be brought to book. There had to be someone's head on a stake. There was this sense of 'How dare you perform so poorly on the big stage!'

I understood the argument about people spending good money to follow the team to France. Their disappointment was massive and sincere. But no one was more disappointed than those of us inside the camp. No one messed up deliberately.

In November 2008, I agreed to do a lengthy interview for RTE television. It was sold to me as a look back on my career as Irish coach. Yet the questioning proved uniformly hostile, focusing entirely on the last eight of my 78 Test games as Irish coach. I thought that pretty much summed up the blame culture.

The need for blood on the floor.

I texted some of the Irish players when they won the Grand Slam under Declan Kidney this year. I was genuinely delighted that they'd finally got what I considered to be their due. And I texted both Paul O'Connell and Brian O'Driscoll when the Lions' captaincy was announced. My respect and admiration for these guys will go with me to my grave and nothing, I can assure you, that happened in my last eight games as Ireland coach could ever change that.

It's funny, I was flying to America on 31 March with a check-in time of 5.30 a.m. at Dublin Airport. Travelling with a single bag. The guy at the Aer Lingus desk told me that the bag was a kilo and a half too heavy.

'You'll have to take something out of it,' he said.

'I can't,' I answered. 'I don't have anywhere to put it.'

'Well, you'd better do something,' he insisted 'because if the baggage handlers see it's over the limit, the whole bag will get tossed in a bin.'

So there I stood, just after dawn at check-in, discarding shirts from my bag. All week I'd been listening to politicians preach the importance of everyone working their way through the depression. And, as I stuffed my shirts into a nearby bin, those words seemed incredibly hollow now.

I remember thinking that, if this attitude was the road to recovery for Ireland, then heaven help us.

3

POVERTY, CHASTITY AND OBEDIENCE

Maybe the first time I truly got to know my father was sitting at his wake.

He died very suddenly in the week before Christmas of 1999 after a virtual lifetime wrestling with a heart condition. My mother, Rena, sat by his corpse, talking about him with such radiant love that, in the grief, her words spun beautiful pictures. I was spellbound. Like so many Irish sons, the affection between my father and I had never been freely expressed.

I knew Paddy O'Sullivan just as a good, kind man whose health kept tugging at his quality of life. A heavy smoker in his younger days, he was on a lot of medication virtually from his forties. Dad suffered from high blood pressure, high cholesterol and an ailing heart. In one sense it was a surprise that he lived to the age of 68.

I will never forget the moment I realised that he was gone. It was a horrible, filthy December day and I'd just spent the afternoon watching Munster play Bourgeoin at Musgrave Park on the TV (which I'm pretty sure Dad did too). I was due to fly to Bristol the following morning in my capacity as assistant Irish coach to see Kevin Maggs play for Bath.

The forecast was for severe frost that night and it dawned on me that a 6 a.m. journey from Moylough to Dublin could be treacherous. So I told Noreen that I'd hit for Dublin early and just packed an overnight bag. I was sitting down for a cup of tea when the telephone rang. It was my brother, Kieran.

'Eddie!'

The moment I heard his voice, I knew that my father was dead. It was surreal. As brothers, we weren't in the habit of phoning one another without a reason and I just sensed that Kieran's reason had to be bad news.

'My father's dead,' he said, unwittingly declaring private ownership.

It turned out that Dad had gone to bed in the late afternoon. My mother managed a drycleaners just two minutes down from the house. She loved it. It gave her an escape from the worry of nursing him, a worry that was now constant. I think, near the end, she could just sense Dad slipping away. We all could. His heart was getting weaker.

This day she came in, called out his name and there was no answer. She found him lying cold in the bed, the blankets barely ruffled. He had, it seemed, slipped away in his sleep.

On one level, it was a relief. We all knew that he was nervous about his health. One of his brothers had died in his fifties from a heart attack in the US and another would, later, die after a stroke. There was a clear line of coronary trouble on that side of the family. I think my father worried about how his end would come, so for him to die peacefully felt an odd blessing.

Dad was an electrician by trade. He had started out working as a line-man for the ESB and, whenever there were storms, we became accustomed to him being out in the worst of it, climbing poles, repairing lines.

Home was Youghal, a small seaport in East Cork, lying on the estuary of the Blackwater river. I was the oldest of six children (Kieran, Maeve, Grainne, Eoin and Aideen in that order) and, as it happened, the only one who would pursue a life elsewhere.

Our childhood was happy. But we were working-class people and in 1960s Ireland that meant people with few privileges. Myself, Kieran and Eoin went to Youghal CBS where corporal punishment might as well have been part of the syllabus. Routinely, beatings were administered with either a leather or a cane.

The cane was the worst. You might get four or five of the best on each hand, go back to your desk and clamp your burning palms around the metal bar of the desk for comfort.

The worst thing was that punishment came almost as an assessment of your academic ability, which, for me, was bad news. I was an average student, though I could certainly see that others had it worse. Some of the slow learners – kids who would be in remedial classes today – really took the brunt of the Brothers' anger, their lives made miserable by the ignorance of the time.

I remember, especially, one maths teacher. He would march through the classroom, calling out numbers, getting us to add and subtract at breakneck speed for our 'mental arithmetic'. The wise thing was to put your hand up every time. A hand down was like a target on your forehead.

This Brother carried a big, wooden duster around with him and, if you gave a wrong answer, he would smash the duster down on the top of your fingers. Whatever it did for our arithmetic, it worked wonders for our reflexes.

This probably sounds more traumatic than it was. Corporal punishment was just an accepted part of schooling in those days. It wasn't ideal, but it didn't really do us any lasting damage either.

Put it this way, to the best of my knowledge, none of my classmates turned into axe murderers,

Indiscipline was never a problem in the school. Kids would, quite literally, never step out of line. You were getting a bad enough pounding for not knowing your Irish to understand that acting the maggot just wasn't an option.

During my first year in the secondary school, a really nice Brother came to talk about religious vocations. And, for whatever reason, I got it into my head that I wanted to be a Christian Brother. I was 13 at the time and there was a 'house of formation' for the Brothers in Dublin where, incredibly, I would spend the next two years of my life.

My parents were very staunch Catholics, so this was a proud thing for the family. I remember I was due to travel up by train from Kent Station in Cork with some other boys but, when they didn't show, my father decided that he would not let me travel alone.

For him, this made for a particularly awkward day. We didn't have a car and, by coming to Dublin with me, Dad condemned himself to a midnight return to Cork, at which stage he would have to hitch a lift to Youghal. The turnaround in Dublin's Heuston Station had to be brief for him to make the train back and it was literally a case of him stepping from one platform onto another.

So the point of separation was almost brutal. Just a handshake with the Brothers there to meet me and – literally in seconds – my father gone.

The house of formation was on the south side of the city, near Dun Laoghaire. A big, granite place on Kill Avenue that has, since, become an art college. Actually, there were four buildings, separated by a double yard. The Brothers themselves lived in the front building, which was an old monastery. Then there was a church, a big recreation hall and, along the back, classrooms.

The dormitories were over the recreation hall and I'll always remember one of the kids could literally see his front door in Sallynoggin from a window by his bed.

To me, home might as well have belonged to another galaxy. I didn't cry that first night in Dublin until I got into bed. But then the tears came in a flood. And that was pretty much how I would deal with my loneliness in Dublin. Privately.

As much as I could, I tried to remain stoic in public. Maybe it was a survival mechanism, because the regime was tough and rigid. Rise at 6 a.m., morning prayers, Mass, breakfast, chores, then study. The classes started at 9.15 and, in a very long, busy day, there was little time for recreation. I suspect they were believers in the doctrine 'The devil makes work for idle hands.'

We did get one hour for games when classes finished at 3.30 and that was always my favourite part of the day. But it would be over almost as soon as it started and we'd be back in for afternoon tea, then study until 8 o'clock and eventually the bell which would signal time for the Rosary. We'd be in bed by 9.20, ten minutes before the lights went out.

It's probably fair to say I knew pretty soon that the Brotherhood wasn't for me. At the end of the first year, my parents came to visit and that was a mistake. It just stoked the fire of my homesickness and I remember literally aching with loneliness as they left to catch the train.

The only regular communication we had was a weekly letter, which the Brothers always opened. It was their way, I suppose, of monitoring any bad news. Yet, on the one day my letter wasn't opened, I read it to find that my paternal grandmother had died.

I knew from the previous week's letter that she had been ill, but it was a shock to read the finality of those words. I wasn't inclined to tell anyone in the college because I didn't have any close friends in the place. So I kept it to myself. I do remember playing billiards one night with a chap from Cork and, out of the blue, I just spat out three words like pieces of gristle.

'My grandmother died!' I said. He looked at me with a vaguely blank expression and said, 'You should tell one of the Brothers.' I never did.

It was a strange time in my life. I didn't feel close enough to anyone really to talk about it and my parents, probably sensibly, decided not to drag me home for the funeral. At the end of my first year, I had told my mother that a clerical life wasn't the life for me. Her response was simple.

'Are you sure?'

'Pretty sure.'

'Well, if you're only pretty sure, you're not a hundred per cent. You should go back. You're in the middle of your Inter Cert cycle. If you come back to Youghal now, it's going to be different. Just finish your Inter, then decide.'

I had no problem with that. I could see her logic and, to be fair, no one was going to force me to stay against my wishes. Deep down, I think I just wanted to alert them to the fact that I wouldn't be staying long-term. In the Brothers, they continuously promoted the vows of poverty, chastity and obedience. Mentally, I was trying to tick each box and found I was struggling with every one of them.

My time in Dublin was a mixed blessing. Academically, I thrived. The discipline of Carriglea Park ensured that, by the time I did the Inter, my grades were uniformly good. But I think Dublin also fed a habit of keeping things to myself. Of concealing emotion.

The principal of the school was a giant of a man from Mayo with a great, bellicose voice and a devoutly anti-English outlook on life. He taught us Irish grammar through the medium of terror. One kid in the class was so scared he wore rosary beads around his neck. In fact, on one particular day I remember him quite literally wetting himself with fear.

The principal also taught us history, so our take on Cromwell et al. was, to put it mildly, pretty lopsided. Looking back, we were desperately vulnerable. Most of us were miles from home and had only minimal contact with our parents.

This same man would have us in church at half six every morning, to hear him deliver a homily. His subject could be anything, but the puritan tone was constant. The country, he'd tell us, was 'Gone to Hell in a hand-basket!' Young people had no respect. Sex was out of control.

For me, sport was the salvation. I was very small for my age, but I was decent at Gaelic and soccer and, in a sense, that was how I forged my personality. The school actually competed in Gaelic football and I scored a late goal once to win an important league game. The following morning in his homily, the principal lauded me from his pulpit for saving the school's reputation.

It was probably the high point of my time there.

By and large, we were an enclosed order. The only time we left the school apart from games was on Sunday afternoons when we were brought for a walk to Dun Laoghaire or Killiney, marching two abreast down the pavement in uniform, a strange army of formal children.

There was one young Brother who I always suspected saw the regimentation as damaging. In late spring, he'd bring us on hikes to the Sugar Loaf or Three Rock or, on one occasion, Kippure. We'd be dropped in minibuses out to Kilmacanogue and the deal was that we walked all the way home. By the time we got back, our bodies were almost seizing up with fatigue. It was exhausting. And absolutely wonderful.

We did make an annual pilgrimage too to Callan in County Kilkenny, to the home place of Ignatius Rice, the founder of the Christian Brothers. But, other than that, nothing. Just study, prayer, sleep.

It was a pretty draconian existence yet, in fairness, there was never a sense of being trapped there. Plenty of boys packed it in, usually at the end of a school year. That said, it was like an admission of failure to do so. It carried a certain stigma. We all took great delight in my second year when a kid who had come up from the Gaeltacht region of Kerry, a fluent Irish speaker, decided to jump ship after about six weeks.

The principal had virtually adopted him as his pet, mentioning him often in the morning homily as a virtual prototype of what the rest of us should aspire to be. It was like a small victory when he left. A triumph for the sinners.

Returning to Youghal CBS was pretty seamless after my Inter Cert. I was happy to be back with old friends. But the education system was hopelessly one-eyed at the time. Coming out of primary school we had been streamed into two very separate groups. The 'A' stream would do French and Latin in secondary school. The 'B' stream, woodwork and mechanical drawing.

In other words they were already establishing your place in the food chain. The bright kids would go on to white-collar work. The rest would be tradesmen. It was an appalling betrayal of a kid's potential to grow.

Although I'd got a really good Inter, I was pitched straight back into the 'B' stream on my return to Youghal. The system led to some awful injustices. One good friend of mine was streamed 'B' as well. He got seven honours in his Leaving Cert but, because he had no languages, he couldn't go on to university.

There was no art on the syllabus in Youghal, yet I'd got an 'A' in my Inter Cert in Dublin. So my mother came up with the idea of doing art as an additional subject for my Leaving Cert. I did it with the help of a wonderful man called Tony Breslin. Tony was a well-known potter in the town and a qualified art teacher. For two years, I made a weekly trek to his studio for tuition.

It was nice being home with family and friends. Nice living under the same roof again as Mam and Dad.

The strange thing is it would be about a quarter of a century later under that roof – standing in the sitting room, my father's corpse laid out before us – before I learnt what my first trip to Dublin had taken out of him. The train back was delayed and he had arrived in Cork at around 1 a.m., which would have been the easy part. It took him something like three or four separate lifts in the dead of night to get home to Youghal.

He finally got in around 5 a.m., sat down on the couch and cried his eyes out. And then, as dawn broke, he pulled himself together and went straight back out to work.

Standing over his lifeless form that day in 1999, my greatest regret was simply that I hadn't known.

4

LEMON SALAD

If God lost the first battle for my heart, you could say that the sea lost the second.

We were fishing people. My mother's family held a salmon licence and most of our summers were spent trying to make it profitable. That made for hard days and – often – nights in a fourteen-foot boat, watching nets and trying, essentially, to out-wit the tide.

It wasn't quite Hemingway's old man trying to haul in a giant marlin, but it did have its worries and its dramas. Actually, at times, it could be downright frightening. My uncle and grand uncle got turned over once while I was in school. It was a really bad, gale-swept day in April and I vividly remember being in the mechanical drawing class at the CBS. The school grounds ran right down to the water's edge and, looking out at all the 'white horses' that day, it wasn't hard to imagine people getting into trouble.

Suddenly word came through that two boats had gone down, one of them containing uncle Liam and grand-uncle Jimmy. In Youghal, there was always that strange, unspoken fear of the sea that stalks all fishing communities. And this was one of those days that made the blood run cold.

The boats were fishing in what we called 'the low water' (you fish the tide down until it turns) just off Green Park and both crews managed to scramble to safety onto the rocks beside Youghal lighthouse. It turned out that my grand uncle had got caught up in the nets and uncle Liam, who would have been in his late twenties at the time, literally lifted him one-handed out of the water with an almost superhuman strength that I can only imagine came from absolute terror.

The fishermen had a saying that someone 'nearly had his lemon salad last night' if one of them almost drowned. I could never quite decode it, though salad is cold and lemon bitter, so maybe it's self-explanatory.

Incredibly, grand-uncle Jimmy couldn't swim a stroke, despite being a merchant seaman and fisherman all his life. He was of a generation that believed, if you went overboard, swimming just prolonged your agony. Once in the water, you were as well to let nature take its course.

It was a brand of fatalism I could never embrace.

I spent a lot of summer days fishing with my uncle Michael and first cousin, Michael junior. There were two ways to fish in Youghal, in the harbour or off the beach. In the harbour you just drifted with the tide, taking turns to run your nets, a fleet of boats running one after the other.

The other way was to go off the beach, two boats to a berth, running weighted nets side by side and turning an angle to trap the fish. That was always the hardest fishing. You had to fish the tide down which meant you could be out on the water, two to a boat, for 14 to 16 hours a day.

This would be a Monday to Friday stint, June to August and tough, tough work. Most of the hardened fishermen would knock off on a Friday afternoon and, basically, drink their way through the weekend. Us young guns would happily take up the slack in their absence. The finances worked this way. My uncle owned the licence, the boat and the nets. You might catch 50 salmon a week, weighing an average of 8 lb each. That's 400 lb of fish and, at maybe 50p a pound, it would work out at £200.

My uncle would take a third of that and maybe another £5 for petrol money. The remainder was split between the hands.

On a good week, you could walk away with £65, which was good money in the 70s when Youghal began to take a terrible pounding from the economic downturn. The major employer in the town was the textile industry, through Seafield Gentex, Blackwater Cottons and Youghal Carpets. Then there was Murray Kitchens too. These factories would run three shifts a day, seven days week.

The town was built on these businesses and it seemed the only thing to do on leaving school was to take your place on the factory floor. All of my uncles and most of my aunts worked in the textile industry, but my father broke the cycle. Having started in a factory, he went to school at night to become an electrician.

It was a point that my parents endlessly impressed upon us. Our futures did not have to be on the factory floor, we didn't just have to go with the local flow. So, they encouraged us to do our Leaving Certs and find a trade. My two brothers both became electricians in the end, actually training with my father.

The logic of Mam and Dad's thinking would come home forcibly through the 70s and 80s when the textile industry, essentially, went to the Far East and – within a very short space of time – the four major factories in Youghal all went to the wall. That absolutely gutted the town and virtually all of my uncles became unemployed overnight.

In many ways, the fishing kept the town alive after that, feeding the local economy.

Over the years, I would take a lot of summer jobs in Youghal as well as the fishing. They ranged from my very first job, working in a fish and chip shop, to harvesting grain, to making cheddar in a cheese factory and, finally, to working in a pub. Briefly, I even flirted with the thought of opening a chip shop myself. There always used to be a queue down the street from the chipper at pub closing time and it seemed to me that a man could make a decent living out of selling chicken suppers.

I was so taken with the idea, I considered leaving school early. The idea, though, didn't survive my mother's consternation and Youghal was spared the culinary delights of 'Eddie's Diner'.

Fishing was the one constant though, in all honesty, I never seriously considered it a career option. The life was hard and fraught, the rewards relatively modest. There were a lot of tactics and, on occasion, little swindles involved. Night-time in the harbour offered opportunity. In the darkness, you could row somebody out by quietly putting your nets maybe 40 yards outside the fella who had the slot in front of you. This was a calculated gamble. If he found out, chances were he'd row across, jump in your boat and probably punch you senseless.

If not, he'd certainly get you on the quay when you came in.

The sea became eerie at the optimum time for fishing. In the harbour, the best time to catch a fish would be when the light was turning and the fish just couldn't see the nets. In the bay, when the tide would drop, you might be sitting in pitch blackness, not a ripple on the water, the nets sagging onto the sea floor like worn-out hammocks.

In that situation, we'd sometimes go up onto the beach, light a bonfire and cook breakfast. It may sound romantic and I suppose it was compared to the winter seasons of old. My grand uncles often spoke of being out on the water in January, using hand-lines to catch pollock and cod, their boots literally freezing to the bottom of the boat. I could never imagine how they endured that because, even on summer nights, the boat could be a bitingly cold place.

Dawn was always welcome. The first place you'd sense its arrival was at the bottom of the boat where you'd be able to just about recognise the outline of your feet, long before there was any trace of light in the sky.

My cousin Michael and I became regulars on the night shift. When things were going well, we'd hang onto a berth for dear life because it could be worth up to 50 salmon a week. So I might slip out on my own at midnight, then Michael would come along the beach at 2 a.m., I'd take him on board and we'd stay there till maybe three the following afternoon.

Sometimes it felt like we were playing poker with the salmon. A game of bluff between us. They'd see the nets and circle out of curiosity until, eventually, nosiness would get the better of them. They'd poke the net and you'd see a cork go down. The trick was to splash the angle with an anchor and force them into the trap.

You'd be exhausted at the end of a night stint. I remember coming back in with Michael once and standing upright in the boat as we passed a place we called Perks' Corner. Perks' was a family-run amusement park that would draw people in their hordes during summer. You could get ten to fifteen trains leaving Kent Station on Sunday mornings and pouring into Youghal for the beach and what became known by Cork people as 'the Merrys'.

Anyway, passing Perks', I closed my eyes and the next thing I knew Michael was shouting at me to fend the boat off the quay. I had been asleep for nearly ten minutes. Standing up.

Like so many other women in the town, my mother dreaded us being out on the water. She never slept much until we were safely in the door. But then her grandmother and mother would have been through exactly the same before her. It was simply a Coveney and Delaney way of life. A tradition. There were no safety systems. We didn't fish with buoyancy aids because of a worry that they'd get caught in the nets. On good summer days, you'd be stripped to the waist, but then you'd have these heavy wader boots from there down. On bad days, you wore oilskins.

By and large, if you went in the water, you didn't get back out. It was *sayonara*.

Actually, if your boat turned over at night, probably no one would even know you were in trouble until daylight. So you lived on your wits. You knew, with all the stuff you were wearing, that you'd go down like a stone. Sometimes a big wave might catch you broadside and your life would literally flash before you.

I remember one day especially. I must have been 16 at the time and I went out with Michael (14) and my brother, Kieran (15), to fish a 'low water'. It was June but a strong wind was blowing from the south and it was only when we went down to the harbour and ran our nets that we realised just how strong. Conditions were horrendous.

Before long, the three of us pretty much realised we didn't want to be out there. Kieran was the first to call it. 'Will we head in?'

'Yeah, maybe we should.'

Deep down, we knew that this equated to chickening out. With an outboard motor, it was only about five minutes into the quay, down past the Christian Brothers' school. I remember the nose of the boat actually smacking the quayside as we landed. And the stern form of grand-uncle Jimmy standing there to meet us.

'Where are ye goin?' he asked.

'Ah, we're gonna come up.'

'Sure, there's another two hours of low water out there.'

'Yeah, but it's fairly rough down there.'

'Get to hell back out if ye know what's good for ye!'

Jimmy wasn't going to let his grand nephews take the kind of option that just wasn't in his own DNA. So out we went again, moored up and waited our turn, the three of us absolutely petrified. I think we got five salmon on our first run, then – by a pure fluke – timed our second run perfectly to pull in another dozen.

Every other boat in the fleet was coming home with twos and threes. And here we were now, three kids, swinging home with nearly twenty. Jimmy was there on the quay to greet us.

'Well, how did ye do?'

'Seventeen.'

'Not bad!'

These were hard men with great stories. Jimmy was part of a proud maritime tradition on my mother's side of the family tree. My great-great-grandfather, Captain Lynch, had been Master of *The Youghal Citizen*, lost off the Saltee Islands on Christmas Day 1895. My great-grandfather, Mike Delaney, was 'boy' on that ship and thrown onto the rocks to safety before it went down. He became a Royal Marine Reserve who served on *The Donegal* during the First World War.

I had a cousin, Michael Fitzgerald, who served in the British navy before coming home to fight on de Valera's side in the Civil War, for which he was – apparently – executed at the age of 21. Another escaped from prison during that war, took the ship to America and settled in Long Island where he ran bootleg whiskey for the mafia during Prohibition.

You could certainly say that my mother came from interesting stock.

Grand-uncle Jimmy brought all of these men to life with his stories. Mike Delaney, his father, was a kind of hero to him. As a kid I remember meeting him. He stood just four feet ten in his bare feet, smoked a pipe and was intimidating as a bear. Jimmy often told of how Mike was once on shore leave in the West Indies and fought a giant local on the quay.

The place was jammed with onlookers to see the expected slaughter. 'You'd think there was nothing in Mike to look at him,' Jimmy would say with a chuckle. 'But he beat the local to a pulp he did!'

Mike was the kind of man Jimmy could look up to. Hard and unromantic. Jimmy himself had lived an interesting life too, sailing the world. I could sit listening to him for hours without any danger of being bored. He once caught a barracuda in the Panama Canal with a primitive hook made in the ship's engine room.

Those kind of stories gave him a strange ferocity in our eyes. He was in his seventies now, but nothing seemed to frighten him. So, when he stood on the quay that day hunting us back out into the storm, we weren't inclined to argue. 'Fuck this . . .' I remember thinking.

But I knew better than to say it.

5

BANNED

There were certain house rules for a kid in 1960s Ireland and I fell foul of probably the most infamous.

'The Ban', as it was called, forbade members of the GAA community from any involvement in so-called 'foreign' games, like rugby and soccer. Mere attendance was deemed sinful and it was quite a common occurrence for someone to be reported on by friends, in the very best *Stasi* traditions of neighbourhood watch.

My 'crime' was to play a soccer match for Youghal against Lismore and it took less than 24 hours for news of this impure deed to reach the school gates. When it did, myself and a friend were called to the principal's classroom.

'Well lads, is it true ye played a soccer match in Lismore yesterday?'

'We did, sir!'

'I've bad news for ye then. Ye're banned from playing Gaelic football under the regulations.'

The procedure was cold and unequivocal. We were heretofore prevented from playing in any of the school leagues. The attitude was: 'If you commit the crime, you do the time.' And we had certainly been guilty as charged. We played a game of soccer. Confirmed sinners at the age of ten.

I loved all sport but that pretty much finished me with Gaelic football. It also fed a little belligerence within. The school leagues were run on two pitches directly across the road from where we lived and, when I'd see the teams arrive, I'd go behind one of the goals and mess around with a rugby ball. I suppose it was my way of telling them what they could do with their suspension.

I did actually win an East Cork Championship at wing-back with Youghal some years later, but GAA never really held the same lustre for me again after falling foul of 'The Ban'. The town had three or four soccer teams and I played Sunday mornings with Sarsfields, named after Sarsfield Terrace, the estate my father grew up in.

This was strictly a social exchange, though, the team sheet all but index-linked to the hangover profile carried through from the night before.

I also got into karate around this time. Maybe it had something to do with the popularity of Bruce Lee movies in the early 70s, but a club started up in Youghal and I really got into the discipline. We trained two nights a week and I managed to reach purple grade, about two thirds of the way to a black belt.

I also did a bit of gymnastics in the CBS and was pretty decent at the basics – handstands and cartwheels. And in secondary school, I took to the boards, participating in a few musicals. I once played the leading lady in *The Mikado* and spent many subsequent years beseeching my mother to burn the photographic evidence.

To be fair, I had a competitive streak in me that just about any performance forum could probably have fed.

My mother's brothers, Liam and Bernard, both played for Youghal RFC though, so the club held a natural appeal for our family from an early age. They played on a pitch called Frogmore and, to begin with, the players changed in the Devonshire Arms Hotel. That arrangement was later moved to Aherns Seafood Restaurant, where a set of showers was put in at the back of the pub and the players would be driven up the hill to Frogmore in a fleet of cars.

Kieran and I would happily skulk down in someone's car boot to make the journey with them.

One of the abiding memories of my childhood is of peering in the window of Youghal Carpets and spotting the great Tom Kiernan sitting at a desk. I was maybe eight at the time and Kiernan, an accountant by trade, was Ireland's rugby captain. It was a huge thrill to see someone so famous working in our town. Though he would be in Youghal only for a short spell, Kiernan went out to Frogmore every lunchtime to practise his place-kicking. It was a matter of immense local pride.

Kieran and I both played rugby pretty much as soon as we were allowed to. Unfortunately, we were drawn to the same position. Hooker. This led to skin and hair flying in training matches where neither of us would give the other an inch. Almost uniquely for the 60s, Youghal had a vibrant under-age structure and by the time I was nine, we were playing full-scale fifteen-a-side games.

Our first coach, a local baker called Brendan Murphy, pretty much gave us free rein and – for Kieran and me – this was taken as a licence to beat the crap out of one another. It got so bad that my mother eventually came up and asked Brendan to put an end to it. And he did, by turning us into halfback partners.

Henceforth, Kieran would play all of his rugby at scrum half. He was injury prone but ferociously competitive and I always reckoned unstoppable from ten yards out. He was twice leading try scorer in the Munster Junior League and even played senior for a time with Highfield. I used to liken him to the great All Black number nine, Sid Going.

The only problem with Kieran was that you'd have to send him a letter to get the ball. Kicking wasn't his strongest point and the only time he passed was when he had nowhere left to run.

When I came back from Dublin after doing my Inter Cert, I was very keen to step up to the mark with Youghal. With the under-16s, I now came under the coaching influence of twin brothers Sean and Jim Hogan, who were on the firsts. I actually played my first senior game with the seconds when I was just fifteen. Norman McDonald, the captain of the team, became my minder. Norman was an open side and any time I hit the deck, he'd literally dive on top of me and take a shoeing rather than see the new kid injured.

I was playing fullback at the time and weighed no more than nine stone. It was a scary environment for a kid to step into, but I was pretty quick and reasonably skilful. As a fullback, I always reckoned that those two ingredients could get me out of most trouble that arose.

I played Munster Junior Cup against Tralee when I was only 18 and, believe me, that competition was no place for the faint-hearted. Tralee were coached that day by former Irish out-half, Barry McGann. In fact, I had the honour of playing against McGann once, for Cork Counties against Cork Constitution.

It was a Cork Charity Cup match and we were opposing fly halves. Him a full-blooded, if slightly rotund, legend. Me, a snotty-nosed sixteen-year-old novice. Cork Con stuffed us and McGann gave me a lesson in game management. He was a beautiful footballer and, on the day, set up an emerging Jimmy Bowen for a bagful of tries.

My sporting ambitions pretty much began and ended with Youghal back then. I had no grand visions – on or off the pitch – beyond the home place. It's funny, but there was a rather quaint approach to career guidance in those days. I remember a large, cardboard box, loaded with leaflets, being put up on the window of the classroom. The idea was that you'd have a look through them and, hopefully, take away something that appealed. I took away two: Physical Education and Architecture.

PE was probably the sexy choice. Well-known Irish sports personalities like Tony Ward, Brian Mullins, Jimmy Deenihan and Pat and Mick Spillane were already high-profile residents of Thomond College in Limerick and, for many aspiring PE students, that institution soon acquired an almost Mecca-like status.

I knew that, without French or Latin, I couldn't take the conventional route into Third Level education and sign up to University College Cork or any of the big Dublin universities. That possibility had been streamed away by the local CBS! But Thomond was a possibility. Thomond didn't require a language. Actually, Thomond ticked all the boxes, so long as I got five honours in my Leaving Cert.

And here, I had reason to be thankful for my mother's prescience.

It had been on her initiative that I added Art as an extra subject in the 'Leaving' and, sure enough, it delivered the crucial, fifth honour. This, mind, did nothing more than enable me to apply for a place at Thomond. I still had quite a few miles to travel.

From memory, there were 5,000 applications and 500 people interviewed that year for just 50 places. I was chasing a long shot. Even when I got called for interview there was no real sense of achievement. A friend of Dad's drove me down, the two of them chatting in the car for the whole journey in what I recognised as a pretty pointed tone. They were trying to soften the blow they presumed was coming.

'Jasus, Eddie, you'd be doing well to get into this place . . .'

'Yerra, you'd probably need some pull . . .'

The interview was essentially a series of tests, the first one psychological where applicants were given a quick reality check. A lot of people were trying to get into Thomond, just to pursue their sporting careers really. It had a certain cachet. Looking back, it was like Ireland's very own Fame Academy. So the people on the interviewing panel were mistrustful of a lot of people's motives. And probably with good reason.

The psychology lecturer cut to the quick immediately. 'Remember, if you get into this college, you are going to become a teacher,' he said. 'If you don't want to be a teacher, you should probably leave now!'

We went from psychology to oral Irish, then down to the pool to swim a length and into the gym for a variety of skill tests. Everything was fine, nothing terribly taxing. Then came time for gymnastics and, suddenly, I was in my element. I remember some of the other applicants looking at the mat as if it were a tangle of live snakes. I jumped straight on and started walking around on my hands. Then I did a cartwheel.

There were maybe 20 people in the room and, almost instantaneously, I felt I had nailed the thing. In the car on the way home, I genuinely sensed I would be getting a college place, even if my father was still trying to let me down gently. 'Listen, don't be getting your hopes up . . .'

I think it was about two weeks later that the letter arrived in the post. 'Eddie,' my mother shouted up the stairs, 'I think it's from Limerick!'

I charged down, suddenly fearful that my optimism might have been misplaced. But the news was good. Thomond had liked the handstand.

6

BOY TO MAN

If you judge a man by the company he keeps, I had become virtual royalty by the autumn of 1978.

Limerick changed everything in my rugby life. I even got a bird's-eye view of maybe the most lied about day in Irish sporting history, Munster's defeat of the All Blacks. Not alone did I sit on a wall in Thomond Park that celebrated November day (unlike most of the half million others who claim to have been there), I'd even watched Munster prepare the ambush.

It worked this way. In college, among those I befriended was Tony Ward. He was already well on his way to becoming a major international rugby figure, yet you'd never have known it from the way he dealt with people. 'Wardy' was likeable and utterly helpful and we would eventually come to share a house together.

To begin with, I was slightly in awe of him. He would make his debut for Ireland in the Five Nations of 1978 and over the next few years become one of the most recognisable faces in Irish sport. So he was probably the coolest guy on campus without ever giving the impression that he knew.

College life was wonderful. If you didn't have a class, there was always a game of five-a-side soccer available in the sports hall. But the syllabus was tough too. It was a four-year course with a big drop-out rate and, from memory, I think only 28 made it through from the beginning to the end of our class.

Along with physical education, I did physics, chemistry, maths and biology. It was a very heavy workload with continuous assessment while, physically, I was stretching myself to the full. With such a schedule, it was quite common for your system to get run down. I remember getting a huge boil on my knee that, once cleaned out, came to resemble a bullet wound.

But, above all, Thomond was a fun place to be and very tightly knit compared to other colleges. My friendship with Wardy pretty much developed from those five-a-sides. He was aware that I went home at weekends to play rugby for Youghal and took to enquiring about our results on Monday mornings.

At the end of my third term, he invited me to play in a sevens tournament at Garryowen. Thomond were entering a college team and reckoned they could make good use of my pace. We won the tournament, I got a bucket of scores and – at the presentation – I was approached by a Garryowen club official who had clearly liked what he'd just seen.

'Where do you play?' he asked me.

'Youghal.'

'Well, would you like to play for Garryowen?'

'I wouldn't mind.'

That was the beginning and end of the conversation. I thought nothing more of it. It was May and I went home to spend the summer fishing. Actually, nothing more was said until the following September when we returned to college and Wardy brought up the subject. He told me that Garryowen were genuinely interested, that the enquiry hadn't been flippant.

I wasn't fully convinced that I'd be able to make the step up to senior rugby, but the offer was being made and, if nothing else, it appealed to my vanity.

I decided to break the news that weekend when I went home to play for Youghal by going to our coach/captain, Paddy 'Boukie' Lane, before the game. Boukie immediately called for quiet in the dressing room. 'We've a bit of an announcement to make,' he said. 'Eddie's been invited to join Garryowen!'

The room erupted with applause. This was considered a great honour for Youghal RFC, a home-grown player joining the big boys. There wasn't an ounce of recrimination at me leaving. The vibe was universally warm and generous.

By now I had played in another Charity Cup match for Cork Counties, a representative honour for junior clubs. We trained for the game down in Barrackstown, Fermoy, as luck would have it, the same venue Tom Kiernan had chosen to train Munster for that game against the All Blacks.

I would travel down from Limerick on Wednesday nights with Pa Whelan and Larry Moloney, two of the Garryowen lads in Kiernan's squad. They'd do their session on one pitch, we'd do ours on another, directly adjacent. It felt slightly surreal, the conditions were so basic. The floodlights were poor and the grass always seemed a little higher than ideal.

There was a suspicion that Kiernan specifically wanted it that way. For a two-month lead-up to the game, he 'beasted' them over and back across that pitch in Fermoy. If Munster were going to be anything against the All Blacks, Kiernan was going to make sure they would be flying fit.

Driving to training, Pa and Larry would be going on about how hard Kiernan was pushing them. Through the session, they'd be looking across enviously at us juniors practising our 'skills' with the ball while they were being run into the ground. The two lads would be absolutely knackered for the drive home, Larry especially. He was a phenomenal athlete, who held

Munster schools records for sprinting and the long jump. But there was a view, too, that he could be lazy. Larry was a fullback who, it was joked, needed a written invitation to come into the line. When he did, mind you, he'd just turn on the gas and destroy you.

I played with Larry subsequently and he had the capacity to take your breath away with his acceleration.

There was, of course, a sense of utter disbelief when Munster managed to beat the All Blacks. I went in afterwards and met Wardy and Dave Mahedy in Jury's Hotel. People were, quite literally, walking around in a daze. The unbeatables had been beaten. Tommy Kiernan's plan had worked.

I had always gone home at weekends until I joined Garryowen but, now, I immersed myself in the social scene. We rented a house on Castletroy Park, myself, Wardy, Mahedy (who would train many teams to success in different sports over the years), Dave Phelan and Gerry O'Loughlin. Wardy and Mahedy, who were now in their final year at college, seemed almost joined at the hip. I pretty much took my lead from them, given they had a two-year advantage on me in terms of experience.

There was a real college atmosphere in the house, with plenty of parties. On Thursday nights, we might head for a disco at the NIHE (National Institute of Higher Education), stopping on the way at the Hurlers' bar. There were also regular discos held in the college sports hall.

All the years mixed socially and there were certain rituals. One decreed that, on your birthday, you got thrown into the pool. It was a lunchtime ceremony held virtually every day. Lectures would end at midday and some poor sap would be dragged down, kicking and screaming to the diving pit. The smart thing was to come in T-shirt and shorts, thereby limiting damage, though, latterly, this led to the victim simply being stripped naked.

The biggest mistake was not to bother showing up at all. Then, your locker would be placed at the end of the diving board and, of course, the only certainty about going out to retrieve it was that both you and your locker were going to end up in the sink.

Our house parties were raucous enough, though I never came across drugs of any type. I think people were too motivated athletically to be interested. Certainly, on a personal level, I was developing serious rugby ambitions.

In my first year at Dooradoyle, I was on the under-20s team, but struggled to make the seniors. And even with the 20s, I was consigned largely to the wing because of the presence of a bright young out-half called Greg Dilger.

I was getting frustrated. One of my difficulties, I felt, was that I had no pedigree. I hadn't come through the conventional route of Munster schools rugby. On a lot of occasions, I found myself vying for a place with a big, blond centre-wing who had starred for Rockwell and Irish schools called John Duggan. He was a golden boy. I was an upstart.

I expressed my frustration one night at training to Pa Whelan, the club captain. He reassured me that my chance would come. 'Yerra, just keep the head down . . .'

There was a kind of cyclical routine to that frustration. I'd be on the Garryowen senior team until January or February, then the old warhorses would come out of hibernation for the Cup. And, suddenly, a lack of experience would be rolled out as the reason for my omission. I felt I was in a 'Catch 22' situation.

During the Christmas holidays of 1978, two men from Sunday's Well called in to see me in Youghal. They had watched me play in that Charity Cup game for Cork Counties and seemed to know of my frustration now with Garryowen.

'Would you be interested in playing with Sunday's Well,' I was asked.

'Well I don't know, I'm in college in Limerick and . . .'

'Look, we're playing Terenure on Saturday, why don't you play for us at out-half?'

I agreed immediately. In a sense, I was being a little devious in that I wanted to put Garryowen on the spot. If they saw that there was a demand for my services, maybe they'd be more inclined to play me. And the game, after all, was just a friendly. There would be no paperwork. No registration. What was there to lose?

So I played for Sunday's Well at a frosty Musgrave Park that Saturday, scoring all their points (two penalties and two drop goals) in a 12–6 win over Terenure. I specifically remember a moment with the game winding down. We were 9–6 ahead and had just been awarded a scrum on their 22. I was feeling pretty bullish and told the scrum half to get the ball out to me as fast as humanly possible. He was having none of it.

'No, I'm going to have a cut here!' he said.

'Give me the fucking ball!' I roared. I just sensed that this was my moment. Everyone in the ground would have known I was going for the drop goal but, as far as I was concerned, nothing short of a stone mason with bricks, mortar and a few days to kill was going to stop that ball going over. And so it happened. I nailed the kick.

What I hadn't bargained for, however, was a report on the game carried in the following Monday's *Cork Examiner*. It was written by Charlie Mulqueen and carried a headline that clearly identified me as the star of the day. Alarm bells immediately began ringing in Garryowen.

I remember sitting down with my father and discussing the pros and cons of signing up with Sunday's Well. He was inclined to advise against it. I was still in college in Limerick after all. Where was the sense of travelling to Cork two nights a week for training when Garryowen was literally just up the road? Dad's logic was pretty bombproof.

Pa Whelan came to me too and told me I'd be playing the next match a few weeks later, ironically against Terenure in Dublin. There was an international on the day before that game and most of the team turned up at Lakelands badly hungover. I didn't. I arrived in the whole of my health, but still played poorly.

No matter, I decided to turn down the overtures from Cork. I'd stay and fight my ground with Garryowen.

I vividly remember my first senior game for Garryowen. I was playing on the wing against Old Crescent out in Rosbrien. For some reason, Wardy had what we used to call a 'brain fart' and decided to run the ball from practically our own line. I got put away around the 22 and just bolted like a horse from a burning building. I was 19 and running out of pure fear.

All I could hear over my left shoulder was the voice of Seamus Dennison (famous for a crunching tackle on Stu Wilson in 1978 that is still spoken of today) shouting 'Run you little fucker, run!'

I was kind of glancing back, looking to make a pass, presuming that someone would nail me. But no one did. I made it to the line, collapsed in a heap and, as I was picking myself up, there was the great Dennison to greet me with a bear hug. I was absolutely chuffed. I presumed he was about to tell me how well I'd done. But he just caught me by the collar and shouted, 'If I ever see you looking over your shoulder again, I'll kick you up the ass!'

For a few years now, I had been on a serious mission to bulk up. Because of my size, I knew I needed more ammunition and it was in that pursuit that PJ Smyth became an important figure in my life. PJ was a lecturer in rugby and athletics at Thomond. But he was also a sports psychologist. Pretty much from my first day at college, I became aware that this guy had a lot of interesting things to say.

By now, he had finished playing with Garryowen. But he was still a phenomenally fit guy who just had the gift of holding your attention. A few of us really came under his influence at

Thomond. He worked with us on individual skills, like side-stepping and swerving, and directed us towards the benefits of weight training and, latterly, plyometrics.

As a student, he had helped me with a weights programme but plyometrics, at the time, amounted to a little known secret used by a few coaches in Eastern Europe. As I began to establish myself at Garryowen, PJ introduced them into my training programme. I remember working on my own one summer in Galway and PJ brought me to see the national sprint coach, Ciaran Coakley.

He had a look at my running style and came to the conclusion that I was too high on the ground when sprinting. A specific plyometric bounding exercise was drawn up, essentially to reinvent me as an athlete. And the improvement was absolutely staggering.

I started scoring tries the following season that, sometimes, literally startled me. I was five foot six now and thirteen stone of muscle. And I could run a 4.4-second forty yards, which is NFL standard in America. As well as being able to run around people, I was now an extremely difficult target to get under.

The plyometrics transformed me as a rugby player. When I got the ball, I'd have only one thing on my mind – pin my ears back and head for the corner. I finished as leading try scorer in Munster that year with 28 in all competitions, my confidence absolutely soaring. I'd go into the sports hall with PJ and we'd set out crash mats. He'd be the cover tackler and I'd be trying to score in the corner. I'd be given less and less time, less and less space. It didn't matter. I always felt capable of scoring.

Garryowen were beaten in the first round of the Cup in 1980 and it meant our season was over at the end of March. So we decided to put together a sevens team, coached by PJ, captained by Wardy. There was a big tournament run annually in Limerick, which carried a first prize of representing Ireland at the Heineken Sevens in Amsterdam. That became our target.

The team to beat at the time was Waterpark. They'd won all the big sevens tournaments and, sure enough, we came to meet them in the final. It was a rout. We won 35-0, skating through the entire tournament without conceding a try. It was exhilarating to be part of it.

By the time I left college (1980) I felt I had become a serious athlete. My place on the Garryowen first team had been cemented, though I still knew I had plenty of road to travel. I had ambitions to play for Munster and, if the opportunity arose, possibly even for Ireland.

You see, at Dooradoyle, I had become used to the company of 'stars' like Wardy (though he had moved to Dublin now), Pa Whelan, Seamus Dennison, Larry Moloney, Willie Sexton and Mick Sherry. I wasn't in awe of anyone.

A rugby life in Limerick had taught me that I couldn't afford to be.

7

HOOP DREAMS

I never fulfilled my ambition to play rugby for Ireland, but the disappointment wasn't scarring.

I was a hard-hat player, a nine-to-five operator who knew what he had and understood the difference between it and a God-given talent. In many ways, I was a manufactured foot-baller. I became a very decent winger who, at my best, might have sneaked in for a couple of international caps if circumstances allowed. But we'd have been talking one or two, not a broad collection.

People like Trevor Ringland, Keith Crossan and Moss Finn were on the scene. Unless all three were hit by a meteorite, my chances were always going to be limited.

Remember, I had been an out-half most of my under-age career, but turned myself into a very fast, blocky runner. I had good foot skills and, between the weight training and plyo-metrics, pretty much managed to get the most out of what nature had given me.

With PJ as coach, Garryowen broke a 28-year famine by winning the Munster Senior League in 1982, beating a very strong UCC team that had internationals Donal Lenihan and the aformentioned Finn on board. The following season, we won it again, this time defeating Shannon in the final, with me scoring a controversial try. Just as I dived over in the corner, Irish international Colm Tucker hit me like a dumper truck. Tucker was one of the most athletic men I'd ever seen at the time, a man mountain with extraordinary talent.

I remember grounding the ball just as he arrived and the ball, flag, me, everything being tossed up in the air. The referee immediately gave the score which proved a cue for bedlam. There was feverish debate after about whether I had actually grounded the ball until the *Limerick Leader* hit the streets the following Tuesday evening with a photograph by Eoin South clearly showing me get the ball down.

I was probably at the peak of my powers by now and Garryowen's success catapulted me onto the Munster team. Yet, Munster then and now were two starkly different brands. Back then, they would play a mere handful of games a season, though those games – at least – tended to draw decent crowds. That said, my first cap was a brutally anonymous, short-lived affair, ten minutes against Combined Universities in Cork. I tore my hamstring and went down like a sack of potatoes.

The injury meant that I missed the first game of the Interprovincial Championship against Leinster, returning subsequently to play Connacht in Galway. This was a hell of a Connacht team, captained by Ciaran Fitzgerald and with internationals like Robbie McGrath and John O'Driscoll on board. They had already surprised Ulster in the Sportsground, so the normally spartan Galway venue would be absolutely heaving for the game.

We stayed the night before in the Corrib Great Southern Hotel and that was my introduction to the human force of nature, otherwise known as Moss Keane. Moss was a demolition

derby over dinner, throwing butter at people, constantly messing. If you threw something back, chances were he'd just
upgrade his weapons and return fire. And you're sitting there
thinking 'Where's this going, Moss?'

He wouldn't have known me from Adam at the time. I was a
complete greenhorn, he was a Munster, Ireland and Lions legend
about to make his final appearance for the province. All he would
have known about me was that I was new and almost certainly
worried.

Walking out of the dining room, he kind of startled me by
coming over.

'Where are you off to now?' he asked.

'Nowhere in particular, Moss.'

'C'mon, we'll go for a walk then.'

I'll never forget him for it. All he saw in front of him was this
young whippersnapper from Cork, but he knew that if I went
back to the room I'd just be playing the match over and over in
my head. So we walked down towards Galwegians and back
again, killing maybe an hour.

Moss didn't have to do that but it showed the man behind the
cartoon if you like. To this day, people just see him as this huge,
light-hearted figure who never takes anything too seriously. But
there is a depth and intelligence to Moss that he likes to obscure
in banter.

I scored one of the best tries of my career the following
afternoon, burning my opposite number – an Irish sprint
champion – on the outside. This was particularly satisfying as the
same individual had a rather high opinion of himself, so much so
he even gloated about a last-ditch, try-saving tackle made on me
in that Heineken Sevens final back in 1980. Yes, the one we won
35–0! So there was now just a hint of settling an old score.

The game had been on a knife-edge with about twenty
minutes remaining when Wardy ran a double-switch and put me

around the corner. I hit it on the money and scored in the corner. I remember looking up and seeing the touch judge, Mossie Moran, standing over me with both hands pinned behind his back. 'That's a good one,' he said.

It was the culmination of everything I had been working so hard on in the gym. I felt pretty much unstoppable at that moment. Connacht fell apart afterwards and we won by twenty points, Tommy Kiernan – to my great delight – stepping into the dressing room afterwards and declaring the try as good as any he had seen.

Our last game in that interpro series would be against a Jimmy Davidson-coached Ulster at Ravenhill. Jimmy was under massive pressure, as they'd followed up the humbling loss to Connacht with a defeat to Leinster. Had Ulster lost, Jimmy was almost certainly gone. But a Keith Crossan try with virtually the last play of the game secured victory and the coach's future.

Ulster actually won their first interpro title in nine years the following season and, incredibly, either won or shared every subsequent championship from there to the onset of professionalism in 1995. On the back of that success, Davidson would deservedly become Irish coach in 1988.

His Ulster team recorded a famous victory over Andrew Slack's Grand Slam Wallabies at Ravenhill in 1984. This was the all-singing, all-dancing side of Mark Ella, David Campese, Roger Gould and Michael Lynagh, so Ulster's 15–13 win was quite an achievement, especially given that none of the home nations managed to beat them on that tour.

In Munster, we had a 'cut' off them ourselves at a fog-enshrouded Thomond Park, but were all but blown off the park by the eccentric English referee Roger Whittington. I scored the first of our two early tries though, with visibility down to less than fifteen metres, it wasn't a score captured for posterity by any camera lens. Michael Kiernan just put a grubber kick through and I was onto it like a buzzard on a carcass.

The score was met by virtual silence as many people in the ground had absolutely no way of knowing we had even scored. In fact, running back after the touchdown, someone in the crowd asked me what had happened.

'We scored.'

'Who got it?'

'Me.'

John Barry got another try and, with Wardy landing a conversion, we should have been off to a flier. But Whittington was never off our case and four Australian penalties had us pretty frustrated. He was a notoriously fussy and finicky man, known for his perfectly combed hair, creased shorts, and starched collars.

There was one quintessentially Munster moment in the game as Gould was lining up an Australian kick at goal. He was a bit of a perfectionist, so the process took some time. While he was waiting, Whittington took out this pristine handkerchief and daintily blew his nose. Then he started fixing his hair. And a voice of lovely, raw Limerick mischief came knifing from the stand.

'Ah ref, you're gorgeous!'

You could have heard the laughter in Shannon and, in hindsight, maybe it didn't do us any favours. We lost the game 19–31 and one of the Australian tries should never have been awarded, the 'scorer' being held up by the combined efforts of Packie Derham and yours truly. Had there been a TV umpire available, he would have seen that the ball was actually touched down on Packie's head!

That said, it was a privilege to play against those players, particularly the jet-heeled Ella. The guy was absolute class. He didn't so much run as glide across the ground. Compared to the rest of us, he might as well have been on roller-blades and it wasn't long after that tour that he made the move to rugby league.

The previous year, I had got called up for an Ireland 'B' team that was butchered by Scotland at Melrose. That Scottish team had the Hastings brothers, David Sole, John Jeffries and Iwan Tukalo on board, the spine of a future Grand Slam team. They were far too strong for Ireland and I spent the entire game on the bench. Probably my good fortune.

Off the field, my life had taken on an entirely different complexion. Maybe six months after leaving college in 1980, I did a stint as PE teacher at the Vocational School in Tipperary Town. The position was available full-time but, to teach in a Tech, you needed to take an Irish exam, called 'Ceard Teastis'.

I hadn't taken it.

Before this, immediately after graduating, I had spent six months with Wardy trying to set up a health studio above his sports shop in Limerick. I was supposed to be manager, but it never quite got off the ground and, in the end, we parted company.

Failing to get the job in Tipp Town left me pretty much at a loose end until a chance meeting in Limerick one day with a guy from a year ahead of me in college, Eamonn McGinley. I had played rugby against Eamonn. He was teaching in Blackrock now and wondered what I was doing. I told him the grim truth.

'Nothing, I've got absolutely nothing!'

'There's a job going in a place in Galway!' he responded.

The PE job was in Mountbellew, which to me might as well have been on the far side of the moon. I had never heard of the place. It turned out another graduate from college had been appointed to the post on a probationary basis, only to then turn it down when a permanent position came up in Dublin. So I rang the school, the Holy Rosary College, a co-ed convent run by the Sisters of the Christian Retreat, a French order.

They had just been awarded a PE post by the Department of Education but, having been let down already, they were extremely sceptical about dealing with flighty college graduates. All the nuns in the school were Irish and the principal, a formidable woman from Kerry, was determined not to suffer fools.

I agreed to an interview in Ballinasloe and, in my ignorance of the geography, needed a bus and a train to get there. Still, the interview seemed to go well. The following morning, the nun rang me in PJ Smyth's office.

'I'd like you to take the job,' she said.

'Grand,' I responded. Deep down I was beginning to get second thoughts.

'Now you will take it, won't you?' she persevered.

'What do you mean?'

'Well I want your word that you won't pull out because, if you don't show, I will lose the appointment and the school won't have a PE teacher. So don't let me down.'

'I won't,' I said. 'I'll take the job.'

The following day, I got a phone call inviting me to interview for a PE job in Presentation College Cork. This would have been my dream destination. The power in Munster rugby at the time was very much in Cork. If I took the job in Pres, I'd almost certainly have played my rugby with Cork Con. And, given the politics of the time, playing with Con would have given me a better shot at an Irish cap.

I desperately wanted to go for it but, on principle, I couldn't. I had given my word to the nuns and my father's gospel kept ringing in my ears. 'You word is your bond,' he always said. 'Don't ever break it.'

So I was headed for Mountbellew, soon as I found it on the map.

I then went out and bought a Fiat 127, before getting a crash course on how to drive it from Liam Hennessy that Monday on the campus in Thomond. The following day, I set off on what felt like a great safari for the West, Liam delegating his brother, Deasun, to ride shotgun by my side. Just one snag. I had to collect Deasun in Cappawhite along the way.

This entailed leaving Limerick at six that Tuesday morning, picking up Deasun and driving across the mountains in a real pea-souper of a fog. In other words, my first day at the wheel turned out to be on a treacherous road in virtually zero visibility. It was absolutely nerve-racking, if not downright reckless.

It felt like it took the whole day before touching down in Mountbellew. I remember going into the school and introducing myself to the secretary, only to be told rather curtly, 'You're late for the staff meeting.' So I walked into this room, maybe sixteen teachers inside and introduced myself as the Holy Rosary's first PE teacher. The expressions I encountered suggested that they were underwhelmed.

The move to Mountbellew presented an immediate difficulty for my rugby career. I was still playing with and – to be honest – struggling for fulfilment with Garryowen. Now the front door of my digs in the West to Dooradoyle was exactly 78 miles, over largely tortuous roads. The journey would take me through New Inn, Bullaun, Loughrea, Gort and Ennis.

Back then, the club trained Tuesdays and Thursdays, the Tuesday session resolutely physical. I remember Garryowen captain Jerry O'Mahony coming to me and asking me if I was committed to the club for the coming season. I suspect they were just beginning to see potential in me. I told Jerry of my doubts about commuting from Galway and we managed to reach a compromise.

Jerry said, 'Look, we know you're a good trainer. What if we agree that you don't have to come on Tuesday nights. And we'll only expect you on Thursdays before a league match or if we're playing a team like Lansdowne or Wanderers in a friendly. The rest of the time, we'll trust you to train on your own.'

I agreed to stay on that basis, saying with a shrug, 'If you don't pick me, you don't pick me.'

Looking back, it was a close call. I genuinely did consider just packing in rugby altogether. With PJ at the helm, we then went on to have two momentous seasons at Dooradoyle, with successive League title triumphs. But then PJ left the club and went to America, furthering his studies at USC (University of Southern California). And the moment he went, Garryowen's back-play swung into dramatic decline. In fact, within a year of him leaving, our skill levels had plummeted, making it an increasingly solitary experience to play on the wing for Garryowen.

I would teach in Mountbellew from 1981 to 1988 and, to begin with, I have to say I enjoyed the distance between it and Dooradoyle. Limerick can be a very intense place to play rugby. Here, they barely knew about the existence of the Munster Senior League, let alone gave a damn about who won it.

I started off on a year's probation with the Holy Rosary and soon found that I didn't always see eye to eye with the principal, Sister Dympna. She actually indicated that it wasn't her intention to keep me beyond two years, but the then Minister for Education, Gemma Hussey, changed all the school quotas. It meant that the school was actually over quota now. In other words, if they let me go, they wouldn't get a replacement. Like me or not, Sister Dympna was now stuck with me.

I suspect her difficulty with me came from the fact that I immediately brought rugby onto the curriculum in a resolutely Gaelic football area. This clearly went against the grain. I was young and pushy, always peddling new ideas. Facilities were terrible in the school and, until now, PE had been a rudimentary one-hour shift on Wednesday afternoons.

The one thing the school did have was a wonderful basketball programme. It was run by a Clareman, Jerry Nihill, who was heavily involved in Irish teams and whose own son, Cian, has more than half a century of international caps today. We had no gym in the Holy Rosary, so the programme was run outdoors in the school yard and, if the weather was bad, out of a tiny facility the size of a Fiat Ritmo in the local Agricultural College.

The boys and girls trained together and, out of that programme, five boys and three girls went on to play Irish schools. One kid, Tommy Higgins, had been born in Philadelphia, but moved back to Mountbellew where the family had a garage. He went on to play basketball for Ireland and minor football for Galway.

Jerry put me in charge of the girls' programme. I had no basketball background, other than the knowledge taken from a pretty cursory, ten-week introductory programme at Thomond that taught the basic laws and systems of the game. But I was hungry to learn. And, crucially, I was inheriting a group of highly skilful kids who were equally hungry.

They trained with and played against the boys and, to put it mildly, the boys wouldn't cut them any slack. This really stood to them in competition, making the girls mentally tough. We played in the under-15 Connacht Championship which was run from two divisions, North and South. The two strongest schools were both in the South, ourselves and Mercy College, Tuam.

Mercy were strong and I always reckoned our best chance of beating them was in a one-off game. So we'd never show our hand against them in the South. We'd run bogus offence and defence systems knowing that we could afford to finish second in the South because we were always stronger than the best team in the North. In other words, unless we made a complete mess of things, we'd always be facing Mercy in the Connacht final.

It became a very intense rivalry but, for three years in a row, we beat them in the decider. You could see that this was getting to them. Mercy would always feel they had our measure in the

South, then it would come to the Connacht final and we'd bamboozle them with completely different offence and defence systems. The girls bought into this strategy totally.

We actually won the All-Ireland in 1983, beating a big, strong team from Dingle in the final at Sexton Street in Limerick. The Dingle girls considered themselves tough, but they weren't tougher than Mountbellew boys! And that was the barometer our girls used.

I remember calling time-outs to break Dingle's momentum that day. I knew if it was a pure game of basketball, our girls would win. Two of them could shoot the lights out. If we could find them in space, they'd make baskets. One of them, Fionnuala Gallagher, would go on to secure a Home Internationals title for Ireland with a magical last second play. Nothing she ever did surprised me.

The one thing I learned in basketball was that the coach could have a profound impact on a game. For that reason, you had to be aware tactically. You couldn't bluff it. The right tactical decisions could, literally, change the course of a game. You could open up opportunities by running particular offence systems. Defensively, you identified threats and worked a system to close them off. You had to put the right player in the right place to make the right shot. Jerry Nihill was a huge help in getting me up to speed. And the more I learned, the more I wanted to learn.

I remember thinking, We don't do this in rugby. We just run around with our hair on fire. 'Hurry up, lads, try harder. GET STUCK IN FOR FUCK'S SAKE!' We aped the GAA in that. We talked in clichés.

'Don't crowd the square, lads!'

'Let the ball do the work, lads!'

'Take the points, the goals will follow!'

All bullshit. Meaningless. Now here I was coaching under-15 girls in basketball, discussing whether we're playing against a 1-

3-1 zone, a 1-2-2 or a 2-1-2. Talking about a game in entirely logical terms, working out systems. And, for me, that was a kind of epiphany. We were identifying weaknesses in the opposition and designing game plans to exploit them

And I couldn't stop thinking to myself, I could make this work in rugby!

8

MONIVEA

The rugby missionary that is Padraig McGann came blowing into my life like a human storm.

I had found a place to live in Moylough, maybe three miles from Mountbellew. It was resolutely GAA country and a gentle, bucolic escape from the intensity of trying to win things with Garryowen. I loved that, the sense of two very separate threads running through my life.

Then Padraig tracked me down.

He had got my name from George Spotswood, in the Irish Rugby Football Union. George was head of development with the IRFU and would have had my details on file through club registrations. Padraig had heard I was living in East Galway and the night he came to my door, I can't say I was bubbling over with enthusiasm. But he had a gift for getting things done and never baulking at an obstacle.

'I'd like you to do a bit of a coaching for me!' he said, as if he was just asking for help to push a stalled car.

'Where?' I asked.

'Monivea!'

'Jesus, I'm playing with Garryowen, I'm on the fringes of the Munster team, I'm having to commute up and down to Limerick…'

'Listen, I don't care,' he said, impervious to the shriek of violins. 'We'll train whenever you're available.'

'But I do my own training on Tuesday nights and generally have to go to Garryowen on Thursdays and…'

'Doesn't matter, you tell us when and we'll be ready!'

'Em, OK.'

'And you might give us a hand with the mini-rugby on Saturday mornings!'

'Well that would depend on where I'm playing that day. I might be able to squeeze in the odd hour maybe…'

'That'll do.'

I couldn't say no. As I would discover with Padraig, it simply wasn't a word that existed in his vocabulary. And I'll never forget my first Saturday morning in his world. I drove up to this bleak, wind-exposed pitch on a hill above Monivea and stood there waiting for people to arrive. There wasn't a sign of human life anywhere. These, remember, were pre-mobile-phone days and you half got the feeling that you had become the butt of a practical joke.

Next thing, two antiquated old buses came spluttering up the hill and disgorged about 130 kids into the countryside. It was like the barbarian hordes descending. I watched them wash towards me and just two words came into my head. 'Holy fuck!' If I needed anything here, it was a couple of border collies.

Then McGann walked across with a fertiliser bag containing maybe five rugby balls and a load of two by one laths for markers. 'Off with you!' he said.

It turned out that he ran his buses all over the Monivea region, collecting these kids from every crossroads. They came because, after training, he'd bring them all back down to the village for a bottle of orange and a packet of crisps. Local people thought he was certifiable, this eccentric man selling his odd passion. But you'd have to be blind not to see he had something magical too.

I split the kids into groups and ran relay skills. Once I set them racing against one another, they were happy. I couldn't try to start a game of any sort because it would have been like trying to box water. So, to begin with, it was all a little chaotic. But, over time, we put a little structure to it. Padraig delivered more balls, more markers, even a few fellas to help me.

Monivea, at the time, had nothing. There was this little purpose-built set of changing rooms beside McGann's pub in the village, from where teams would drive the mile and a half up to the pitch.

But Padraig was a virtual evangelist. The very fact that he was running mini-rugby in a place like Monivea in the early 80s spoke volumes for his innovation. He was an extraordinary force of human will-power who believed in the notion of a 'Field of Dreams'. Build it and they'll come.

Monivea played in the Connacht Junior League and I would coach an under-16 team to the club's first silverware, the Connacht Cup. The out-half for that team was a big, raw-boned kid called Tomas Mannion who went on to win two All-Ireland Gaelic football medals with Galway. We built that team around him because he was virtually unstoppable with the ball.

I was dealing, essentially, with raw diamonds here. Most of the Monivea players were farmers. They were also, first and foremost, hurlers. And the problem with that was, if they got a decent run in the hurling Championship, I might not see them on the rugby field before Christmas. They were, however, hard and fearless and the hurling meant they had very good hand-to-eye co-ordination. And, though they had a poor concept of rugby technique, they had an inherent toughness that meant a little information could go a long way.

Once I taught them to tackle properly, we'd have car wrecks all over the pitch. They'd cut each other in two. These lads wouldn't start training for me until maybe 8.30 p.m. because they'd have been working the farm all day. And, to begin with, they might arrive into the field with a feed of bacon and cabbage on board. But, after a couple of nights depositing their dinners in a ditch, they got the message that a man couldn't really train properly on a full stomach.

I pushed them very hard. In fact, the more I explored their potential, the more excited I became about coaching and its possibilities. You see, I took it as a challenge to present the Monivea players with interesting sessions that made them want to come back for more. The alternative for them was to put their feet up on a cold winter's night. If I didn't get it right, that's exactly what they'd do.

Unfortunately, not everyone shared this enthusiasm for learning. Actually, the rugby led to a degree of tension in the local community. I became aware of a view in the parish that I was trying to pull the players away from hurling, which was tantamount to pulling devout Catholics away from the Church. One night I was having a pint in the village and one of the locals abused me from a height. It was made very clear to me that I was an 'outsider' who it was felt was harming the parish.

The attack shocked me. I honestly couldn't see anything negative in what I was trying to do with Monivea. On the contrary, the players' enthusiasm thrilled me. I remember one night after Christmas, the hurling championship over, having 47 guys at training. Conversely, I might have got no more than five at a session in mid-October.

My life with Garryowen had begun to unravel a bit through PJ's departure for America and, with it, any lingering notions that I might actually play for Ireland. Starved of possession on the wing, I began to realise – almost subconsciously – that my priorities were beginning to change. I was enjoying the teaching in Mountbellew and looked forward to few things more than pitching up for training at that big, gaping field on the hill in Monivea.

It was as if someone had flicked a switch in my head. By now, I was married. I had been teaching a karate class at night in the school and, in April of 1982, Noreen Mannion joined the class. We clicked immediately and, after a whirlwind romance, married that September.

It was like finding a soulmate. Noreen had little interest in rugby, but she became a massive support in my career. She claims that I turned to her one day and said, 'I don't think I'm ever going to play for Ireland but, one day, I'd love to coach them!'

In the end, the decision to take a break from Garryowen wasn't really traumatic. I had stopped enjoying my rugby. It was beginning to register that, maybe, there were things outside the game that could be every bit as fulfilling as chasing Munster Senior Cups.

One of them was music. Noreen comes from a very musical family. Her brother, Tomas, is a primary school teacher who can play virtually any instrument you care to name. Noreen herself is a talented harpist.

The family are probably best known for their pedigree in cycling. Noreen's father, Martin, was a household name through the 60s, winning events the length and breadth of the country. Four of his brothers, Paddy, Mick, Jim and Pete, followed suit and – for a time – the five Mannions were considered a pretty formidable team.

Martin, sadly, died a relatively young man from a heart attack, but he is still fondly remembered around the country. His widow, Mary – an extraordinary woman – would run the family construction company out of Moylough for roughly the next 20 years until Martin Jnr rook over. No mean achievement for a mother of six children in the 60s.

In 1979, Tomas put together a group of musicians from Moylough as a kind of challenge to the renowned Ceoltas Ceolteoiri Eireann who had a virtual monopoly at the time on international tours for traditional Irish music and dance. The Moylough group went on a tour of England, about 25 people in total, performing at Irish clubs up and down the country. In 1981, they expanded to do a tour of America, their ambitions steadily growing.

Two years later, they were going to America again and – with Noreen travelling – I would have loved to go. But – it being my first year involved with Munster – I had to stay at home. It was a no-brainer. Opportunities were beginning to open up for me in rugby. It would have been madness not to pursue them.

In 1985, however, they organised a two-month world tour, taking in Singapore, Australia, Hawaii and America. I'd been an interpro for two years now and reality was beginning to bite. I realised the dream of an international cap was pretty much already gone. And I suppose, deep down, I had begun to feel a little disenfranchised.

The tour felt like the opportunity of a lifetime and I just decided to take a year out of rugby. I remember the traditional letter arriving from the Munster Branch, enquiring about my availability for the season. It was one of those letters a player usually responded to on automatic pilot. You ticked the 'yes' box.

But this time I ticked 'no' and, within days, had Munster chairman of selectors – Benny O'Dowd – on the phone to me. Benny was completely at a loss as to how anyone would actually make themselves unavailable to play for their province. I told him my reasons and. from the tone of his voice, I could deduce that he was less than impressed.

As well as being a roadie on tour, I played a bit of bodhran. Now I'm well aware that real musicians wouldn't regard this as a musical instrument. I've often heard it said that the best way to play a bodhran is with an open-ended penknife. But I loved the buzz of the performance and, while my main job was to ensure that all of the equipment got safely from one venue to the next, playing the bodhran on stage with so many genuinely gifted musicians was a massive high.

We played two concerts in Singapore, then on to Perth, Adelaide, Melbourne, Sydney, Brisbane and Hawaii. After that, we had a stack of dates in America – San Francisco, Los Angeles, San Diego, Seattle, Chicago, Philadelphia, Austin and Dallas. The first part of the show had a mythological dimension, part of it called 'The Battledance'. The second was, essentially, just one, long, riotous *seisun*.

In Chicago, Michael Flatley came to see the show. He'd just been crowned the world Irish dance champion and came on stage to perform with us. You could see, immediately, that the guy had phenomenal talent. The next time I saw anything close to what he produced that night in Chicago was the interval act at the Eurovision Song Contest in Millstreet, the night Riverdance was born.

I had to take leave of absence from my teaching job to do the tour as the Department of Education was very rigid at the time. You had to be almost on your knees, praying they wouldn't penalise you for loss of service. So it meant taking a financial hit, one that – being honest was worth every single penny. That tour proved the experience of a lifetime.

Having taken a break from Garryowen, I effectively became player-manager with Monivea, which, though it meant the plunge into junior rugby, enabled me to become even more hands-on than before. It also meant I could start playing out-half again, running the show and having some fun.

My first year playing for Monivea, we got to the Connacht Junior Cup final. Our semi-final was against Galwegians who, traditionally, would have seen Monivea as little more than road kill. A lot of their team had been regraded from senior, so they wouldn't have seen a lot of our lads having any business being on the same pitch. They beat us up hill and down dale the same day, but just couldn't transfer that dominance to the scoreboard.

Leading by three points in the dying seconds, they had a scrum in front of our posts. It was, almost certainly, the last play of the game and their out-half – one Eric Elwood – just needed to hump the ball into the next field. But Eric was no more than nineteen at the time and imbued with the fearlessness of youth. He decided to go for a drop goal.

I saw him slip back into the pocket, immediately read his intentions and – BANG – nailed him. I picked up, popped the ball to the one real flier in our team, Pat Blade, and he ran 80 yards to score under the sticks. Bingo. Monivea were in the final where Creggs would be our opponents.

To beat Creggs, I knew we needed a dry day. Sadly, we didn't get one.

It just bucketed down on the Sportsground that day and a real grind of a game closed out at 3–0 in their favour. I was gutted. We had constructed a decent backline at Monivea, but we needed a dry ball to make it count. Padraig had lured the Connacht prop Pat McGrath back from Wegians to play in that Cup campaign with us and I'll always remember his observation, 'Jasus, O'Sullivan, you've that backline humming!'

The Blade brothers were a key part of it, Pat on the wing, Johnny in the centre. That day in Galway, Johnny kept coming to me, complaining that he needed a drink. He was saying that his mouth was very dry. Actually, I remember him asking me at one point if I had any sweets that he could suck on.

And I'm there saying, 'Jesus, Johnny....'

Maybe three weeks later, he was playing a county hurling championship match for Monivea in Athenry. A blistering hot day and he's at corner forward. Johnny spots a bottle of water behind the posts, walks over to get a drink and collapses. They said he was dead in seconds.

It always struck me that Johnny might just as easily have had the heart attack that day we were playing Creggs. He was your quintessential hard, country hurler. He would, literally, go through a wall for you. Actually, chances are he wouldn't even notice the wall. In a sense, I think I was a little in awe of people like Johnny Blade. I mean I always thought I was reasonably tough on a rugby field. But I was nothing compared to these guys.

The Monivea boys brought this natural physicality to everything they did. I remember having to hold guys back at training because they'd be literally hurting each other. The key was keeping things under wraps, then 'releasing the hounds' on Sunday. I loved working with them because they were so genuine. They'd question nothing. They just assumed you had the answers and, so, took on board anything that I'd say. To that extent, they were a coach's dream.

It turned out that Johnny Blade had a heart defect he knew nothing about. A brother of his, Tomas, would die the same way many years later. When I think of the players I would coach across the years, I can't say I ever came across a more genuine, open-minded group than those Monivea juniors.

And, over time, my work with them got me noticed in higher places. Around 1984 a development officer's job came up within the IRFU. I applied, was granted an interview, thought I did well, but the job was offered to an Ulster man, Willie Gribben. I found the experience quite intimidating. There had been maybe eight guys on the panel, among them Tommy Kiernan.

As it happened, Willie decided not to take the job, discouraged

– I think – by the need to move to Dublin. And his decision led to me being offered the position. One of the conditions of the job was that you'd have to give up playing and, on that basis, I had pretty much decided it wasn't for me anyway. I just wasn't ready to hang up the boots.

As it happened, I hadn't entirely cut my ties with Garryowen. Actually, I went back playing with them for a season in 1986. They were at a pretty low ebb, which probably explains why they came looking for me to play number ten. We got to the Centenary Cup final against Shannon, a fair achievement given our predicament at the time.

In the semi-final, we beat Young Munster in a game we had no business winning. With almost 80 minutes up on the clock, it seemed a small miracle that we were still within striking distance. From memory, we were three points down, facing into a scrum in the middle of the pitch. Referee Johnny Cole from Shannon told me afterwards that he had decided to blow the next time the ball went dead.

The ball squirted out of the scrum into my hands, I set up a ruck and the ball was moved swiftly to our left winger, Mervyn Long. Mervyn went bolting down the wing, then did this crazy cross-kick into the middle of the field. I was chasing like a dervish and, freakishly, the ball bounced up over the head of their covering centre, interpro Francis Brosnan (all six foot five of him), into my hands and I put Ger Griffin in under the sticks.

Shannon thumped us in the final with my good friend Niall O'Donovan playing at number eight. To this day, I joke with him that I still have the stud marks all over from the number of times he just ran over me from the back of the scrum. That Shannon team had a fantastic, controlling scrum half, Sonny Kiely. He played like another flanker and, with Niallo at eight, they were a formidable combination. The ball hardly ever went beyond them.

The joke used to be, 'When is Sonny going to stop kicking the ball?'

'When Niallo learns how to!'

In 1988, my last year before breaking away from teaching, two more development officers' jobs came up within the IRFU. I didn't really pay any heed, though I at least knew I was now on the Union's radar. That summer, I had been invited up to King's Hospital to help run a youths' week with Willie Anderson, John Murphy – the new development officer – and Ray Coughlan. The week was very much a reactive strike by the Union as rumour had been floating around that Tony Ward and Bill Beaumont were ready to set up a summer camp of their own in Dublin.

The idea of individuals actually making profit out of rugby in Ireland was anathema to the Union. They were determined to see it off at the pass. The week in King's Hospital was well received, maybe 150 kids of all ages being coached from dawn till dusk. Actually, it was during the same camp two years later, at Clongowes Wood, that I first set eyes on a cocky, young, blond-haired kid called Ronan O'Gara. He could almost make the ball talk and was out on the pitch this beautiful evening, a fourteen-year-old running the show, pulling all the strings, cocky as you like.

And I remember saying to Anderson, 'Willie, if that little fella doesn't play for Ireland, we've done something very badly wrong as development people.'

After King's Hospital, I was asked if I might make a presentation at a Munster Branch coaching course in Limerick two weeks later. Certain wheels were beginning to turn.

That course ended with a dinner in the Glentworth Hotel at which Tommy Kiernan, the President of the Munster Branch, suggested to me that I go after one of the development jobs with the Union. I was unconvinced. I knew I would have to request a career break from the school and I couldn't be confident how that would be received. But when someone like Kiernan was recommending....

I went to the principal the following day, presuming that she would be hostile to the idea. To my amazement, she wasn't and I put in an application. Eventually, three of us were appointed, myself, Anderson and Declan O'Leary. I was given responsibility for developing the game in Connacht and North Munster, which would involve visiting schools and clubs, helping coaches.

The Union supplied each one of us with a Ford Orion car as we'd be on the road seven days a week. To me, it was a job made in heaven. I jumped in with both feet.

Around this time, I was still mucking around as a player with Garryowen, though very much in wind-down. In 1989, I moved to Corinthians in Galway but never enjoyed it there. I found myself, essentially, on the outside of a clique and it began to dawn on me that I was getting far more pleasure from the coaching side of the game.

There was also the fact that Katie was born that December. I had been a bit of a road-warrior for a long time now and my priorities were changing. Funnily enough, I had been capped by Connacht that September, called up as an eleventh-hour option on the wing to play Scottish Districts at the Sportsground. We were duly hammered.

That Christmas I decided to retire as a player. There was a GOAL charity match in Corinthians on St Stephen's Day and I just told them afterwards that I wouldn't be togging out again. It was a completely unemotional decision. Just a case of 'Thanks for the use of the hall, I'm out of here!'

My work as a development officer was now beginning to open doors for me. I had been taken on as fitness advisor for the Irish under-21s, coached by Johnny Moloney with Ciaran Fitzgerald as his assistant. And I had also written a manual for the IRFU, called 'Fitness for Rugby'.

It was around this time, too, that a larger-than-life figure first stepped into my world. The All Blacks were touring Ireland and I had gone in to Corinthians, to watch them train on the eve of their game with Connacht. I got talking to this guy about the upcoming game and Irish rugby in general. It struck me immediately that he had a voracious appetite for information.

George Hook was, at the time, assistant Connacht coach. One year later, he was offering me a job.

9

THE WEST

Billy Glynn's plan was maybe too good to be true.

He was talking a twin-track approach for Connacht and Galwegians, with me at the helm of both. For the first time, Galway would have an authentic AIL team, capable of competing in Division One. There was talk of selling Glenina (Galwegians' home pitch) and building everything up from the ground again. New team, new facilities, new ambitions.

Having coached Blackrock in Dublin for four years and finding myself spending more and more time away from home, I was easily seduced. The option had been there for me to give 'Rock another year but I was getting to spend just one day a week in Moylough. I'd arrive home late on Thursday night and be gone again early Saturday morning. My family life was virtually non-existent.

Returning to the west would also enable me to resume teaching in Mountbellew, where my leave of absence was now elapsing. It made sense on every level.

This was 1995 and the dawn of professionalism. No one really had a clear sense of where the game was heading and virtually the whole rugby community seemed to be playing a guessing game. For the first time, players would be paid to play for Connacht, though the coach's position remained amateur. I left 'Rock on good terms and, to this day, have good friends there. But the thought of starting some kind of rugby revolution in Galway was simply too tempting to reject.

Glynn's ambitious vision, sadly, never really got off the ground.

The proposed investment into Galwegians didn't materialise and, on a personal level, I never felt accepted in the club. Why? I honestly don't know. I was just never comfortable there. Even in the bar after games, other than players talking to me, I found myself pretty isolated. Maybe it had something to do with the fact that I had spent a few months of my playing career with Corinthians.

Results didn't help. We lost most of our games in Division Two, albeit usually by a single score. The reality was that we had a very, very average team. One of our locks, John Dillon, had played Gaelic football for Galway in the 70s. He was now in his mid-forties. The other second row I had lured out of retirement. As with Buccaneers, our out-half, Eamonn Molloy, was actually an inside-centre. Our results reflected our resources, though we did win the Connacht Senior Cup in April 1996.

The only real pleasure in the job for me came from the training sessions. Every night we'd have up to 35 players training in Glenina, good guys eager to learn and utterly indifferent to the cliques in the clubhouse.

With Connacht, we did record one pretty memorable victory against Fiji in the Sportsground. It was a game we approached with apprehension, given the steady drain on our resources back to London and Leinster. We were basically on our knees. This was November of 1995 and I remember John Callinan, Chairman of the Connachct Selectors, was so concerned about our prospects that he proposed changing the fixture to one involving a Connacht President's XV, whereby we could invite players in from outside.

There was a fear that we could get absolutely destroyed and embarrass the province. But I reckoned inviting 'outsiders' in could damage morale when it came to contesting the interpros. It would give the wrong message.

The game was on a Tuesday and we assembled in Galway on the Friday night. We trained all day Saturday, Sunday and Monday. Fiji were probably the best running team in the world at the time, so we came up with a game plan to maul everything. When the forwards were finished mauling the ball, the backs would maul it further. When they were finished, they gave it back to the forwards.

It was an off-the-wall gameplan, but we had to have something to keep the ball out of their hands.

I remember Eric Elwood came into camp, having just been dropped off the Irish team. He had been told rather undiplomatically the reason for his demotion was that he 'couldn't move a backline'. Now I was telling him that the last thing I wanted to see him do was pass the ball!

On the morning of the game, I pulled back the curtains in my room in the Great Southern Hotel and you could see there wasn't a ripple on Galway Bay. The sun was spilling down out of a perfect sky. And all I could think was: Bugger, we could get butchered here!

But, by lunchtime, the day had changed. The clouds rolled in and the rain started coming down in stair rods. And we just mauled Fiji into the Galway mud, beating them 25-5 for Connacht's first victory over a touring international team.

For some reason, around this time, there had been a paradigm shift in the IRFU's attitude towards me and I was also invited to coach the Ireland under-21s. In fact, the day after that defeat of Fiji, I was on an early morning flight to coach the under-21s to victory against England at Northampton. This was a big thing. There was no pay involved, just the privilege of doing the job. I almost bit their hands off. Galwegians saw it as a bit of an honour too, so there were no apparent negatives. At least, there shouldn't have been.

We would win Ireland's first under-21 Triple Crown, sealing the deal by beating Wales in Wicklow with a team comprising future senior internationals like Malcolm O'Kelly, Kieron Dawson, Justin Bishop, Conor McGuinness, Brian O'Meara and Denis Hickie. But I ran into trouble when one of the squad sessions in Dublin clashed with a Connacht League match. Galwegians lost that game to Corinthians and my absence triggered fury within Glenina.

I had told the club in advance that my international commitments would mean me missing some games, but never an AIL fixture. To me, the Connacht League wasn't exactly big potatoes. Trouble was, they'd lost to Corinthians, an unpalatable fate at the best of times within the club. People were screaming for my blood.

I was brought for coffee one morning by John Sherry, the chairman, and essentially given a bollocking. This just compounded my sense of not being quite accepted at Glenina. Maybe I was reading too much into things, but I just didn't feel people were on my side.

George Hook, meanwhile, had reinvented himself in America. He was trying to develop a coaching programme for the US Union and came to me in a bit of a panic. He knew I had experience of running clinics for the IRFU and wanted me to design a 'level one' coaching course for America. I showed him how to do it and the following season he brought myself and a guy called Bartley Fannin out to the US to help him do some coaching.

By now a decision had been made to appoint provincial

directors in Ireland and it seemed I was a shoo-in to get the job with Connacht. I was in regular contact on the phone with Glynn, looking to agree a deal. But the money being offered was poor. They were basically willing to pay me pretty much the same as I was getting as a PE teacher.

My argument was simple. I had already turned down an offer from Ulster and, if I was going to leave teaching, I could hardly gamble all on taking a one-year coaching job for the same money. It was time to choose – teaching or full-time rugby – and I told them I needed a three-year contract. To begin with, the soundings coming back were positive. I came home from America pretty confident the deal was done, only to be called to a meeting with Glynn, Treasurer Eamonn Feeley and President Willie O'Flynn. Again, I argued my case. Again, I thought I had agreement.

Then I got a phone call from Feeley. 'It's one year or nothing,' he said.

'Then it's nothing!' I replied.

This left me in a pretty invidious position. I was already in Dublin with the Connacht squad, due to fly out the next day to Sweden on tour, and I now felt I had no option but to resign. Glynn was effectively the Connacht team manager and I was communicating with him largely down the telephone line from the study of George's home in Foxrock. So I rang and told him my decision.

The next day, I broke the news to the players at the Skylon Hotel, not really knowing where it left them. Little did I realise that, thousands of miles away in Hamilton, New Zealand, Warren Gatland was already packing a bag.

The story goes that, after his meeting with me, Glynn went walking down the street, bumped into Galwegians clubman Joe Healy, told him his news and the two immediately went into informal emergency conference there and then on the pavement.

And lo and behold, a light went on in Joe's head that prompted him to spit out the immortal words, 'What about Gatty?'

Warren had done a good job in a previous stint with Galwegians and, I knew, was well liked within the club. It was hard to believe that Warren was able to simply hop on a flight and head for the training camp in Sweden without being given some advance notice of his employment but that's reputedly what happened.

The day after I rejected Connacht's offer, I got a phone call at home from Galwegians to say that I was surplus to requirements at Glenina too. The call was made by Mick Deasy, a cousin of Bobby, the then President of the IRFU. It lasted no more than fifteen seconds.

'Eddie, this is Mick Deasy here!'

'Howya, Mick?,'

'We've just had a committee meeting and decided we no longer need you to coach Galwegians.'

'Cheers, Mick.'

End of conversation. Within 24 hours, I was out of both jobs. Bobby Deasy has always vehemently denied he had anything to do with it and who was I to confront the President of the IRFU? Now, my only remaining toe-hold in Irish rugby was coach of the under-21s. I remember putting down the phone to Mick Deasy, turning to Noreen in the kitchen and saying, 'I've just got fired from Galwegians!'

She was shocked. I wasn't. What I felt was pretty deep hurt. The first I knew of Warren's appointment would be when I heard it on the radio the following day. And all I could think was: 'Well doesn't that just stack up very conveniently?'

On reflection, I think Gatty's shadow was always over me at Galwegians. Maybe it's why I felt an outcast. It didn't help, admittedly, that we only won two AIL games in my season as coach there. On reflection, we were lucky that there was no relegation out of Division Two at the time. But anyone with eyes in their head could see that the playing talent just wasn't there. The promised investment had never happened.

Some weeks after my departure as Connacht coach, I went in to the Sportsground to watch them play Leinster. I did so in my capacity as Ireland under-21 coach as one of the 21s, Richie Governey, was playing out-half for Leinster. Connacht won again, just as we had done two years previously. Except, of course, this time Gatty was the hero.

I was standing behind the road-end goal, chatting to a now retired Noel Mannion. A photographer from the *Connacht Tribune* took a picture of the two of us there in the bitter cold, car headlights in the background. And the paper used it that week over a caption 'Out in the Cold'. Pretty much how I felt.

Still, that Christmas of 1996, I got a call to work with the touring Eagles in Wales as a consultant coach. I had been recommended to the head of US Rugby, Jack Clark, two years earlier by Tom Harty in Blackrock. Tom was assistant liaison officer to 'Locky' Butler for the Americans when they toured Ireland in 1994 and, apparently, described me to Jack as this 'lunatic coach' who watched games from the roof of the 'Rock clubhouse.

Suitably intrigued, Jack asked to meet me. He was always on the lookout for coaches and, as he puts it, made a 'mental note' after linking up with me in the Burlington Hotel a couple of days before the Eagles played Ireland.

I was happy to go to Cardiff now. It meant heading straight down to Dublin from an under-21 squad session in Belfast and flying to Wales where I would ring in the New Year with the American team.

It was an experience that stood to me long-term as Clark liked what he saw and, realising I wasn't exactly submerged under offers of work in Ireland, started pulling the strings to get me contracted into the US game.

It couldn't have happened at a better time because I had a bad second year as under-21 coach. We did turn it around in the end with a dramatic, last-minute victory against Clive Woodward's England in Greystones. But a more physically mature French team had beaten us easily and Wales, with twelve survivors from the year before, kicked the living crap out of us. Beating England through David Wallace's last-second try salvaged a bit of pride, but it wasn't exactly front-page news.

It was also a bit of a smash-and-grab job. We got two tries basically in the last five minutes to steal it, Richie Governey kicking the winning conversion on the buzzer. One of our scores, though, was wonderful, a line-out win on halfway and the team basically mauling England all the way into their in-goal area.

That was a good England team. Woodward, in fairness, had some really nice wrinkles in his game. They asked questions of us that day and, only right at the death, had we found the answers.

I remember that day specifically for the frustration of Simon Easterby at not being able to line-out. He was a real stand-out player but the AC joint in his shoulder had separated on club duty with Harrogate and he came to camp injured. The poor guy was in tears he was so desperate to play. 'Give me an injection, anything!' he was saying.

Even our victory didn't really console him. You could see that in the dressing room. The celebrations went right over his head. To him, he had just missed out on what would have been one of the greatest days of his life.

Easterby would become a real warrior in an Irish jersey over the next few years. A man for the trenches. He thought nothing of putting his body on the line and I can't think of any player more highly thought of in the Irish dressing room.

Funny, nine years later when we beat England at Twickenham in their first home game as World Cup winners, I remember walking around the dressing room shaking players' hands, congratulating them. Easterby's head was down from pure exhaustion.

I put my hand on his shoulder. He looked up and said, 'That makes up for Greystones!'

The Union had, by now, been advertising full-time provincial directors' jobs and I applied for all four. But it was made clear to me that Gatland would get the Connacht job and I was aware that the other three provinces were all pretty settled on who they wanted. It seemed obvious that I wasn't on anyone's wish list.

So the day after that England game, I rang Ray Southam – a New Zealander working as the IRFU's Director of Rugby – and told him I was withdrawing my applications. Maybe it was belligerence on my part, but I wanted to make a point. Southam sounded shocked.

'Do you mind me asking why?' he asked.

'Because I'm off to America!'

'You're doing what?'

There was this pregnant pause. Had I said I was taking a bicycle into space to do a lap of the moon, he might have found it more believable. I suspect he thought I might actually have been making it up. England were playing Ireland at Lansdowne Road that day, but I was in my car headed for Moylough.

Jim Glennon was the under-21 manager and I had told him over breakfast that morning. Just two of us in the dining room. 'Jim, you might as well know, I'm going to America.' His expression had mirrored Southam's tone. He seemed incredulous.

'Fair play to you,' he said eventually, 'for taking such a leap of faith.'

We still had one game to play and our last outing of the championship (and my last as coach) was against Scotland in Watsonians. Governey, our out-half, had played so well against

England, he was promoted to the Ireland 'A' team, who were due to play immediately after us. So I gave Ronan O'Gara his first under-21 cap. I'd seen him play with Cork Con and believed he was the real deal.

We absolutely demolished the Scots, ROG giving a masterclass. With the backing of the wind in the first half, he kicked brilliantly into the corners and opened up the Scots with some sublime passing. Turning into the teeth of a gale for the second half, he kept everything tight, massaging the pack up the field with his kicking. This was a real 'old head on young shoulders' performance and it made for a wonderful result for me to finish on. By now, the players knew I was headed for America.

The following day, Ireland – coached by Brian Ashton – took their ritual pummelling at Murrayfield (we had now gone thirteen years without a win there). It was a miserable, wet, wind-lashed day and we encountered severe turbulence that night on the flight home. ROG was sitting next to me and, as we began a fairly hairy descent into Dublin, he was asking me about the US.

'Are you looking forward to it?'

'Well, it's a pretty good opportunity for me.'

'Do you know where I was born?'

'Where?'

'San Diego!'

'You're kidding.'

'No, technically I could play for America!'

'Jesus,' I said, laughing, 'I'll have to keep that in mind.'

10

BUCCANEERS

We were a perfect fit, the mavericks and the outcast.

Buccaneers sprang into my life with startling impact just after I returned home from my first season in America. A phone call from Gerry Kelly, now CEO of Connacht. Would I like to ride a rollercoaster?

It was 1997, winter looming. With little or no overlap between the seasons in America and Europe, I could effectively do two jobs without any conflict of interest. Buccaneers had just been promoted, undefeated from Division Three of the AIL and celebrated by hunting their New Zealand coach out of town. He wanted them to run the ball. The players reckoned it would be more profitable to keep it up their jumpers. Artistic differences.

Buccs were just three years old as a club, an amalgamation of Athlone and Ballinasloe. They represented a philosophy utterly alien to some of the stuffier houses of Irish rugby. I chuckle these days when I hear Pete St John's ballad about the Great Irish Famine, 'The Fields of Athenry', being declared a Munster rugby song.

It isn't. It's stolen property.

When Buccs won, we'd lock the doors of the dressing room and bawl out a rendition of 'The Fields', the chorus being picked up by supporters outside. It would be defiantly loud and raucous. These boys weren't just challenging tired stereotypes in Irish rugby. They were pitching old-school arrogance on its head.

I was delighted to take up the baton with them, if only because it would keep me visible at home. The American project was big and exciting. But it was an obscure, unseen world as far as the people who mattered in Irish rugby were concerned. I did know that Eddie Coleman, later to become President of the IRFU, was in the habit of ringing George Hook to see how I was getting on.

Eddie, for some reason, seemed to have it in his head that – if I never came back – I would be a loss to Irish rugby. In time, I would have reason to be grateful for his interest.

Funnily, for someone who had left the country feeling unwanted, I now seemed to have become viable currency again. Just after arriving home, I got a call from Dion Glass, inviting me to become Ulster coach. One year earlier, Ken Reid had made pretty much the same phone call.

In both instances, I had to say no. When Reid rang, I felt I had a commitment to Connacht. Now I had to tell Glass that I'd signed a contract with US Rugby. I liked Dion. He was an IRFU committee member and I knew that Ulster were going through a difficult transition. He wondered would I even consider giving them a dig-out for a few months while they pursued a new coach.

I couldn't. I'd been away from home for six months and the idea of setting up base in Belfast was just unthinkable now.

The Buccs offer, though, ticked all the right boxes. It was virtually on my doorstep – maybe half an hour from Moylough to Athlone – and wouldn't interfere with my American commitments.

We trained Tuesday and Thursday nights on a uniquely wet

pitch at the front of the old clubhouse. It was probably the only pitch in the world where water ran up a hill. The higher you went, the wetter it got. Training would start at 8.15 p.m. because the Rigney brothers were coming from Portlaoise and a few others from Galway.

They were predominantly strong men who knew where they wanted to go. With the Rigneys, Noel Mannion, Joe McVeigh, Jimmy Screene, Martin Cahill and Eoin 'Tayto' Brennan, Buccs had the makings of a great pack. My assistant was Davy Henshaw, a brilliant guy who had played tighthead for me with Connacht. I quickly realised that the differences the players had with their former coach had been actually well founded. Buccs didn't have a backline. They had a seven-man Band-Aid.

Put it this way, if I had gone in there with the same game plan I used at Blackrock, we would have been wiped out. At 'Rock, we had so much talent behind the scrum, we ran everything. It was exhilarating, even if the weather would cost us two All-Ireland Leagues.

But the 'Buccs' backline was all round pegs in square holes. Our out-half, Eamonn Molloy, was actually a solid inside-centre. Our backs coach, Ciaran Slevin, was playing in the centre. We had one flier of a winger, Mick Devine, who we tended to lean heavily on. Mick was from Shannonbridge, a smart footballer I'd worked with at Connacht and a guy I always considered underrated.

Actually, in my first year with Buccs, I saw him do something that I'd never seen before and certainly haven't seen since. We were playing Terenure and he ran right up to and around Girvan Dempsey with some remarkable footwork.

Mick's younger brother, Cormac, was pretty much one of the Buccs' family. He was a smashing kid, maybe 14 at the time and absolutely rugby mad. He came to all our games and would be down on the touchline trying to work out opposition line-out calls so that he might give me some useful information for the half-time talk.

Cormac played rugby with Garbally College and lived for the game. But, one day in training, he collapsed and died. It happened about five in the evening and, by the time this devastating news reached us, we knew that Mick was already in his car on the way down to training from Dublin.

I will never lose this image of him pulling into the car park. Normally the place would have been a hive of activity but, this night, everyone was just sitting in the dressing room numb.

Mick got out of the car, sensing immediately that something wasn't right.

'What's wrong, are we not training?' he asked.

We brought him inside and told him that Cormac had been taken ill at school, that he was in hospital in Galway and we were bringing Mick straight there to see him. We felt we just couldn't tell him the awful truth. But halfway in the road to Galway, there was no longer any need. Everyone's body language reeked of tragedy.

Mick got agitated. 'Lads, tell me the fucking truth here.' And they did.

Our game that weekend was cancelled but, two weeks later, we faced Galwegians in a top-of-the-table-clash. Deep down, I don't think anyone had really regained an appetite for rugby. Cormac's loss just left a gaping hole. No one's heart was really in this.

Yet there was a context to this game and it couldn't be ignored.

Buccs were a very well-run club, though still new and rough around the edges. There was great energy in the place. Their facilities are wonderful today but, back then, they were demonstrably outsiders. The new clubhouse had yet to be built and the old one was a bit of a bomb shelter.

We had one professional player, Mark McConnell, on

contract from the Connacht Branch. Galwegians had fourteen. It was like being part of a stubborn revolution, the authorities just about accepting us on sufferance. We were the poor relations, the rest of the world pitted against us. And I suppose I liked that. I certainly sensed that, because of my own history with Connacht and Galwegians, I was now seen as a bit of an anti-Christ coaching Buccs.

You will gather, then, there were palpable tensions. McConnell had broken a bone in his foot and, thus, only became available to us later in the season. He was living in Galway, so I sat him down one night in the club with Gerry Kelly and asked him to move to Athlone. The following day he rang to say that, not only was he not moving, he was transferring to Galwegians.

The problem was that all of his mates in Galway were Galwegians people who'd have seen us as having horns and a tail. It got so heated that Noel Murphy, an IRFU committee member, had to come to Athlone one night to try to resolve the issue. A deal was eventually brokered that he would stay with Buccs. But continue living in Galway.

By the time the Galwegians game came around, McConnell was ready to play. He was actually a terrific second row who would probably have been capped for Ireland down the line had he not sustained a serious knee injury. I decided to bring him straight in, dropping Donal 'Plugs' Rigney. It was a contentious decision. Plugs was good, but he could be a bit of a hothead. Leaving him out, I knew, wouldn't exactly be universally popular in the dressing room.

There was a minute's silence in Glenina that day and we all wore black armbands in memory of Cormac. Mike decided to play and the game, as you might imagine, was hugely emotional for everyone connected with Buccs. I heard, subsequently, that Galwegians had brought in Warren Gatland to coach them that week, seeing as how fourteen of the players were his with Connacht. Given our already besieged circumstances, that just added to the sense of hurt.

They beat us too, by a single score as it happens, getting away with murder in the line-outs. I couldn't wait to get out of the place. But coming out of the dressing room after, the Galwegians scrum half Diarmuid Reddan (brother of Irish international, Eoin) asked me to go in for a drink. I could think of nothing I wanted to do less.

'I can't, Diarmuid,' I said.

'You're coming in,' he argued.

'Really, I couldn't stomach it.'

'I'm bringing you in, end of story,' he said.

It was a decent gesture and, inside, Eric Elwood came straight across and bought me a pint. They were good guys and I appreciated the point they made in being seen to talk to me. But, bottom line, we'd lost in a place and on a day we desperately wanted a victory. Galwegians had been promoted.

The defeat pitched us into a home and away play-off against Willie Anderson's Dungannon, who were facing relegation out of Division One. They came to Athlone and beat us 17–7. The tie looked over. I had a drink with Willie in the bar after and he seemed cock-a-hoop. And, by now, I had a problem.

The second leg was to be played on the day Katie made her Communion. So I told a white lie. I told the club I had an appointment in America. Only Noel Mannion knew the truth and I had him sworn to secrecy.

I gave the team talk that Thursday night and I remember driving out the gate, wondering what fate awaited them in Dungannon. They had trained really poorly and, in the talk, I hadn't spared them. Now they were headed north, already ten points down to face a Division One team. The general expectation was that they'd be butchered.

We went into Ballinasloe as a family that day and I remember walking around, wishing that I might become invisible. I was desperate for news of the game, but couldn't draw attention to myself by asking. So I was back in Moylough by the time Mannion rang with the news.

'You're not going to believe this . . .'

'Tell me!'

'We won!'

'Serious?'

'Butchered them, 27–10. We're in Division One, Eddie.'

'Holy Jesus!'

I was desperate to talk to people about it, but I couldn't ring anyone. I was, after all, in America! That night, sitting at home in Moylough, imagining the party kicking off down the road in Athlone, was utterly surreal. And I couldn't help thinking that somewhere high above us all, there'd be a beautiful smile on the face of Cormac Devine.

We strengthened our hand for the following season, bringing in people who could make a difference. One was Stephen McIvor. He was a smart scrum half I'd once had a run-in with at the Sportsground. It was after that Connacht–Munster interpro of Christmas 1995, maybe 200 people watching them fillet us to pieces. Munster just sewing it in, calling dubious 'injuries' (back then tactical substitutions weren't allowed). Rubbing our noses in it.

Pissed off, I walked into the changing room after and there's McIvor standing at the door to the showers, with a towel around him. Freezing. 'Do you know how to turn on the hot water here?' he asked.

'I'm not a fucking plumber!' I responded.

When Buccs approached him to sign, that was effectively all he knew about Eddie O'Sullivan. He was a little hesistant. But we actually got on quite well in the end and, with Simon Alnutt as his halfback partner, we now had the weaponry to make the most of a decent pack. McConnell went back to New Zealand, but we got a very bright number eight from Waikato, Martin Steffert.

The plan had been simply to survive in Division One and, as luck would have it, our first game up was against Galwegians. It was early December in Athlone and we demolished them. Suddenly the whole Buccs phenomenon began to gather impetus. Strangely, I also missed that game, this time making a real as distinct from imaginary journey to America, where the bulk of the Eagles players were playing in the Inter Territorials in Tampa, Florida.

But Buccs were becoming the talk of the AIL now. It wasn't uncommon for us to draw crowds of 5,000. When you think about it, we drew on a very broad support base. The nearest senior rugby club was in Galway, fifty miles away. North of us? Sligo. East? Dublin. South? Limerick.

People just bought into the whole Buccaneers thing and we came to our last game, home to Lansdowne, with the winner through to the AIL semi-finals. Lansdowne were coached by my former Connacht assistant, Michael Cosgrave. We beat them in a very tight game and that's the first day I can vividly remember 'The Fields' being sung in the dressing room and the crowd picking up on it outside. Slowly at first, then gathering pace and eventually absolutely manic.

One of the supporters actually grabbed the PA's microphone and started singing. I remember climbing up on scaffolding to do an interview for RTE and having to abort because of the noise. They were extraordinary scenes.

Our semi-final was away to Cork Con and, on a remarkable Sunday afternoon, maybe 6,000 packed into Temple Hill. Almost half of them wore the black and amber of Buccs, a sight that would send a tingle down your spine. Sadly, we made one mistake in defence that day and Ronan O'Gara opened us up with a pass. Game over.

I didn't know it then, but that was to be my last game as Buccs coach. By the time I came back from America the following September, I was about to get some bigger fish to fry.

11

'FUCK SAKE HIGGY ...'

To say that George Hook and I go back a long way is a bit like observing that Israel and Gaza have a history.

I can't pretend we were ever bosom buddies but there was a time in our lives when we worked compatibly together and even, dare I say, saw much in one another to like. But I found there was a pattern to life in George's world and it was a pattern of largely one-way traffic. Today, he is one of the most colourful media figures in Ireland with his own radio show and a place on RTE TV's studio rugby panel.

He has made his name on a booming mix of metaphor and analysis that often strays into the land of ridicule. Good luck to him. George has always been an engaging speaker and, for a guy who has been to more than his share of bad places, it's hard not to admire the resilience that has enabled him reinvent himself so many times.

He has written openly of how what he calls 'The Black Dog of Depression' impacted on his life. That took courage. I, personally, saw evidence of that 'dog', so I understand the wretched hold it can take on someone's life. For George to have the career he has today is a credit to his fortitude, not to mention his family.

He is a household name in Ireland now, a man whose opinion carries weight. And, in the latter days of my time as Ireland coach, that opinion was delivered with a serrated edge. I was, apparently, 'like the Fuhrer in a bunker in Berlin' as he described me.

It wasn't George's criticism I had difficulty with. It was the tone I found offensive. In my opinion George thinks nothing of ridiculing someone in his role as media pundit and I simply cannot respect that.

We don't speak now and, from what I can gather, he still believes that I have never given him due credit for the role he played in my career. On that, I will leave you to make up your own mind.

Our first meeting in 1989, on the side of that pitch in Corinthians, gave me the immediate sense of a man on a mission to be a top-rank coach. Declan McDermott was in charge of Connacht at the time but stepped down after the interpros to be replaced initially by Ciaran Fitzgerald and, ultimately, George when 'Fitzy' was diverted to the Irish job.

Apparently, I was one of the first people George rang after his appointment. To be fair, he had great ambitions for Connacht and didn't want the business of choosing his assistant left up to the Branch. So we met for lunch in the Corrib Great Southern Hotel and, as I would discover, lunch was George's thing. He liked to do the full metal jacket, three hours, four courses, leisurely coffees.

George's version of the lunch is that we were pushing salt cellars around the table, exchanging strategies. Mine is that the strategies flowed largely in one direction. He had a lot of vague notions floating about in his head and I kept challenging him to elaborate.

So, what's your policy at the breakdown?
The line-out?
What defensive system do you want to run?

Being strong on theory, weak on practice, George almost threw his lunch up. When you peeled back the skin of his arguments, quite often there wasn't a whole lot inside. But he was bright enough to know if someone might be of value to his ambitions. That was a strength of his, the ability to identify people who could do a decent job. The wisdom to delegate.

To be fair, George transformed the whole experience of playing for Connacht. Annsbacker became our sponsors and their backing enabled us to become the best-dressed team in the interprovincial championship, Connacht having – for years – worn these awful, shiny green tracksuits with logos the size of dinner plates. Now, for the first time, Connacht stayed in decent hotels too.

George simply made people feel good about the experience of playing for the province. He created a palpable buzz.

His coaching background had been limited to a stint with Belvedere under-19s and some time spent with St. Mary's, but the players liked him. George was interesting and innovative and he introduced video analysis long before it became fashionable. To be fair, he gave me a lot of latitude as his assistant too. I think George recognised that, technically, I knew what I was talking about. Pretty quickly, ours was a good working relationship.

There were slight teething problems to overcome, given my position as a Development Officer with the IRFU. George was, effectively, borrowing me from the Union. But it made sense for me to work with Connacht. I lived in Galway, my job gave me an intimate knowledge of the rugby scene in the west. If certain people were unhappy with the arrangement, they couldn't deny its logic.

Our first game as a partnership was against Spain in the

Sportsground on a beautiful September afternoon. Simon Geoghegan made his debut for the province that same day and, like everyone else in the ground, my very first glimpse had me thinking, 'Fuck me, that guy is good!' The Connacht out-half was a young Eric Elwood, yet to mature into the man who would anchor Ireland's backline through the early 90s. Eric, at the time, was a little headstrong and error-prone.

George would be apoplectic when Eric made a mistake, rounding on him in the dressing room, all but reducing it to a personal issue between two people. It was the wrong approach to take with a young player and I always suspected that Eric never liked or quite trusted George because of it.

We conceded a couple of bad tries in that game with Spain and the following morning George's analysis could have been pay-per-view. In fairness, he'd have done his homework. He outlined the areas of breakdown on video and shone a pretty stark light on the culprits.

One of Spain's scores was a pushover try from a five-metre scrum, the entire Connacht back row breaking away when the imperative should have been to stay bound. 'Fucking heads popping up like ducks at a shooting gallery . . .' as George put it. One golden rule had been broken. Then he identified another.

At one point, we had been fifteen metres out from the Spanish line when Jamesie O'Riordan got a touch of what we called 'white-line fever' at the back of the maul. In other words, he took off on his own, lost the ball and we eventually scrambled the Spaniards into touch at a corner flag 80 yards down the pitch.

Jamesie, a soldier by profession, was devoured without salt the following morning.

'Jamesie O'Riordan,' George boomed, 'a fucking cadet in the Irish army, do you know that in the Battle of the Somme there were 50,000 men lost for 80 yards of ground and you fucked away 80 yards in the Sportsground yesterday ON YOUR

OWN!' The players loved it. It was entertaining and, at the same time, tactically relevant. And we could all sense that we were putting a pretty decent Connacht team together.

It was George who would convince David Curtis to come to Connacht from London Irish. He brought in guys like Tim Coughlan, Steve Jameson and Billy Mulcahy. He could track raw diamonds like Kenny Lawless, a fantastic scrum half who seemed to slip under the radar at Clontarf, or Kevin Devlin, one of the best open-sides I've ever coached, picked up at Skerries.

He was, you see, a good reader of a player and an astute selector. But George took defeat far too personally for his own good.

We almost beat Munster in the interpros at Thomond in that first year, which would have been a massive scalp. The chance was effectively lost when our giant second row, Aidan Higgins from University College Galway, was deemed by referee Owen Doyle to have knocked the ball on at a ruck on the Munster line just before Eric Elwood went in under the posts. It was a heart-breaking call but, being honest, probably a correct one. 'Higgy' just tried to pick and score, but nudged the ball forward, however faintly.

We had the game won if the try was allowed, but Doyle called us back for the scrum. Chance gone.

The defeat tore George to pieces. I already sensed he had ambitions to be Irish coach and beating Munster at Thomond in his first season as Connacht boss might well have pushed him right into the frame. Successful provincial coaches like Mick Doyle and Jimmy Davidson had already made that step up, so he wasn't outrageous in believing he might be just one floor under the penthouse suite. George was inconsolable that night in the Royal George Hotel. We went out for a Chinese meal, but it was to no avail. He just spent the night replaying the fateful knock-on.

'For fuck's sake Higgy . . .'

Leinster were next up and, with the Sportsground under snow, the game was moved at short notice to Corinthians. On a bitterly cold day, we should have won again. Curtis, Geoghegan and Jim Staples combined to create a wonderful try from 80 yards out but, somehow, we managed to shoot ourselves in the foot again, allowing the game just to slip away.

This was torture for George. Had Connacht won at Thomond, then beaten Leinster, it would have been headline news in Irish rugby. Instead, we were left brooding over two near misses. Nearly men.

Elwood had played poorly against Leinster, slicing a lot of his line kicks and – on the bus – George ripped into him, saying that he may have been kicking the ball 70 yards, but 50 of those yards were in the car park!

So we're headed for the team meal and everyone has a direct line to George loudly berating Eric for 'not fucking listening . . .' It wasn't the way to do things. George's problem was that he saw losing, a game as failure and couldn't help but transmit that to his players. Everything became personal in his world. Mistakes weren't easily forgiven.

That said, it was now an exciting time to be involved with Connacht. For me, working with a backline that contained Elwood, Curtis, Geoghegan and Staples was a genuine thrill. True, the London-based players wouldn't train with us. We'd just see them the day before a game. But it was never an issue.

These, remember, were still resolutely amateur days. The notion of a player being available to train every day was pretty much pie in the sky. If Connacht had a game at the weekend, we'd train at St Mary's College in Dublin on the Tuesday or Wednesday (most of the players being Dublin-based). After that, we'd convene in the Corrib Great Southern on Friday evening at maybe 6 p.m. and, depending on traffic, do a session under lights.

It seems almost quaint in recall, but these were pre-European days. The province wasn't exactly at the epicentre of a rugby player's life in Ireland, not – mind you – that the international team was either. Ireland struggled badly to make an impact in that season's Five Nations, Davidson – as coach – guilty I suspected of one crucial error. Jimmy tried to coach Irish rugby as distinct from the Irish team. In many ways, he was years ahead of his time, looking to sell a gospel of skill development when few if any people were listening.

The mood surrounding the Ireland team was ugly as we finished just ahead of wooden spoonists Wales in the 1990 Five Nations. Yet Ireland had – at least – completed the campaign with a 14–8 defeat of the Welsh at Lansdowne Road, so Davidson's resignation caught everyone by surprise.

We were all gathered in Belfast for a training camp that May, Jimmy's fitness coach – Colin Boreham – in charge. Just after lunch, at the team meeting Jimmy came into the room and announced he had something to say. 'Lads,' he began, 'I've had a great time as Irish coach, but I think it's time to take a step back now . . .'

You could have heard a pin drop.

Davidson's decision had repercussions on many levels, not least my own. He was replaced by Ciaran Fitzgerald, with Johnny Moloney as assistant – a reversal of their positions with the under-21s. And Fitzy, having liked the work I'd done with the 21s, now seconded me into working as fitness coach for the senior Irish team.

This didn't exactly win me any new friends within the IRFU. Again it would have been perceived as a conflict of interests. I was, after all, on the Union's payroll first and foremost as a Development Officer. To some, I was getting ahead of myself.

I had a three-year contract that was up for renegotiation in 1991. I remember going to a committee meeting, sitting in front of all these people who would have appointed me in the first place, and asking them what the long-term plan was. It soon dawned on me that there wasn't one. Actually, I could detect a certain anxiety at the meeting. It was acknowledged that the Development Officers were doing good work, but there was no obvious career path awaiting the likes of Willie Anderson or me within Union structures.

Those structures were still broadly amateur, predicated on an amateur mindset. I remember going to a review meeting and coming out with a small salary increase, but no sense of anything long-term in the pipeline. And it struck me that I might have to consider where exactly my life in rugby was taking me.

Career-wise, I wasn't yet quite out on a limb. I had taken a five-year career break from Holy Rosary, so the teaching job was still there for me. I still had that safety net beneath me. But, deep down, I was feeling a little restless.

George, by now, had decamped to England as coach to London Irish. He wanted me to fly over and back to London, as his assistant. We were still coaching Connacht, so the web was becoming more and more tangled and I knew the Union would never tolerate me working for so many different masters. So, eventually I jumped ship.

George had recommended me to Kyran McLoughlin for a coaching job at Blackrock College on the basis that, if I was working in Dublin, travelling over and back to London wouldn't be any great inconvenience. Blackrock is one of the great institutions of Leinster schools rugby but, at the time, the junior school – Willow Park – was struggling to cope with numbers. There was also a sense that, though the senior school was winning cups, they weren't doing it in the expansive style so coveted in 'Rock's history.

The coaching was still being done by priests and the brothers of the Holy Ghost, though many had already passed retirement age. Fewer and fewer of the schools' players were graduating to the club now, many slipping away into the arms of Lansdowne and Wanderers under-19s. If there wasn't quite a sense of crisis in Blackrock, there was a palpable unease.

The position on offer was, effectively, two jobs. One with the club, the other with the school. My role with the club amounted to being assistant to Conor Coakley who was, himself, assistant to first-team coach Michael 'Bomber' Brown. With the school, my task was essentially to put a whole new structure in place at Willow Park.

The bursar was Father Jerome Godfrey, a fantastic rugby coach in his own right. His room overlooked the pitches in the college and, over time, he could see all the older brothers struggling to keep a rein on these huge flocks of kids.

One of the first things I did on accepting the position was to buy 120 rugby balls and 500 markers. I then came up with a scheme of bringing back guys who had played senior schools Cup for Blackrock as a kind of surrogate coaching team for the juniors. Many of them were now pursuing Third Level education at UCD. We paid them the equivalent of pocket money for their time.

Alan MacGinty, now Principal of the senior college, was Junior Cup coach. Himself and Brother Joe Gough brought me right on board, giving me a little access to an outstanding group of young players who, in their second year (1993), won the Leinster Junior Cup, hammering St Mary's 33–3 in the final.

It was 'Rock's first JC triumph since 1987 and the team boasted wonderful talents like Ciaran Scally, Leo Cullen, Bob Casey, Tom Keating, Dave Quinlan and Barry Gibney. Scally and Gibney were probably the two gems you would pick out of a pretty special bunch, but both would have their careers cut short by injury.

Actually, the first time I saw Gibney – a phenomenal back–row player – play Junior Cup, I remember remarking that he wouldn't have looked out of place with a silver fern on his chest.

Club-wise, I graduated to assistant coach when Coakley – a guy with a wonderful rugby brain – was, tragically, diagnosed with motor neurone disease. One year later, we won promotion to the First Division of the All-Ireland Rugby League and Bomber decided to step down. Being honest, we had been lucky to go up. In a key game with Terenure we must have collapsed twelve scrums on our own line without the punishment of a penalty try. Terenure, understandably, were distraught. The loss of that game cost them their place in the top flight.

Bomber's departure meant that I entered my third year at 'Rock as head coach, the first non-Rock person to hold the position. It was seen in Stradbrook as a significant departure. Actually, it would have been the talk of the bar.

I liked Bomber and had reason to be grateful for his consideration during my first year as head coach with the club. He was an eye surgeon by profession and I went down to his office in the Blackrock Clinic with a severe headache one day. The pain was directly behind an eye and, as I discovered later, he suspected I had an aneurism.

He sent me down for an MRI and the deduction was there was 'definitely something' there. I was then sent for a CAT scan. This revealed a polyp in my sinuses and it was only then that he told me what he had suspected.

'You're a lucky man,' said Bomber.

'Why?'

'I thought you had an aneurism behind the eye.'

He explained to me exactly what that would have meant. An operation where you have to sever the main artery. The loss of the eye. The possibility of brain damage. He had seen it happen to someone else just the previous month.

I was grateful to Bomber for how swiftly he acted when I went to him. He could be a fiery character and we once had words at a floodlit cup match in Belvedere where I felt he was being too hard on the players. But his heart was in the right place. When I was in trouble, he couldn't have done enough for me.

Another key man at the club back then was Mervyn Dalton. Mervyn was actually drummer and manager with Hurricane Johnny and the Jets, a really popular band in Dublin through the 70s. A terrific organiser, Mervyn became team manager at 'Rock and – at the height of the AIL – he'd organise special trains to bring anything up to 1,500 supporters to matches all over the country from Blackrock Station.

Mervyn invested an incredible amount of time into 'Rock, motivated by a simple desire to see the club do well.

As head coach, I immediately prioritised beefing up the pack, bringing in guys like John Etheridge and Dean Oswald to join Mick O'Neill – brother of Dublin GAA star Pat – in adding some front-line bite. It wasn't the most popular policy. We ended up with very few actual 'Rock guys in the pack and I could sense a fair degree of sulphur in the air among dyed-in-the-wool club members.

Victor Costello had left and gone to Mary's. I knew Victor well. He had been playing for Connacht in the interpros and I wanted him to stay. I tried talking him out of the move, but to no avail.

Yet my biggest problem at 'Rock by now was dealing with one of the stars. I had already worked directly with Neil Francis through my role as assistant coach to Ireland. He was a phenomenally gifted second row but, by and large, 'Franno' was a lazy trainer and inclined to suit himself. I knew and Franno knew that he'd have to change his ways for us to have a viable working relationship. And change just wasn't in Franno's plans.

Over time there was a bit of a stand-off, some of the 'negotiating' a bit surreptitious on his side. Francis could just about live with me as assistant coach but, as head coach, I was probably his worst nightmare. Bottom line, he knew I wouldn't take his bullshit and it came down, ultimately, to the club having to make a decision between its coach and one of its favourite sons. Franno left for Belvedere.

By now, I knew I was a bit of a pariah in the eyes of the Union. I was, essentially, a professional coach and they'd left me in little doubt of my standing within 62 Lansdowne Road after Ireland's tour of New Zealand in 1992. Fitzy, who was now under serious pressure as Irish coach, brought me on that tour as fitness advisor. The game was still amateur so, in a case of lost earnings, there was a facility to apply for refunds to the Union.

My application was rejected.

In fairness to Father Godfrey, he made nothing of it and paid my salary in full. But I knew that most others on that tour had been fully compensated by the Union. They were laying down a marker here and I had no doubt which side of it they saw me on. It was around this time too that the National Coaching and Training Centre had opened for business in Limerick. I attended a meeting aimed at identifying how the centre might help the Irish rugby team. The NCTC made their presentation through a guy I had been in college with, John Kirwan.

At the end of it, the Union's representative, Noel Murphy, piped up, 'So, what you're saying, John, is that you can help us in a way that we won't need a fitness guy of our own anymore?'

I knew there and then that I was surplus to requirements and wrote a letter of resignation soon after.

Connacht's story was changing now. George's too. The establishment of the 'Exiles' meant that English-based players now had a representative outlet on that side of the Irish Sea. It led to a crippling drain of talent back out of Connacht, the likes of Geoghegan, Staples and Curtis cutting their ties with the west.

Worse, a lot of the Leinster players we had recruited began to slip away too.

Then George got the bullet at London Irish. I had been flying over once a week to help him and, being honest, found the commitment draining. I mean I was coaching at Willow and 'Rock, I was assistant to George with Connacht (which was still a purely amateur position) and now found myself on a flight to Heathrow every Monday afternoon, taking training at Sunbury, then jumping on an 11 p.m. flight back into Dublin.

Eventually Aer Lingus would drop the late flight home, so I'd come back on a red-eye on Tuesday mornings, heading straight to Willow Park. It meant that I was seeing less and less of my family at home in Moylough.

Things seemed, by now, to be getting a little ropey in George's world. To be fair, he would write with a fair degree of candour in his own autobiography about this period in his life and a struggle with depression. After London Irish, he moved to Fylde, who'd just been promoted from Division Three to Two in England. George's job was to get them into the top division, but he inherited too many uncommitted players.

I think he had a few piss-heads on board who, basically, got the crap knocked out of them every weekend and consoled one another at the bar. I'd be talking to him every week and the defeats began eating through him. Eventually, he imploded.

Connacht were due to play the touring Wallabies in November of 1992 and, maybe ten days before the game, I got a call from John Callinan, the chairman of selectors. He sounded worried.

'Have you been talking to George?' he asked.

'Why?'

'Have you tried to ring him?'

'No.'

'Well I can't get him and nobody at Fylde knows where he is. Ingrid [George's wife] doesn't know either. Nobody knows.'

Fucking hell, I thought.

The days began ticking now and nobody had a sighting of George. The team to play the Wallabies was chosen, as was the norm, by a selection committee. We arranged a training session at St Mary's in Dublin six days before the game. Everything was in place except the Connacht coach.

I will never forget the scene. It was like something out of a movie. A gloomy, foggy November evening, the sky on the ground, the floodlights giving off this kind of timid, defeated glow. Australia were bearing down on us and there was still no sign of George. I'm sitting in the car with the chairman.

'What are we going to do?' he asks me.

I have no answers. What can I say? We need everyone on deck for this one, but we don't even have the coach. 'There's only one thing we can do,' says John. 'You've got to coach the team.' I ask him what we would tell the players and he said to leave that up to him.

Next thing, this vision appears through the mist. It's George. He's in an open-necked white shirt, sleeves rolled up. This is the middle of November and he could be dressed for the beach. God alone even knows how he's got here. There's no sign of a car or taxi. John rolls the window down.

'Jesus, George . . .' he begins.

'The line-outs, we must sort out the line-outs,' George interjects, as if he's just skipped out of the dressing room. The scene is absolutely surreal. John tells George to get into the car, so he sits into the back seat. He's still on about the line-outs. 'The line-outs are the key.'

I lose my temper. 'George, shut up and listen . . .'

John says to him that he's not coaching Connacht any more. A naturally gentle man, he's trying to be diplomatic. The news seems to confuse George. It's just 'the line-outs, the line-outs, the line-outs . . .' John tells him his priority has to be to go home

112

to his wife and kids now. That Connacht rugby can wait. It subsequently emerged that George had gone missing in London for ten days. Just locked himself in a hotel room, watched TV, contacted no one.

John drove him down to Dr Jack Ormonde, George's GP and a St Mary's clubman, the rehabilitation starting from there. We didn't see George for months. It was left to me to coach Connacht against the Wallabies, Charlie Couper – the forwards' coach – appointed to help me.

George's absence meant that I had to take the pack for a session. Prior to this, I had been seen fundamentally as a backs' coach and I remember the Connacht forwards looking at me as if I had two heads. I was nervous, but I wanted to innovate. I also felt I had a plan.

It worked this way. We had three jumpers – Noel Mannion, Steve Jameson and Tim Coughlan. As a one-off, I wanted to stack them, essentially put the three jumpers in one place. Remember there was no lifting back then. I felt if Bill Mulcahy threw to the three of them – be it at the front, middle or back – one was bound to get it. And that's exactly what we did.

Also, we made out line-out calls in Irish to really confuse the Australians.

On the day, the Wallabies just couldn't handle that. If they stacked the front, we stacked the back. The key was doing it at the last second, so they didn't have time to react. Another tactic I used that day was to break Mannion off the scrum altogether and put him on the case of their number ten. Most number eights broke off anyway, but spent most of that time just scratching their asses.

With Mannion taking the out-half, our ten took twelve, twelve took thirteen, thirteen took the fullback. It meant that Australia had no overlap. Generally teams tended to drift defend and I knew that a good team like Australia would open us up if we did that. They'd just ride a tackle and get an offload. This way, there was no drifting. It was man on man.

Every player knew exactly what he was doing that day, who would go to the rucks, who wouldn't. Years later I met the Wallaby coach – Bob Dwyer – in America and he told me, 'Fuck you drove us mad that day.' He said it was their first time coming up against that one-out defence and they couldn't break it.

Australia won the game 14–6, but all the plaudits came spilling Connacht's way. The expectation had been that they'd roll right over us. In fact, in that morning's *Irish Press*, their rugby correspondent – Karl Johnston – had speculated that the Wallabies could put a hundred points on us. To be fair, he wasn't saying anything the bulk of pundits didn't believe.

The galling thing was that we might have even won the game. Three of Australia's points came from a penalty signalled wide by both touch judges only to be overruled by the Welsh referee. Then Aidan White had what looked a successful kick for us marked wide. Worse, Australia's only try came from a sliced clearance by our captain, Mick Cosgrave. It was a galling day of might-have-beens.

We beat Leinster at the Sportsground in the subsequent inter-pro championship, using the same defensive system. Jim Glennon was Leinster coach and they came with the intention of moving us around the paddock where their supposedly superior backs could then make hay. We smothered them to death. The beauty was that, with no overlap, our defensive line could afford to be very aggressive. Leinster didn't know what hit them.

It was quite a shock, Connacht beating Leinster. The following season, George was back in the whole of his health again, me resuming duties as his assistant. I had no issues with that. It was good to see him well and I certainly believed that we made a decent team.

But, gradually, the provinces were becoming a dead duck

now. The power of the game was moving to the clubs in the AIL. You could have 5,000 for a 'Rock game at Stradbrook even though SkySports would be covering it on TV. Within a few seasons, the AIL was the only show in town.

My last year with Connacht, we played Munster at the Sportsground the day before Christmas Eve. I doubt there were 200 people in the ground. Walking down the line at one point, I bumped into the Munster coach – now their Chief Executive – Garret Fitzgerald.

'This is like flogging a dead horse, Eddie,' he said to me.

'You can sing that!' I responded.

Little did we know what the Munster brand was destined to become.

At Blackrock, I was determined to break out of the stereotype of being seen strictly as a backs' coach.

I had studied Ciaran Fitzgerald's work with the Irish pack and taken on board a lot of information. Fitzy was a very good set-piece coach. By 1991, he had established Ireland's scrum and line-out as the equal of anything in the Five Nations. During training, when Johnny Moloney would be away doing his thing with the backs, I filled in as a scrum half for the line-out sessions. Every day was a learning day.

No question, I harboured an ambition to coach at the highest level now. And, to do this, I felt the broader my experience, the better my chances of being marketable. Was I thinking in terms of Ireland? Probably. I felt if I was going to step into that kind of arena, I was going to have to know more than anybody else. I mightn't have to actually coach the Irish pack, but I needed to know what was going on in there.

I felt I couldn't have this black box theory of expecting things to work without actually knowing exactly why. I had to be able to ask the hard questions.

You see, I knew I had become regarded – essentially – as a backs coach and a fitness guy. I was pigeonholed. So, at 'Rock, I devised a pretty unique way of training because I wanted to be hands-on in every department. Most teams trained Tuesdays and Thursdays, the firsts training separate from the seconds. I wanted firsts and seconds training together. My split was between backs and forwards.

I chose a former Irish prop, Job Langbroek, to work as my assistant. Job was a dyed-in-the-wool Blackrock man, a genuinely solid character who worked with Davy Stockbrokers. His coaching experience was nil, but I knew his intelligence would compensate for any deficit. I first broached the subject by asking Job to help me with the seconds. He was reticent, suggesting that maybe the place for him was coaching the 'third As'.

I assured him that I'd be at his side throughout and that, frankly, the business of coaching seconds wouldn't be that much different from coaching third As anyway.

Today you wouldn't get away with the system I put in place, because players' skill sets have broadened so much. But, at the time, it always struck me as farcical that such a high percentage of training was unopposed. Teams running the ball from everywhere, stock-piling training-ground tries, learning nothing about themselves. In other words, people were working in a comfort zone. I insisted on Blackrock players fronting up at training, backs against backs, forwards against forwards.

It worked this way. The backs all trained together on Monday nights, the forwards Tuesdays. On Thursday nights everyone trained together. Job would be in charge of the seconds at the weekend. I'd be in charge of the firsts. Together, we developed a solid squad ethic.

In my first year as head coach, we lost what amounted to the AIL final against Garryowen in a quagmire at Dooradoyle. There were rumours that Garryowen had watered the pitch because our success in the League was built on an explosive backline. We had Alain Rolland (now a top international referee), Alan McGowan, Martin Ridge, Brendan Mullin, Niall Woods and Nicky Assaf behind the scrum. And the real rabbit in the hat was David 'Jinksy' Beggy, a flier at fullback who was just coming out of a successful Gaelic football career in which he won two All-Irelands with Meath.

There were no actual semi-finals or finals in the AIL but, by some strange quirk of fate, the last round of fixtures always seemed to throw up an all-or-nothing showdown between the top two.

By just getting ourselves into contention, we had taken everyone by surprise. Many journalists had predicted relegation in our first year in the top flight. There was certainly an assumption that we'd struggle. I remember our first game of the competition had been against St Mary's before a full house in Stradbrook. They had a cracking team and would have been one of the pre-tournament favourites.

The game was a humdinger. I remember watching the second half from the roof of the clubhouse and we sealed victory with the last play of the game. We had a scrum in the corner and ran a set-play that became known as 'Sullivan's'. I had used it at London Irish to free up Geoghegan who was tending to get double-teamed. This involved using him off the blind side.

In a sense, I had taken it from my basketball days. It struck me that if a team ran a three-up drift defence against 'Sullivan's' and we got it right, there could be only one outcome. We'd be in under the bin.

Ironically, Geoghegan's famous try against England at Twickenham in 1994 was a version of the same move, except it was Richard Wallace who went through the hole. Against Mary's, we ran the move in the last seconds, Woods went over under the posts and Stradbrook almost burst its moorings.

Mick Doyle was among those eulogising the game the following day through his column in the *Sunday Independent*. That start would give us the impetus for a storming campaign.

One of our best victories was against Shannon at Thomond Park. It was a dry day, which frankly was a virtual prerequisite for us to play. We knew Shannon ran a four-up defence, leaving the winger free on the outside. Shannon had a name for never losing at Thomond but that day, in front of a full house, we gave them a bit of a hiding. You could say we stormed the Limerick fortress.

The following season we again came desperately close to winning the League. This time, as it happened, Shannon beat us at Stradbrook in the decisive contest. Both teams were warming up on the bottom pitch beforehand, the rain bucketing down. And Niall O'Donovan, now the Shannon coach, looked over to me and shrugged. 'I think the Gods are on our side today.'

I couldn't help sensing that he was right.

We gave as good as we got, the pack fronting up, the backs keeping things sensible. But one key moment turned the game against us. Jinksy came through a hole at full pelt only for the ball to hit him on the shoulder. If he held it, he was under the bin. Instead, the ball was hacked back down the field, with Billy O'Shea – the Shannon centre – standing about ten yards offside. To our horror the ref let play go, signalling a manic race to the far end of the pitch.

Brendan Mullin and O'Shea dived across our try-line together, the ball skidding dead. It seemed impossible to tell who got the touch, but the referee ran in from the 22, signalling a Shannon try. He had made the call from a good thirty yards distance, yet even people directly behind the goal admitted afterwards that they couldn't honestly make the call. To me, it was an appalling decision.

In the conditions Shannon were never going to lose it from there and – sensibly – they just played out time.

It was to be the first of four consecutive League titles for them and, being honest, they were worthy champions. Naturally, I'd love to have played them on a dry day but, if you were going to win the AIL, you were never going to get ten dry days. We were sickened, but we took it on the chin.

At the end of that season, there was a bit of a push to get me into the senior school at 'Rock, but it was a little half-baked. People were still grumbling about the style of rugby they were playing. Yet, I felt I needed a mandate for anything to happen and spoke to the principal and president. 'I'm not a politician,' I said. 'I'm a rugby coach. It's up to you guys to clear the path.' I wasn't going to play the Messiah.

They couldn't pull it off in the end and I didn't lose any sleep. The wheels were already in motion to bring me back to the west.

12

OUTSIDE IT'S AMERICA

I am sitting in a hotel room in Colorado Springs, drawn to the sodium glow of a laptop screen.

It's a brand new computer and, beyond the significant achievement of having managed to switch it on, I haven't a clue how to use it. I'm fiddling half-heartedly with buttons, like a kid on Christmas morning with a complicated train set. There's a wall-high mirror in the room and it keeps catching my eye. The man sitting on the bed looks utterly lost. Maybe a little frightened even.

The enormity of what I've done is just beginning to hit home. It's Saturday night and I've been on the phone to home. Noreen put the kids on, Katie (seven) and Barry (four), and it's as if hearing their voices started tugging me down emotionally. I miss them and feel the physical ache of homesickness. And I am only three days in America.

Deep down, maybe I also feel a sense of injustice about being here. I finished up in school last Tuesday afternoon. There were no farewells, nothing. The staff room was half empty. I just gathered up my stuff, took one last look around, and walked out the gate. It was 3.25 p.m. And, maybe at that moment, I realised that that was my safety net gone. I was pretty much on the high wire now.

Driving home, I remember thinking, Fuck's sake, you'd better make a go of this. Failure in America would probably mean me sinking without trace.

In my heart of hearts, I knew there were people in Ireland – certainly in Connacht – who were glad to see the back of me. I had become something of an embarrassment to them. I mean I had established a decent track record as a coach with Connacht, Galwegians, Blackrock and the Irish under-21s and, now the only place in the world I could get a job was 5,000 miles away.

When the word broke that I was leaving Ireland, I had no doubt that certain people breathed a sigh of relief. I put six years into Connacht either as head coach or assistant, without receiving a single penny. Actually, when I resigned in 1996, they said they couldn't even pay my mobile phone bill. So they split it in two and gave me half. I was teaching in Mountbellew and the province's rugby team was now being coached by a New Zealander. I had become the elephant in the corner.

To some, I sensed I might as well have been taking a job on the moon now. America was completely off the radar at our end of the rugby world. I'm sure there was a view that I'd probably never be seen again. And probably, '*Good riddance.*'

I was now assistant technical director of US Rugby, second in command to George Hook. I had two jobs, effectively, which would require me living in two separate places. In Colorado Springs, my role was to help George establish a coaching programme for US Rugby. I'd work for blocks of time with him, then fly back to San Francisco, slipping across the bay to Oakland into Cal Berkeley (The University of California, Berkeley), where I would work as assistant coach to Jack Clark with the US Eagles national team. Essentially, George and Jack were my two bosses now.

A slight complication was that they didn't speak.

The base from which we ran the coaching course was in a beautiful location at the foot of Pike's Peak, about one hour fifteen minutes south of Denver. The US Olympic Committee had a huge training centre there and US Rugby enjoyed associate membership even though rugby, of course, was not an Olympic sport.

George had begun building an instructor base around the coaching programme and – over time – would appoint fourteen people on a geographical basis. It was a sincere and sensible strategy. Unfortunately, some of his choices were pretty calamitous. We would find ourselves trying to teach these people how to run level-one clinics when, at best, maybe three or four were actually up to the job.

For now, though, I probably wasn't inclined to ask enough questions. I was tiptoeing through my introduction.

The Eagles were preparing for the Pacific Rim tournament, the staple of their season against Canada, Hong Kong and Japan. Three games at home, three away. Jack gave me the job of coaching the forwards and my first day taught me a valuable lesson. Deference would get me nowhere.

Whenever there was a 'time-out' called, this group of coaches would – almost literally – leap into action. Torrents of information came flowing in within seconds and, not wanting to cut across anyone, I struggled to get a word in. This was the American way. One in, all in, no hesitation. In the car, on the way back to my hotel, Jack spat out a leading question.

'Sully,' he asked, 'when are you going to start working for me?'

'Sorry, Jack?'

'When are you going to start working for me? You hardly opened your mouth today.'

'Jesus, Jack, I didn't really want to cut across anybody.'

He looked at me as if I was a swimmer worried about getting

wet. 'Listen,' he said, 'we need your information. And we need it today, not tomorrow or next week. You've got to start giving it to us.'

The whole thrust of my work with George was educating coaches. We had to produce coaching manuals, some of which we simply plagiarised. After all, I had been putting together level-one and level-two manuals for the IRFU in the early 90s, manuals that now fitted the American system perfectly with small adjustments. I did develop a foundation manual from scratch, as well as a level-three course. But a lot of the stuff we needed was already at my fingertips

George was the front-of-house man, the guy selling the sizzle if you like. It had been the same with Connacht. We complemented one another in that way. He didn't have a nuts and bolts approach to the game so he would defer to me when the head gasket needed changing. He was the car salesman. I was the mechanic.

He was smart enough to deliver a level-one clinic but anything more technical was my domain. Every weekend, we went from city to city, holding clinics. Des Moines, San Francisco, Dallas, wherever, dealing with some fantastically enthusiastic people. I remember arriving in Dallas one day to run a level-two course at the Harlequins club and talking to this guy who had driven from Los Angeles to make the clinic. That's like sitting into your car in Connemara and driving to Moscow. He had spent two and a half days effectively trekking across the Rocky Mountains. I was stunned. If you needed motivation for running a good clinic, that was surely it.

Cal Berkeley has a very proud rugby tradition in America with 24 national titles and a history of playing host to illustrious tourists. They developed a relationship with the All Blacks in the 50s, at which time they were actually capable of giving them a decent game. I had been utterly uneducated on the feeling for rugby in this part of America. It was an eye-opener.

One night in Berkeley, I went for dinner in an Irish restaurant with Jack. We were having a beer afterwards when I spotted a poster behind the bar advertising the upcoming live performance of an Irish musician. His name was Albert Niland, a name I immediately recognised. Albert had been a pupil of mine in Mountbellew.

'I don't believe this,' I said to the barman. 'I know that musician. I taught him back in Ireland.'

'You're from Mountbellew?' he responded. 'My father's from Mountbellew!'

Suddenly, there was a bottle of Jameson on the counter. This guy's father happened to be the bar owner. So I'm sitting there with Jack Clark and his assistant, Dan Porter, telling the story of this gifted kid who had two passions in his life, gymnastics and the guitar. And their mouths are literally hanging open at how tiny the world had suddenly become.

The following morning Berkeley hosted the collegiate rugby championships and we all pitched up feeling the worse for wear. Jack was standing at one end line with dark glasses on. He called me over. 'You little fucker,' he said, laughing, 'you do that to me again and I'll kill you!'

I reached a kind of unspoken agreement not to talk to him about George or vice versa. They existed in two parallel worlds, one not interfering with the other. That suited me fine. I didn't know the genesis of their differences and, frankly, had no real desire to find out.

I'd call home every second day and, being honest, found that ritual difficult. Noreen was fantastic. She was working as a nurse at the time and, knowing how passionate I had become about coaching, supported me 100 per cent. Without that support, I'd probably have been stuck at home in Moylough, feeling sorry for myself. She knew it and I knew it.

The family had become accustomed to me not being around,

but never for this duration (April to October). Katie was old enough to work out timelines, but talking to Barry almost broke my heart. He had no concept of time. 'When are you coming home, Dad?' he'd ask.

'Three weeks, Bar, I'll be home in three weeks.'

'So . . . you'll be home for dinner on Sunday, right?'

'No, no, Bar. Not Sunday. Three more Sundays.'

I remember one day, especially, having this conversation with him and he asked me, 'So you'll be home before I go into third class?' And that really brought it home. He had absolutely no concept of what I was doing or how long I'd be doing it for. And it was tearing me up thinking, What's going on in his head? Does he feel that I've abandoned him?

Maybe the hardest thing was thinking of the burden I'd left Noreen to carry. The role, virtually, of a single parent while I was in America trying to further my coaching career.

That first year with the Eagles was pretty traumatic. We started our Pacific Rim campaign with a good spanking from Canada in Vancouver. From there, we went to Hong Kong. Another spanking. A victory in Japan rescued the season somewhat and we would finish up with three wins, three losses. A mediocre return for what was a decent Eagles team.

After that, Wales arrived on tour and we played two Test games. The first, in Wilmington, North Carolina, we lost by ten points. The second, in San Francisco, we lost, heartbreakingly, by five. That game was on a knife-edge when Welsh out-half Arwel Thomas attacked down the short-side and put a grubber kick through. The ball hit our winger, Brian Hightower, on the knee and popped up into Thomas's hands. He was in under the bin.

Maybe six of that US team were playing professionally overseas, guys like Dave Hodges, Dan Lyle and Tom Billups. We had a decent line-out and could just about hold our own in the scrum. Wales would have been a prized scalp, but we let them off the hook. It was shattering.

There were problems, too, on the development side. Most of the instructors appointed by George simply were not able to do the job. It meant that the whole coaching programme was, essentially, compromised. Over time, I could sense George becoming increasingly stressed and agitated by this fact. He was also coming under increasing pressure over budgets. By 1998, he was heading into a tailspin.

Deep down I suspected he had just had enough of America. He never liked living in Colorado Springs and, right through that summer, was hardly ever seen in the place. There was a new CEO he didn't see eye to eye with so, while George continued working away, he just stopped pitching up at the office.

One of the rare days he did turn up, things pretty much came to a head. Having spent the morning like a bear with a sore head, George picked up his book and announced that he was going to lunch. I offered to go with him, but George said that he wanted some time to himself. This wasn't his form. He liked lunch and he liked company. I didn't think anything more of it though. He said he'd be back 'twoish'.

We shared a fairly basic apartment together at the time as well as the use of a ten-year-old Saab for getting in and out of the office, which George now took to lunch. That weekend we were booked to give a clinic in Long Beach – him a level one, me a level two – and I was busy beavering away on a new manual.

When he hadn't arrived back by three, I began to get a little uncomfortable. These were pre-mobile-phone days, which meant he was, effectively, non-contactable. The minutes kept ticking by . . . 3.15 . . . 3.30 . . . 3.45 and it began to dawn on me that there might be something wrong here. So I got the office assistant to drive me down to our apartment just five minutes away and, sure enough, the Saab was parked outside.

Inside, I found that all of George's stuff was gone. He had abandoned ship.

My immediate worry was that he had jumped on a flight to Shannon or Dublin. This was Tuesday and I needed him on that plane to Long Beach the following Friday. I spent that night and all day Wednesday phoning around, trying to track him down, climbing the walls.

One of the first guys I had made contact with that Tuesday was Bill Schildnicht, an attorney in Pittsburgh. Bill was an extraordinary character who brought rugby into the projects when the steel mills moved out. He had driven me through the place one day and it was eerie seeing so many places boarded up. Out the back of the main streets, these massive projects had been built. They were awash with people of low socio-economic background and all the problems that go with that. Bill brought rugby into this place, selling the game as a unifying tool.

A lot of the kids were at war with one another over drugs, but he got them to play a match one day, selling the view that the guy on the other side of the tracks didn't actually have horns. It was an edgy, often volatile environment. He told me one night he was taking a session and a police car pulled up, the occupants marching out onto the baseball diamond where Bill trained the kids in the middle of the projects and arresting his 16-year-old scrum half. Just cuffed the kid and threw him into the back of the car.

I remember driving up to those same projects with him one Sunday morning and he pulled up outside this run-down house, three women sitting on the wall. He rolled down the window.

'Toby around?' he enquired.

'Who's asking?'

'Tell him coach Schildnicht swung by.'

Next thing, up pops Toby's head from behind the wall. 'Coach, howya doin?'

George used to go to Pittsburgh and help Bill take training sessions, so Bill had a lot of time for him. But, when I rang on the Tuesday, Bill said he hadn't seen George. In desperation, I rang again that Thursday night.

'Bill,' I said, 'I still haven't found him and I've completely run out of options. We have two clinics in Long Beach tomorrow and I can't do them on my own. There's going to be hell to pay if George doesn't show.'

There was a slight pause on the phone. Then Bill said, 'I know where he is!'

'Where?'

'He's right here.'

George came on the phone, very sheepish and apologetic. He said that he'd just panicked, that he'd had enough of all the 'shit'. I got him to calm down and talked him into getting a flight to Los Angeles. So I picked him up from LAX and we drove down to Long Beach that Friday evening, the clinic going to plan even if I was slightly distracted by the small matter of a Gaelic football game back home.

That year I was fitness advisor to the Galway football team and in regular contact with their manager, John O'Mahony. The clinic started at around 8 a.m., Galway's All-Ireland final against Kildare already under way. So I kept ducking out of the clinic to make quick calls home for updates from Noreen's brother, Roddy. Happily, Galway won.

Being honest, I could sense the wheels were coming off with George now. To be fair, he had built up the coaching programme from nothing, but his 'instructors' were falling by the wayside. He was answerable to the National Technical Panel – of which he was a member himself – and, at the time, there was a huge deal of aggravation about our budget. We were, essentially, spending more money than we had. The problem wasn't waste, so much as simply trying to spread the jam too far.

The funding for the coaching came from two sources. The IRB was one and a company called Rugby Imports, run by a Providence, Rhode Island businessman called Bob Hoder, was the other. Bob was absolutely vital to the programme. Without him putting his hand in his pocket, frankly it wouldn't have happened.

It was George's responsibility to draw up the budget and that had never been his strong point. Jack, by comparison, was a shrewd businessman. He operated the Eagles as a virtually separate entity, attracting sponsorship and ensuring that money raised was fed directly into the Eagles programme rather than any administrative maze. Competing in places like Japan, Hong Kong and – eventually – Fiji and Tonga, required big finances. Even the supposedly simple procedure of organising a squad session meant flying players in from New York, Dallas, Utah, places quite literally straddling America.

Jack ran the programme brilliantly, but his control made people within the IRB uncomfortable. Over time, that discomfort rippled down into the Technical Panel.

George was now one of those moving to have the Eagles made as answerable to the panel as he was. It would mean that Jack would have a boss, control of the Eagles' budget being taken out of his hands. To me, this was never going to happen. He was just too highly respected in US rugby and, in my opinion, rightly so.

Whenever the subject was brought up at a meeting, I'd leave the room. I felt the split was placing me in a slightly invidious position. This massive showdown had begun to loom and I wanted nothing to do with it. Approaching September, my only interest was in finishing out the programme and heading home.

We had had another poor Pacific Rim tournament and there was a bit of turmoil in the camp. Lyle, a world-class number eight with Bath, had blown out the ACL joint in his knee, missing the whole 1998 season.

I felt George was being foolhardy in pursuing the political argument. People recognised the good he had done and, at the time, he had a two-year contract extension on the table. I remember sitting in his office one day in Colorado Springs and saying, 'For God's sake, back out of this, George. This is one political battle you can't win. Back away.'

I was never in the habit of bullshitting him and I wasn't going to start now. I told him, if his plan went south, I wouldn't jump with him. 'I don't have a job to go home to,' I said. 'I've a career here to look after.'

But he was belligerent. He said he was going through with it and that's pretty much what he did, the power play eventually falling on its face spectacularly. It never got the backing of US Rugby and, as one of its most prominent voices, George's position became untenable. The two-year extension offer suddenly slipped off the table. He wasn't fired. He didn't resign. His contract just wasn't renewed. A bloodless coup.

I wasn't aware of any of this at that time. I had studiously kept out of the debate and, by the time it all blew, I was back home in Moylough. As it turned out, George had gone home ahead of me. It was the end of September when I got a call from Jack.

'Listen,' he said. 'You know there's been a lot of hassle with George. Well, basically, his contract is not being renewed.'

I had imagined George's contract, like my own, expired the following April. It didn't. I was shocked.

'George's deal is up next month,' said Jack.

'I didn't know that . . .'

'Yeah and I've just got word from the President that it's not being renewed.'

'OK.'

'And she's going to ring you in the next hour asking you to be the new Technical Director of US Rugby.'

'OK.'

This was code for telling me that I was the new Technical Director. The President was Ann Barry from Minneapolis-St Paul and her phone call would have been seen as just a formal nicety. Not so much asking me a question as handing me a job. One, incidentally, without a pay rise.

George took news of my appointment very badly. His view was that I should have jumped ship with him. When I rang him he told me in words of one syllable that I had stabbed him in the back. It was as if our conversation in Colorado Springs two months earlier had never happened.

'Hang on,' I argued. 'I warned you of the implications. I told you where I stood on this.'

None of this mattered now. To George I was a traitor. And that was us finished. We didn't talk for three years, though, when we eventually did, he accepted he had been in the wrong. But, at the time, George believed he had been messed around in America. And, in that context, everyone was to blame.

It was a sad way for it to end, because people recognised the good he had done for US rugby. He had sewn the seeds of something very productive, very positive. His vision had been absolutely vital. And, to begin with, they had been happy to extend his contract. But the failed coup changed everything. I often suspected that maybe George always understood that it might, but had just become a little punch-drunk from fighting constant battles. Everything just wore him out in the end and it was as if he was actually looking for an exit strategy. In the end, he saw himself as a victim

So I'm now Technical Director, saddled with an instructor group that had basically fallen apart. One of my first jobs was to get new people on board as diplomatically as I could. And I'm assistant to Jack with the Eagles, preparing for the 1999 World Cup.

At home, meanwhile, I was into my second year as coach to Buccaneers in the AIL. You could say my hands were full.

The Pacific Rim tournament had now extended to include the South Sea islanders, Fiji, Tonga and Samoa, as a kind of IRB guilt trip. Even with Hong Kong gone, it was becoming incredibly expensive to participate in and would crash and burn within three years.

Heading back to the States in April of 1999, I knew I couldn't continue indefinitely splitting my life on either side of the Atlantic. Noreen said as much. It was as if I had two lives now and it just wasn't fair on the family. We agreed that, after the World Cup, we'd make a decision. Either we'd move lock, stock and barrel to America as a family or I'd just come home for good. Which way the dice would fall, I honestly didn't know. I just knew that something had to change.

Jack had decided to make changes with the Eagles. Having spent the summer working with the backs, I now went back with the pack, with Wallaby Roger Gould brought in to work with the backs. A scrum coach, John Moore, had already been brought in from Wales. We began to turn things around but our Pacific Rim schedule was absolutely dreadful.

Our first three games were Japan at home, Canada and Samoa away. Ordinarily, we would have played the Japanese game in San Francisco, then fly an hour and a quarter up the coast to play Canada in Vancouver. For some reason, we agreed to play Japan in Hawaii. Still not too bad for Vancouver, except the Canadians decided to move that game to Toronto.

It meant that, in a ten-day window, my itinerary was Denver LA–Hawaii–LA–Toronto–LA–Fiji–Samoa–Fiji–SanFrancisco–Dublin. By the end of it, I felt I'd been to the moon and back.

Already jet-lagged, we lost to Japan in Hawaii (we had further to travel than they had), won in Toronto with the last kick of the game, then lost in a hell of a game to Samoa. After that, I had gone home for ten days, returning for victories over Tonga and Fiji in San Francisco.

Our World Cup preparations now began in earnest with a trip to Australia. We put out a young and pretty weak second string against a New South Wales Development XV and paid the price with a heavy defeat. But then we went up to Queensland and, had the referee given us a fair crack of the whip, we'd have beaten the Queensland Reds – coached by John Connolly – on a wet night in Ballymore. It was a great performance by the Eagles and we flew home feeling pretty good about ourselves.

As RWC 1999 approached, we'd been offered two warm-up games, one in England, one in Wales. I told Jack I was a little apprehensive about playing an English team that had the capacity to rout us. The game in Cardiff would be against Wales 'A' as part of the official opening of the Millennium Stadium, which was fair enough. But England I really didn't fancy.

Unfortunately, my worst fears came to pass. They beat us 106–8 in a terrible slaughter at Twickenham, ripping the guts out of our team. Everything we had won back psychologically in the Pacific Rim tournament and tour of Australia now basically lay on the ground as dust. It was gut-wrenching.

I will never forget sitting in the stand, watching this relentless white wave come crashing over us. It was men against boys, professionals against amateurs. They ripped us to pieces and, in hindsight, I'm not sure we ever fully recovered. After that, Wales 'A' beat us in Cardiff as well.

Brittle confidence had always been an issue with the Eagles. We'd had to pre-qualify the year before through a process that pitched us into games against Argentina, Canada and Uruguay in one week. Having to win just one of the three, we lost the first two and – depleted mentally and physically – just about scraped past the Uruguayans to qualify.

So the house of cards was always threatening to come down

and that warm-up game with England finally delivered on the threat. Remember, you're talking about fundamentally amateur players with precious little Test experience. At Twickenham, every last shred of self-belief was mangled.

It meant that we went to the 1999 World Cup a desperately tentative team. I found it particularly strange standing at Lansdowne Road in an American tracksuit, listening to the anthems, before our opening game against Ireland. On the day we got our selections wrong, were beaten up in the set-pieces, and lost heavily.

After that we went down to Romania in a game we might have won and ended our campaign with a game against Australia at Thomond Park.

We stayed in the Castletroy Park Hotel and, throughout the build-up, I tried to impress upon the American players that they'd have 10,000 people cheering for them wildly. 'We're underdogs,' I explained. 'And, in this neck of the woods, the underdog is king.'

On the day they couldn't believe the atmosphere. Australia beat us comfortably in the end, but – with the crowd behind them – the Eagles played out of their skins. We would be the only team to score a try against the Wallabies in the tournament and, truth to tell, were unlucky not to get two more. We had a maul going over the Wallaby line pulled down, which should have resulted in a penalty try. Then, one of the Eagles was foot-tripped at the side of a ruck with the try-line beckoning. On both occasions referee Andre Watson gave Australia the benefit of the doubt.

It was, at least, an honourable exit from the tournament for the Eagles and a respectable performance to mark Jack's last game as coach. He had announced that he was stepping down and I suppose I would have been considered a logical replacement.

But, for now, my contract with the Americans was up. As they prepared for the long flight home, I was happy to be facing a trip of roughly 5,000 miles less to Moylough. I said my farewells, not knowing if we had a future together.

13

ARRANGED MARRIAGE

The day that sealed my fate as Irish rugby coach was one that, for my critics, bore a perfect symmetry.

Ireland's 12–16 loss to Wales in Croke Park on 8 March 2008 came at the end of a week in which Warren Gatland had happily cranked up the hype machine about our so-called 'feud'. There was a lot I could have said at the time, but losing the game pretty much lost me any platform on which to publicly tackle a few home truths.

The build-up had, predictably, been distilled by the media into a battle between two coaches with a sulphurous history. Warren played along. All week, he was back in *'Et tu, Brute?'* mode, rekindling the story of supposed conspiracy and betrayal that prefaced his departure from Irish rugby. I never took the bait.

I was determined that the game wasn't going to be about me. We needed a win in the Six Nations, pure and simple. Hand on heart, Warren's name did not come up at a single Irish team meeting that week.

The game proved an intense and nervy affair effectively decided by the 'inches' Al Pacino's character, Tony D'Amato, talks about in *Any Given Sunday*. About 23 minutes into the game, Shane Horgan looked to have put us seven points clear only for the TV umpire to rule that 'Shaggy' had grounded the ball fractions short of the try-line. Almost immediately after, Stephen Jones slotted a penalty for Wales. Probably a ten-point turnaround, given the conversion would have been under the posts. I firmly believe we would have gone on to win comfortably had the try been awarded.

But it wasn't and we didn't. Shane Williams scored the only try of the game in the second half and, one week later, Wales secured the Grand Slam with victory against France in Cardiff. That same day, we went to Twickenham with a depleted team and got our asses kicked.

I met Warren under the stand immediately after the game in Croke Park and congratulated him. It was practically the first time we had spoken in six and a half years.

That night, the dinner was in the Shelbourne Hotel and, after the main course, I got up from my table and walked across to his. I could sense the whole room watching. 'C'mon,' I said, 'we'll have a pint.' You could almost hear a pin drop as we walked out together, people clearly curious to see where this was heading. Outside, the bar was mercifully empty. I ordered the drinks and Warren began to speak.

'Look,' he said, 'there was a lot in the papers this week, stuff being taken out of context . . .'

I interrupted. 'First of all,' I said, 'congratulations again today. Ye deserved to win. Ye were the better team.'

'You know,' he began again, 'stuff came out this week different to the way I intended it . . .'

I cut across him again. 'Warren, you know the press better than anybody. You're no schoolboy. You should know how things you say can be spun into a headline.'

'Yeah,' he said, 'well I do feel I was badly done by over here!'

'Obviously you do, that's no secret,' I said. 'And I understand that. But here's the deal. I never did anything wrong to you. When I was your assistant, I worked my ass off to try to make the team a success. I didn't make the decision not to re-employ you. That was made by the IRFU. But it's been hung around my neck ever since, which is grossly unfair. And you've bought into that. It came out again this week and, in that sense, you've wronged me. This isn't about the game of rugby. It's about two guys doing a job. Do you really think the IRFU would give me the job just because I wanted it? You were the guy in possession. They made their own decision.'

'Well,' he argued, 'I know that certain players were gunning for me. That they had big parts to play!'

'Warren, if you've a problem with any player, then you take that up with the player. But that's got nothing to do with me. Now I've told you what I think. I don't hold any grudges against you. That's it. We're having a pint.'

'Fair enough,' he said.

And that was the end of it. We chatted on pretty amicably, about our families, our kids. It was like we were right back at the beginning of our relationship. He talked about the Welsh players, how their skill-set was so good. And I agreed. I said they were like hurlers in Ireland, that they had basic, innate skills. I was actually enjoying talking to him again. All the bullshit had been parked.

And it was at that point that my old sparring partner from Connacht, Billy Glynn, invited himself into the conversation. For me, that was time to go. I'd said what I needed to say. The story of Warren and me had just become an urban myth, like the crocodiles in the sewers of New York. Certain journalists had fed into it and he'd been happy to allow them. Now, at last, I'd got it off my chest.

I went back to my table, satisfied that we had – at least – cleared the air.

I'd known this day was coming from the moment he had been appointed coach of Wales. The press were always going to have a field day. Yes, it had been a controversial decision not to extend his contract as Irish coach in 2001, but there were two sides to the story. I felt that what Warren was coming out with the week of the Welsh game was a fundamental attack on my character. The players, naturally, knew all this was going on in the background. But I just wouldn't let it become an issue in the build-up. I couldn't.

I wasn't going to talk to him through the press. Anything I had to say, I was determined to say it eyeball to eyeball.

The story of Warren and me actually begins in the Irish midlands. I met Eddie Coleman and Eddie Wigglesworth in Moate while the 1999 World Cup was still in progress. Ireland's defeat to Argentina in Lens had drawn the ire of public and pundits alike, the team famously opting for a fourteen-man line-out in one last, despairing bid to rope in the Pumas.

The line-out failed, pitching Irish rugby into turmoil and exposing Gatland – as coach – to serious levels of vitriol.

Philip Danaher had been operating as his backs coach, but made it clear all along that he would be stepping down after the World Cup. So, within two days of Ireland's exit from the tournament, I was essentially offered Philip's job. I knew I couldn't turn it down, though I did have a few small issues of housekeeping to attend to first.

In my role as US Technical Director, I had to attend a youth conference in London the weekend of the World Cup semi-final. After that, I had to go back to Colorado to submit my final report to the board. Jack Clark was in London and we went to the semi-final together.

In fairness to Jack, he always understood that my heart was in Irish rugby. When Brian Ashton resigned as national coach mid-season in the 1998 Five Nations, I had taken a phone call from

Pa Whelan – then the Irish manager – looking to see if I could give them 'a hand out' for the remainder of the Championship. I rang Jack to check that US Rugby wouldn't have a problem with this.

'You're not going to do a runner on me now, Sully, are you?' he said.

'No, Jack, absolutely not.'

'Well, if your country needs a dig-out, you can't say no!'

I told Pa that I had the all-clear and he said that he'd come back to me. But he never did. One week on, nothing. So I rang him and he started to ramble a little. It turned out that Danaher had already been given the job. I was furious that Pa hadn't had the courtesy to phone me and we had words on the phone. I'd known him long enough not to shy away from giving him a bollocking.

This was different now. This was a formal offer and Jack couldn't have been more magnanimous. I knew he saw me as his natural replacement as Eagles coach. It made sense because I knew the system. He was ready to step down and giving me the job would have made for a seamless transition. Yet now I was pretty much walking away from American rugby.

'You've got to take this one,' he said to me in London. 'You can't let this go!' Jack had always joked that I was destined to coach Ireland. 'I hope you're right,' I'd say laughing. 'It's written in the stars, Sully!' he'd say.

Actually, with me out of the equation, Jack's search for a new Eagles boss now acquired a real urgency. At that semi-final in Twickenham, we met Bob Templeton, who had been Bob Dwyer's assistant with the Wallabies at the previous tournament. Jack joked to him 'Yer man here is doing a runner on me back to Ireland, can you think of anyone who'd do a job with the Eagles for me?'

As it happened, Templeton would have heart bypass surgery

back in Australia after the World Cup and, while in hospital, get a visit from Duncan Hall, who'd finished as Leicester coach the year before. Duncan was looking for a job.

'Well, why not throw your name into the hat . . .'

Jack was delighted when he heard this but then, tragically, Templeton died in hospital due to complications. I suspect Jack saw this as some kind of divine signal and gave Duncan the job immediately. It didn't work out. In fact, one of the games that told him it wasn't working was a Test against Ireland in over 100-degree heat at Manchester, New Hampshire. The scoreline? Ireland 83, Eagles 3.

That night, I remember sitting with Jack trying to console him. I had been that soldier. But I was now Ireland's assistant coach.

When I was first offered the job, I asked Eddie Coleman, 'How are Warren and Donal (Lenihan) with this?' Lenihan was now the Irish manager. 'They're absolutely fine. No problems. Everything's been agreed,' insisted Eddie. He told me that Warren would ring me in the next few hours for a chat. Warren didn't ring.

Forty-eight hours went by without a call. I rang Eddie. 'Listen, I've heard nothing from Warren!'

'OK, leave it with me.'

Maybe two hours later, Warren rang. 'Happy to have you on board,' he said. 'Everyone's delighted.' Even to this day he insists that it was his decision to bring me on board. I don't know. I'd certainly doubt I was his first choice.

Lenihan was, effectively, boss and quick to emphasise the point. 'I'm in charge, Warren is head coach,' he said. The dynamic back then was different from today. Head coach answered to manager. And the coaching staff was relatively modest, no kicking coach, no defence coach, no skills coach. Just Donal, Warren, me, a doctor, a physio, a masseur and a baggage master.

I had played with Donal for Munster and against him for Garryowen. He'd also been on the Irish team in 1991/92 when I was doing the fitness work for Ciaran Fitzgerald. I liked him, still do. And he was a brilliant manager.

Straight up, I have to admit that my ambition was to be Ireland coach down the line. Some Irish people see ambition as a dirty word. I don't. While assistant to Warren, I'd do my damnedest to make the thing a success. I didn't want his job. I wanted him to do well but, some day, I hoped I might get the chance to do the job myself.

We got butchered in our first game of the new Six Nations at Twickenham. For me, it felt like a horrible case of déjà vu. I was sitting in practically the same seat I'd been sitting in when England savaged the Eagles in our World Cup warm-up game a few months previously, feeling just the same sense of hopeless disembowelment.

There was hell to pay back home, where one journalist even saw fit to criticise me for the poor performance of the backs despite the fact that I'd had literally no input into the day whatsoever. No matter, there was blood in the water and everyone was taking hits.

Next game up was Scotland. Having helped coach the US Eagles to play Ireland at the World Cup, it struck me that Ireland's style of play held no mystery. Essentially, we tried to make ground through the pack, offloading to the backs only when all other options had been exhausted. This was fine against weaker teams (like America). But Ireland simply didn't have the armoury to pummel opposing Six Nations packs into oblivion.

I gave Warren and Donal my opinion. I felt we had the core of a decent backline and restricting them to static ball when the pack ran out of road meant that we ended up kicking away a lot of possession. I suggested quicker line-out ball to the backs and no back-row moves in the scrum.

'Get the ball straight to the backs and I'll get you over the gain-line,' I promised. 'Get the backs over the gain-line and we can run the forwards off them. If that doesn't work, we'll try something else. But give me one shot at this.' They agreed.

The Scottish game probably needs a context. Ireland had now been humiliated at the World Cup and butchered in their first Six Nations game. People were roaring for Warren's head on a plate. The criticism was reaching that vindictive stage where everything the coach did was being twisted into some kind of Mister Magoo misadventure. Brutally unfair but, sadly, par for the course with the modern media.

If we lost to the Scots, Warren was probably gone. I knew that. And, as heir apparent, I also knew that – in those circumstances – I was virtually certain to be handed the job just two months after leaving America. All I had to do was nothing.

Instead, I tried frantically to make things work. I didn't want to step on anyone's toes, but I did want to help get the team back off the floor. The Monday after Twickenham, I actually met Eddie Coleman in the Berkeley Court. Our selection meeting would be later that night in Cork. He wanted to know what I thought we could do to turn the situation around. 'Look,' I said, 'my view is that if you want to make an omelette, you've got to break some eggs.' I told him what I thought.

'Well you'd better break some eggs,' he said. 'Because this thing is going down in flames!'

I sat into my car for the drive to Cork, turned on the radio and the *Joe Duffy* programme was besieged with callers over some shameful 'rugby' incident in London at the weekend. The reason for the uproar gradually dawned on me. Our reserve hooker, Frankie Sheahan, had headbutted an abusive supporter in Jury's Hotel, Kensington. Driving to Cork, I wondered, could things get any worse?

I made my case for change at the selection meeting. But, if we changed strategy, we needed to change personnel. There was general agreement in the room and we announced eight changes to the team slaughtered in London, with five new caps – John Hayes, Simon Easterby, Peter Stringer, Ronan O'Gara and Shane Horgan.

This may sound arrogant but I always had this theory that, if you showed me a defensive line-up, I could crack it. At worst, I could get you over the gain-line. Analysis was virtually unheard of at the time, but I got a guy in Scotland to do a bit for me on their players. I discovered that if you shut down their out-half – Gregor Townsend – as he ran from left to right, he was inclined to throw a blind pass back infield.

Halfway through the second half, that's precisely what happened. David Humphreys, having replaced O'Gara, latched onto one of Townsend's blind throws, hacked it the length of Lansdowne Road and scored. We won. Everyone was euphoric.

My priority as backs' coach was now to try and get an exceptional young centre we had into places that he could play. Brian O'Driscoll had, essentially, only been getting the ball when the pack had finished with it. He was running into brick walls. Drico was still a relative unknown, but it was obvious he could play.

Italy were next up at Lansdowne and we tore them to pieces inside the first 20 minutes. They played a four-up defence, the winger coming in and taking the fullback, so we just dismantled them by running double skips.

Now we're on a roll. We go to Paris, O'Driscoll scores a hat-trick of tries and we beat the French on their own territory for the first time since 1972. The tries come because we're no longer slaves to the pack. It's exhilarating. That night, we decided that Donal, Warren and me, with our respective wives, Mary, Trudy and Noreen, would head out for a quiet pint. Paris, as you might imagine, was in the grip of a green party.

Donal, in fairness, was never a fella for addressing the masses. He fancied a nice, low-profile evening. But, as we walked down from the hotel, Warren and Trudy disappeared in the throng. Later, on our way back, we were trying to get a taxi close to Kitty O'Shea's pub. It was closing at this point, but we stuck our heads in the door. And there was Warren at the top of the stairs, waving to the crowd like the Pope in St Peter's Square. He loved them and they loved him. The place was mental, so we made a quick escape.

Back home, a change of direction was decided for our last game against Wales in Dublin. Warren wanted, he said, to keep the Welsh 'honest'. So the plan was to take the ball around the sides, keep things tight. It was a close-run thing, but we lost. Anthony Foley might have saved us at the death by just sliding over when one-on-one with Gareth Thomas. But 'Axel' opted instead to 'make sure' and pass outside to Denis Hickie. Thomas practically put Denis into the second row of the stand.

There was a paradigm shift in the Irish set-up immediately after that Six Nations. Lenihan stepped down to take up his role as manager of the Lions, Brian O'Brien coming in as his replacement. But the hierarchical order had changed for good. Warren, as coach, was now unequivocally the number one.

I knew that he was angling now for a contract extension to take him right up to the next World Cup. And I knew, too, that there was a kind of three-way conflict within the Union about how to respond. Some felt he should get a one-year extension, others thought two, and others again felt he shouldn't get any. As it happened, he got two.

We headed off on a summer tour of the Americas for Test games against Argentina, USA and Canada and, from the outset, it was a mess, Firstly, Munster had reached the Heineken Cup final against Northampton at Twickenham. Secondly, to mark the 125th anniversary of the IRFU, a game was organised between Ireland and the Barbarians at Lansdowne Road. Munster played on the Saturday, Ireland on the Sunday and we flew to Buenos Aires on the Monday.

Nothing felt right. We picked up a raft of injuries against the Baa-Baas, including O'Driscoll and Denis Hickie, while most of the Munster lads were still licking their wounds after a heartbreaking loss. Bizarrely, Warren then called an impromptu team meeting as we walked between Terminals One and Three in Heathrow. Just stopped in his tracks and started giving this spiel about it being a 'serious' tour, passers-by gaping.

You could sense players looking at him, wondering what was coming down the line.

On arrival in Argentina Warren gave a marathon press conference that – because of translation issues and the number of journalists (at least 100) – dragged on for almost two hours. He then changed his mind about training without telling me and I missed the session. I was incensed, making my feelings known to Brian O'Brien.

Our second night there, it was decided that everyone should go out for a beer so we headed for an Irish pub. It was as if we were all on a jolly. The Pumas, meanwhile, had us lined up in the cross hairs. They were determined to prove that their World Cup victory in Lens had been no fluke. We were treating the tour like a holiday.

No surprise then. Argentina won. Quite easily (34–23) as it happens.

Next up were my old friends the Eagles. Because of my American connections Warren allowed me take the lead in formulating a game plan. I knew that the Eagles had won two games in a row in the Pacific Rim, but beaten very weak Japan and Canada teams. They were being talked up by coach Duncan Hall into something that they simply weren't.

Eagles captain Dave Hodges, told me that Hall was living in 'dreamland'. Apparently, when Jack asked him about his intended game plan, he declared, 'Tell the Irish and Eddie O'Sullivan to bring whatever gameplan they like!' Hall was flying solo and his players knew it. We won by those 80 points in boiling heat.

From there, we went to Toronto. Fletchers Field. For me, another dose of déjà vu. We stayed in the same, shitty hotel out by the airport that I'd stayed in with the Eagles during the previous year's Pacific Rim. The training pitch was poor. Warren seemed to slip back into vacation mode and I could see it beginning to rub off on the players. Training was shambolic. I went to Briano and he spoke to Warren.

I suppose you could say that there was now a bit of tension between us. Realising, I believe, that people at home were asking questions, he asked me to take training. Some of the players who had come in – like Simon Easterby, Ronan O'Gara and Kieran Dawson – would have known me, because of our involvement with the under-21s, better than they knew Warren.

Maybe he was feeling insecure. His head had been in the guillotine coming out of Twickenham. One slip against Scotland and it was in the basket. He had been falling off the horse at that point and I helped him back on. I had given him a game plan when I could have sat on my hands.

Now, maybe four months on, we were in Toronto and the energy was all wrong. It was the last week of the season and the fellas had switched off mentally. At a time when we needed to be battening down the hatches, everything was getting looser.

Back home, David Humphreys' wife was heavily pregnant with their first child and, on the morning of the game, went into semi-labour. Not unnaturally, 'Humps's' head was already on the plane home. He was in no condition to play, but Warren decided to start him. Humps, not surprisingly, had a poor game.

There was an air of pantomime about us. At one point, we ran a move, throwing two skip passes. A prop who knew he was to be skipped tried to catch the ball and knocked it on in front of our own posts. All the day lacked was canned laughter. In the course of the game, we replaced Humps and Peter Stringer at halfback with ROG and Guy Easterby. Near the end, Guy made a break off the back of a line-out, put Paul Wallace over in the corner and ROG nailed the touchline conversion to secure us a draw!

It would be fair to say the chemistry between Warren and me was not especially comfortable now. I just felt that he never had a clear game plan. He was a very good forwards' coach and, because of that, our set-pieces were excellent. But, beyond that, there was little sense of a coherent strategy. He'd come down in the morning with a few lines scribbled on a piece of paper and, in training, there was no such thing as time allocation. Sessions that were meant to last an hour and a half drifted to two hours and beyond.

He would lose the confidence of some key senior players in 2001. In fact, by the time we played the so-called 'Foot and Mouth' games that autumn, a few of them had had enough. It was as if he just wasn't dialled into the same wavelength. For two years the IRFU had implored him to appoint a defence coach, but he wouldn't do it. The thing was drifting.

It wasn't, by any means, all attrition between us. We were miles apart on rugby matters but we could go for a couple of beers together and actually have a good laugh. I felt that, when it wasn't business, we enjoyed each other's company. Rugby-wise, there was, undeniably, an undercurrent. It was hard for me to believe that I hadn't been parachuted in over his head. And, on that basis, hard not to imagine that he might suspect I was just waiting to jump into his seat.

His dealings with the Union were poor. It seemed that he treated the committee men with contempt, often flatly ignoring them when they'd be in the team hotel. This never made much sense to me. Like or loathe these people, they put a huge amount into the game on a voluntary basis. It seemed to me that all they asked in return was a little civility. With Warren, they didn't get it.

I saw him in a lift one day with maybe six committee men and he studiously ignored them. How hard was it to say hello?

He also tried to lay down certain markers. One Friday I was booked on a lunchtime flight to London and we had a meeting arranged at Lansdowne Road for ten that morning with the squad administrator, Joan Breslin. My flight was at one, so I needed to be at the airport in or around 11.30 a.m. Everyone knew that.

Warren arrived into the office at 10.55, Briano, looking embarrassed, by his side. I was furious. The moment the meeting started, I got up and walked out, slamming the door behind me. I just wanted to make the point that I was there, but wasn't putting up with this kind of bullshit. Later, I said as much on the phone to Briano. I'd been there, sitting on my hands for an hour, waiting for them to arrive.

Briano, typically, did his best to smooth the waters. 'Look,' he started, 'we just got delayed!' Bullshit and I knew it. But he was a clever man manager, very good at not letting things fester. Without him, I suspect there would have been a great deal more aggro between Warren and I.

The 2001 Six Nations was, of course, disrupted by the outbreak of 'Foot and Mouth'. It meant that our games against Scotland, Wales and England were played that autumn.

We had opened with a nervy win on our first Championship visit to Rome. In the build-up, Warren gave an interview to the *Irish Times* in which he was asked about rumours that the team might get an audience with the Pope. His response had been pretty dismissive, something along the lines of not having time for that kind of distraction.

The article appeared while we were in camp in Limerick and, suddenly, all hell broke loose. A high-ranking member of the

Catholic Church contacted the IRFU to express their disgust that the Union would even consider rejecting an invitation to St Peter's. As it happened, the audience had already been agreed to.

Eddie Coleman, President of the IRFU, now had the job of firefighting. He was trying to get hold of Warren, but couldn't get an answer from his mobile. Eventually, he rang Briano. I was standing next to him in the lobby of the Castletroy Park Hotel as he handed the phone to Warren. 'The President wants to talk to you . . .'

'Em . . . oh.'

'I think you should take this call, Warren!'

In fairness, Warren just hadn't realised the sensitivities of the matter. The idea of an Irish team playing in Rome and turning down an audience with the Pope because they were too busy was unconscionable. I could hear Eddie Coleman screaming down the phone, Warren visibly in shock.

We beat France in Dublin in our second game but, then, the Championship was essentially suspended for six months because of the 'Foot and Mouth' outbreak. It was a pity. The team was acquiring real momentum, but it would be September by the time we got to Murrayfield.

In the interim, Donal Lenihan rang to say he was going to suggest to Graham Henry that I should be brought on the Lions tour as a third coach with Andy Robinson to look after the midweek team. I'd love to have gone, but Henry said no. Instead, I went with Ireland on a low-key, one-game tour to Romania.

That September, we went to Edinburgh half-baked and got butchered 10–32. All the talk in the build-up had been about how we were building a squad for the 2003 World Cup and, as ever, the Scots were waiting in the long grass.

I remember sitting in the stand after just fifteen minutes, thinking, This isn't about whether we'll lose, but by how much!

Youghal R.F.C. 1st XV 1978.
I am front row centre, my brother Kieran front row 2nd from the right.

Playing for Garryowen FC 1982.

My first Munster Cap 1983.

Messing with Woody in the team room in Dunedin during the New Zealand Tour 2002.

Words of wisdom from Brian O'Brien.

Sharing a joke with Brian O'Driscoll at training.

Leading the team off after the warm-up before the 6 Nations game v England, Lansdowne Road 2005.

Making a coaching point to Will Greenwood, Geordan Murphy and Shane Horgan during the 2005 Lions Tour to New Zealand.

Discussing team tactics during a team run with Paul O'Connell.

A media feeding frenzy at the 6 Nations Launch, 2007 in London.

With Brian O'Driscoll and the Triple Crown Trophy in the Irish changing room, Twickenham, 6 Nations 2006.

Addressing the squad at training.

Saying goodbye to the 'old' Lansdowne Road, November 2006.

Savouring the moment with Manager, Ger Carmody, after the England game at Croke Park, 6 Nations 2007.

A last minute tactical chat with Ronan O'Gara close to kick-off time.

A funny moment at training with Niall O'Donovan during the 6 Nations 2008.

It was obvious that we had been scouted as they seemed to anticipate every move we made. We'd trained at Boroughmuir and David Humphreys revealed that Gregor Townsend told him that night over a few drinks that they had all our moves.

Again pressure was beginning to build now as we sat down to pick a team for the next game, Wales in Cardiff. Most of the meeting focused on number ten, Humps v ROG. In Scotland, ROG had started and it certainly hadn't been his fault that we lost. But his confidence was in shreds. It was a massive call and Warren insisted we stuck with ROG.

I was uneasy. I felt that if we got off to a bad start in Cardiff, the whole thing could crumple again. After all, it was just ROG's second Championship season. Another bad day could do untold damage to his confidence. Back in my room, that sense of unease just hardened. I felt pretty strongly that we had done the wrong thing, so I rang Briano in the room next door and told him so. As it happened, he felt the same.

So we went down to Warren's room, got him out of bed and talked him into starting Humps. We walloped Wales 36-6.

England then came to Dublin chasing a Grand Slam and, by some miracle, we beat them. I say that because our training in the week of the game was shambolic. By the Thursday we were moving from our Wicklow base, the Glenview Hotel, up to the Berkeley Court in Dublin. I met Keith Wood, our captain, in the corridor.

'Howya doin?' I asked.

'I could be better!'

'Why?'

'I'm really pissed off with the way this week is going.'

'Well, join the club,' I said.

We talked about the shortcomings of the preparation. England, we knew, were there for the taking. Martin Johnson and Lawrence Dallaglio, who represented the spine of their pack, were missing. They were starting Iain Balshaw at fullback, someone we always considered an easy target. They'd given the captaincy to Matt Dawson, another bad decision. Dawson was a terrific scrum half, but he was prone to volatility. Everywhere we looked, we saw potential weakness to be exploited. Yet it felt as if we were just gliding towards the game on automatic pilot.

'Woody' I knew was fed up with close shaves and he could see another one on the horizon. We agreed that we'd try to get Warren, Humps and the two of us into a room in Dublin. And we did, 5 p.m. that Thursday. Warren's room. It was there that we came up with a territorial game plan, forcing them to play in their own half, setting up midfield targets and getting Humps to kick to the corners.

Essentially, we didn't want to get into a fist fight with them. The plan was to just keep moving them around. Woody and I did most of the talking, Warren agreeing. And that's how we beat England, playing them on our own terms, pressuring their weak points. Fittingly, Woody got a brilliant try off a line-out set-piece. It would be the only time in his entire career that he was on a winning team against England.

We didn't win the Championship, but four wins out of five put Warren in a pretty strong position. Through his newspaper contacts, he immediately began agitating for a contract to take him all the way through to the 2003 World Cup. It wasn't the way to deal with the IRFU, but he seemed to feel he was now pretty bombproof.

That autumn the All Blacks came to town and, with Humps outstanding at ten, we stormed into a commanding lead. We led 16–7 at the interval and, when Denis Hickie crossed for a try immediately after the resumption, an historic victory looked imminent. But we then folded like a house of cards, conceding three tries in a ten-minute spell, the Blacks running out comfortable winners. This was now symptomatic of a bungee cord trend with the team, of performances habitually going up and down. That day, we defended like lemmings on a cliff edge, all the Union's worries about the absence of a defence coach coming home to roost again.

The performance against the All Blacks showed we could look a serious team for an hour. After that, the bigger sides knew how to pick us off.

Jack Clark flew to Dublin for an IRB meeting that same week and I got him tickets for the game. Duncan Hall having fallen on his face, the Eagles had no coach at the time. People saw Jack and automatically put two and two together. They assumed that I was trying to orchestrate something. I wasn't. Jack did, I admit, ask me if I was interested in the Eagles post and my honest answer was: 'I don't know.'

If Warren was given the extension he was looking for, I couldn't honestly have seen us working together for another two years. In that case, the Eagles post would probably have attracted me. Yet, if I went back to America, I also knew that the Irish job might have slipped out of my reach forever.

The truth is that I discussed this in my head alone. I never said any of it to Jack, nor to anyone in the Union. Rumour subsequently took hold that all of this was part of a grand plan. Pressure the Union into believing that I was on the brink of jumping ship to America and they might be panicked into giving me the big job now. I remember an exchange I had with Jim Glennon.

'Jesus, you're a smart operator,' he said.

'Why?'

'Getting Clark to fly in from San Francisco when you did.'

'But I didn't . . .'

It was pointless. The impression of tactical shrewdness on my behalf was too tempting for some people to ignore. What I did know was that, in his dealings with the Union, Warren could still be quite curt and aloof. At meetings he was either aggressive or non-communicative. It wasn't clever. It never is wise to cut off the hand that feeds you. I knew that, in some quarters, there was a feeling that we had blown a Grand Slam by going to Edinburgh with our heads halfway up our asses. Now the All Blacks, from a position of seemingly looming defeat, had just upped a gear and brushed us aside.

And Warren's all the time trying to negotiate his contract through a media contact.

There was a series of reviews done on the season and, as was normal, we were all called to a committee meeting in the Berkeley Court to discuss the findings. The atmosphere was businesslike, all the heavy hitters of the Union grilling Warren, Briano and me on where we thought the team was going. Warren's share value was still high and I assumed that he was getting his two years.

Then I got a call to attend another meeting at Lansdowne Road. I arrived early and decided to pull into the Berkeley Court for a coffee to kill time. As I drove in the gate, Warren was walking out past me. He looked ashen. I waved, but he just walked past without responding as if he'd seen a ghost. At the time, I presumed he just hadn't seen me though he would reveal later – in his own version of events – that he had.

I remember thinking, Something odd is going on here.

Down at Lansdowne Road, I was beckoned up to the boardroom, where Eddie Coleman, Syd Millar, Noel Murphy, John Lyons and Philip Browne were waiting. Again there were a few questions about the direction I thought the team was taking. Largely similar, in truth, to those I had already answered. Then, out of the blue, I was asked if I would have any problem working with Declan Kidney. I said I wouldn't.

And, at that point, Eddie Coleman fixed me with a stare and asked, 'If you were asked to coach Ireland, would you accept the job?'

I paused for a second, my heart thumping. 'Absolutely,' I said finally. 'I'd consider it an honour to coach Ireland.' Eddie leaned across the table and shook my hand. 'Congratulations,' he said. 'You're now coach to the Ireland rugby team!'

It turned out they had brought Warren in to the Berkeley Court to tell him that he wasn't going to have his contract renewed. Clearly he had just stepped out of that meeting when I saw him. People say he was sacked. He wasn't. He had been agitating for a two-year extension that the Union just decided not to give him.

I was told that Declan Kidney was downstairs and I was invited to go down for a chat with my assistant! Now, Declan and I had a little history. Nothing beyond the normal tensions between provincial coaches and those running the national team, but enough to make me feel the need to broach it. He was also manager of Ireland 'A' and I was mindful of an incident in which, because of a glut of injuries, he had come looking for some reinforcements from the senior panel for a game against Japan. We turned him down, Ireland 'A' – as we expected – winning the game by 50-odd points without our help, But I knew Declan was annoyed.

There had been another incident involving the IRFU's Fitness Director, Liam Hennessy. He wanted the Irish players to have a proper pre-season, incorporating what was to become a regular trip to Spala in Poland. Naturally, the provincial coaches were fighting their own corners. Declan came to this meeting and, essentially, started putting across his perspective. Maybe it wasn't my place, but I stepped in and we had a lively argument.

Had I now answered 'no' to the Union's question about working with him, would the invitation to coach Ireland still have followed? I'm not sure. I certainly felt no inclination to find out.

Anyway, I went downstairs and greeted him warmly. 'Look,' I

began, 'we may have had some differences in the past . . .' Declan interjected. 'I've never had any problem with you,' he said. I would, maybe, have preferred if we'd cleared the air, but I was happy that we would both be pulling in the one direction now.

On reflection, I suppose, the arrangement was an artificial one. We were both ambitious and, while I think it suited the Union to have us working together, I'm not sure anyone had quite thought out the likely working dynamic between us. Over time, I think the arrangement became difficult for us both.

And, in my heart of hearts, I probably suspected it would from day one.

This was a Tuesday night, but my appointment could not be formally announced until the IRFU had signed off on the small print of Warren's departure. I drove home, got in around midnight, the kids already in bed. Noreen was waiting up and her first words made me quite emotional.

'Your mother would be so proud now,' she said.

Rena had died that June, still heartbroken I suspect by my father's passing. And I knew Noreen was right. My mother would have been so proud. We sat down, had a cup of tea and – for the next two days – I pretty much went into a bunker. Philip Browne instructed me not to even answer the phone. There would be a press conference in Dublin that Friday to formally make the announcement. It would be the day that George Harrison died.

The unveiling itself is a blur. After the conference, I settled into a room in the Berkeley Court with Browne and the IRFU's media liaison officer, John Redmond. For maybe the next four hours, three mobiles and a landline seemed to be ringing incessantly. Media enquiries mixed with calls of congratulation. I took one from Jack Clark, literally cheering down the line from San Francisco.

'Told you, Sully, didn't I?'

The following day I had breakfast with Briano and the two of us drove to Kilaloe for a meeting with Woody at his home. After that, it was straight in to Thomond that evening to see Munster play Llanelli. I was determined to hit the ground running.

Then that Monday morning, the shrapnel began to fly.

14

THE BIG JOB

Fred Trueman famously once observed in an after-dinner speech, 'I'm here to propose a toast to sportswriters and it's up to you if you stand up!'

Given my reputation in some sections of that industry as a controlling megalomaniac, it might surprise people to know that the first thing I did as Irish coach was go in search of help. Straight away, I knew I needed a defence coach and a forwards' coach. Yet, first and foremost, I needed to be sure what senior players I could lean on. And, specifically, if I had a captain.

That's why Kilaloe was my first port of call the day after being officially unveiled as Ireland coach. Keith Wood, I knew, had become pretty demoralised with Ireland's inconsistency and my big fear was that he might decide to retire from international rugby. He'd been seven years playing for Ireland now, roughly half of them wearing the captain's armband. And, in that time, he'd known more bad days than good.

Woody was playing with Harlequins, had a successful PR business in London and, had he walked away from the green jersey at that point, no one could reasonably have blamed him.

When I think of Wood, I can't honestly think of anyone I have worked with in rugby that I admire more. I find myself drawn to Sir Alex Ferguson's observation on Roy Keane after that famous 1999 Champions League semi-final against Juventus at the Stadio Delle Alpi in Turin. Keane was, of course, harshly booked quite early in that game, ruling him out of the final in Barcelona if Manchester United got there. Yet his subsequent performance bore a selflessness that 'Fergie' found utterly heroic.

'I didn't think I could have a higher opinion of any footballer than I already had of the Irishman,' he wrote in his auto-biography, *Managing My Life*. 'But he rose even further in my estimation at the Stadio Delle Alpi.'

That pretty much captures the kind of admiration I had, indeed still have, for Woody. As it happened, injury would greatly restrict his involvement with the Irish team during my time in charge. But what he gave, he gave unequivocally. To this day I remain in awe of what he put himself through to play in the 2003 World Cup, more of which anon.

At the time of my appointment, I couldn't have described our relationship as a friendship. It wasn't. In fact, I remember Blackrock losing an AIL game to Garryowen and Woody saying something sarcastic to me in the showers that really pissed me off. It was just his style. He was opinionated. He shot from the hip and you dealt with that or you didn't. We wouldn't have spoken again until I was Irish assistant coach and, even then, our relation-ship was a slow-burn thing. But I did feel there was a mutual respect between us and, maybe, a legacy of trust too connected to something that had happened in camp during the autumn of 2000. We were based at the Glenview Hotel in Wicklow when Woody took a call to say that his brother, Gordon, had suffered a heart attack in America.

We didn't have much information on his condition, but it

became an absolute imperative to get his sister and partner over there as quickly as possible. Through my contacts in America, I had been able to organise this pretty quickly. In fact, within an hour of hearing about Gordon, we had flights arranged and the girls booked into a hotel directly across from the hospital.

Tragically, Gordon's heart would give out on him again two years later, this time fatally. It was the autumn of 2002 and we were preparing for upcoming World Cup qualifiers with a game against Romania in Limerick. On the Tuesday morning we were at a staff meeting when a phone call came through for Briano. Gordon's partner, Siobhan, was Briano's daughter. I could see instantly from the way he put down the phone that something terrible had happened.

Briano just looked at me and said, 'Gordon's been found dead in his car.'

He was living in Kilaloe, had gone down for a paper and never came back. Siobhan went searching and found him still at the wheel, the car pulled into a ditch. Gordon was 41. Though they weren't married, Gordon was effectively Briano's son-in-law. I could see the devastation in his eyes.

We went down to the team room to find Woody who, in the mornings, was always full of the joys of spring, slagging people, making light of the day ahead. As we arrived, he was just stepping up on the weighing scales. 'Woody, I've some bad news for you,' said Briano. Instinctively, Woody thought it was his mother, Pauline, who wasn't well at the time and would, sadly, also pass away soon after.

'No,' said Briano gravely. 'It's Gordon. He's gone!'

'He's gone gone?' asked Woody.

'Gone gone.'

The two of them got in a car and drove straight to Kilaloe. I went into the team room and told the boys. I can remember Anthony Foley, who would have known Gordon well, almost falling off his chair at the news. The whole squad went to the funeral that week, Woody himself almost missing the birth of his son, rushing almost literally from the cemetery to Dublin airport for a red-eye to Heathrow the following morning.

Within a matter of hours, Nicola had given birth to their first child, Alexander.

I don't think any of us will ever fully understand what Woody was going through at the time. He had been due to lead the team out in Thomond Park that weekend with his nephew, David (Gordon's son), as mascot. Emotionally, he had to be in tatters. Yet not once can I remember even the tiniest hint of self-pity creeping through. The months after that would expose him to an injury nightmare and many long, lonely months of painful, unseen rehabilitation. Yet he came through.

Like I said, the guy to me is a 24-carat hero.

Two other guys I needed to be sure were onside happened to be people I had played against. I met both Peter 'Claw' Clohessy and Mick 'Gaillimh' Galwey that Christmas to ascertain their intentions. My mission statement was to make Ireland a more consistent team and I reckoned these two experienced heads would be vital to anchoring our first Six Nations challenge. Claw was uneasy. He told me that he reckoned he had another championship in him, but couldn't see himself doing the subsequent summer tour in New Zealand.

'We'll worry about New Zealand when it comes around,' I said. 'But you're on board for the Six Nations?'

'One hundred per cent,' said Claw, who would play all five games in that Championship.

I wasn't in the business of making promises, but I did make one to Gaillimh. I knew I couldn't guarantee him a place in the team, but I also knew the calibre of the man. Gaillimh has, I believe, gone into the record books as the most dropped international in Irish rugby history. Yet you would search long and hard to find a more resolutely positive presence in any dressing room.

When I asked him to stay on board, his response was: 'I'm on board alright, but promise me one thing. When the day comes to cut me loose, give me some kind of advance warning. Don't let it be a bombshell that I hear from someone else.'

I gave him my word.

That day came quicker than I expected. Gaillimh would actually captain the team in my first game against Wales and play in the first three but, by the time our fourth game came up – against Italy – I decided not to include him in my match-day 22. We trained in Belfast that week and on the Tuesday, after a session at the RUC grounds, I called Mick aside and told him I needed to talk to him back at the hotel.

He'd been around a long time and was smart enough to know what was coming down the pipe. So, that lunchtime, he came down to my room with Briano, who had, for years, been his mentor at Shannon. I didn't beat around the bush. 'You're not in the 22, Mick, and I don't know if you'll ever be back again,' I told him. Typically, he took it on the chin. Actually, you couldn't imagine a guy handling that kind of situation better.

'Fair enough,' he said. 'I've got a few more caps this year that I didn't think I'd get and I've enjoyed every minute of it.'

It was hugely emotional, both Briano and Gaillimh close to tears. In fact, Mick joked subsequently that he nearly felt more sorry for Brian than he did for himself. I do know that certain journalists pressed him subsequently to have a go at me, to paint himself as being victimised and Galwey just wouldn't wear the idea. A real man's man.

For a forwards' coach, I basically drew up a shortlist of one. Niall O'Donovan was Plan 'A'. I didn't have a Plan 'B'. He was assistant at the time to Declan Kidney with Munster and well established in his own right now as a top-rank coach. He was also a straight talker, which I liked. I have always considered myself a reasonably good judge of people and, from day one, I saw Niall O'Donovan as a top-notch guy.

His demeanour in Thomond that day 'Rock beat his Shannon team in the AIL announced him unequivocally to me as a gentleman. Shannon supporters can be pretty unforgiving and, on this occasion, we had torn their team to shreds. Yet Niallo could not have been more magnanimous. I remember telling Briano of my plan.

His response was that O'Donovan would be a 'fantastic' choice but that, as heir apparent for the Munster job, he might not choose to take it.

Munster and Leinster were playing in that year's Celtic League final at Lansdowne Road and Briano and I drove to Dublin that Friday. The Munster team was staying at the Mespil Hotel and we met Niallo in the lobby. I told him what I had in mind and emphasised that this was not a selection process.

'I want you to be clear on something,' I said. 'I'm not leaving here to go and talk to somebody else. If you say "no", I go back to the drawing board. There is nobody else in the picture for this. This isn't an interview. If you want the job, it's yours. If you don't, I'll fully respect that. But you are my first choice.'

Niallo asked if he would be included in team selection and I assured him that he would.

'Look,' I said. 'The forwards would be your responsibility. By that I mean, I'd be giving you total ownership.' I knew it was a difficult decision. Declan was staying Munster coach until the end of the season but, after that, Niallo would have been the obvious choice to take over. He took 24 hours to come back to me. 'I'll do it,' he said.

The final and most problematic piece of the jigsaw was finding a defence coach. I was pointed in the direction of former rugby league star Ellery Hanley, who had worked with Bath and

England. As a Bath player, Kevin Maggs was my contact. 'Maggsy's' view was that Hanley knew his stuff even if, personality-wise, he could be a little overbearing.

The arrangements for a meeting were made through his agent, but nothing seemed simple. The first meeting fell through, then likewise with the second as fog at Bristol forced Briano and I into taking a flight to London and attempting to drive down the M4 to Bath. The problem? We flew into London City airport, to the east of the city and spent two hours in a virtual car park on the M25. By the time we got on the M4 it was much too late to head to Bristol, so we swung into Heathrow and flew home. A total waste of a day.

I rescheduled the meeting for one week later in Coventry. Meantime, Donal Lenihan had got a list of other potential candidates from the England defence coach, Phil Larder. One on the list was Mike Ford. I had never heard of the guy, but something about his CV appealed to me. It was solid, nothing spectacular. But you could see that he had done a lot of groundwork.

So I scheduled two meetings that day in the English Midlands. One with Hanley, the other with Ford.

Hanley's agent decided to talk to me before letting his client join the meeting. It was hard-sell stuff. All about how Ellery was a world-class coaching talent and a top-rank person, blah, blah, blah. Eventually, I interjected. 'Look,' I said, 'it's actually Ellery himself I'd like to speak to.'

So Ellery arrived, swinging the Mercedes keys through his fingers. He sat down and gave me the whole spiel of what he expected of people he worked with. And all I could think was that this guy's ego seemed bigger than a house. Still, if he was good at his job . . .

I explained the conditions under which he would be joining us. How I'd be head coach and his area of expertise would begin and end with defence. Everything I said just seemed to wash right over him. I almost got the impression that he felt he'd be doing Irish rugby an enormous favour by coming to work with us.

No matter, I decided to broach the issue of money. 'Look, I'm just gonna go over here and talk to my agent,' said Ellery. 'I'll come back to you.'

They chatted in a corner for maybe ten minutes, then the agent came back across. 'What are we talking about financially?' I asked. Suddenly, he started the spiel again. What a great guy Ellery was. How much he was in demand. His track record as a player.

'We've been through all that,' I said. 'I need you to put some hard numbers in front of me.'

He wouldn't. Mister Agent just kept flip-flopping until, finally, I called an end to the meeting. 'Look, I've someone else to meet,' I told them. It wasn't a problem. The meeting ended amicably enough. They were going to get back to me with numbers.

Maybe twenty minutes later, Ford walked into the room with a folder under his arm. No agent, no Mercedes keys. He sat down, put his CV on the table and it struck me instantly how he was just this down-to-earth North of England bloke. The more I talked to him, the more I got a sense that – despite a lack of experience in union – this was a guy with a real passion for what he was doing.

After fifteen minutes of our conversation, the decision was a no-brainer.

The irony is that Mike told me subsequently how he had bumped into Hanley in the hotel lobby that day. They had played together in league and Mike, on realising that they were in for the same interview, pretty much wrote himself out of contention.

But I flew home that night with Mike Ford pencilled in as my defence coach. It wasn't going to be easy, I knew. Asking a guy with no virtually no experience in union to build a defensive system that would stand the test of international rugby was a big throw of the dice. Yet I had liked him instantly on our first meeting.

Within 24 hours I contacted Fordy and we worked out a deal over the phone. He sounded nervous and asked if, maybe, we could fax a signed copy of the agreement to him. Philip Browne duly obliged. Fordy would later admit that he presumed Hanley had simply asked for too much money, but money had nothing to do with it. This was a sixth-sense thing.

The following weekend, I rang Mister Agent while en route from a game in London. He sounded glad to hear from me.

'Look, we've just come up with those figures . . .' he started.

'Well, I'm just ringing to let you know that we've decided not to run with Ellery; we've got somebody else in mind.'

There followed a pregnant pause.

'Hello, hello,' I pressed.

'Em, I don't understand,' said Mister A.

'Well, there's nothing to understand really,' I said. 'We've just decided to go with somebody else. Can you thank Ellery for his time and let him know we wish him every success in the future.'

The phone went dead, Mister Agent seemingly lost for words.

I wasn't exactly taking over a team on its knees. We were in reasonable shape, I knew that. And Warren, certainly, wasn't slow to suggest that the reasons for his departure had little to do with rugby. Despite signing a confidentiality clause, he was subsequently quoted in an English tabloid as saying, 'I just didn't kiss the butts or massage the egos of the right committee guys.'

But we were also prone to bewildering inconsistency during his time in charge. I wanted to rid us of this bungee-cord habit, this tendency for performances to flip from one extreme to the other.

Maybe because of my background in America, I understood the value of analysis. The more you broke performance down into logical parts, the more you could be in control of it. And an absolutely key figure in this regard would become our video analyst, Mervyn Murphy. Having outsourced analysis initially, Warren brought Mervyn into the Irish camp in 2001. It was an inspired decision.

We had both coached Mervyn with Connacht and Galwegians. He was an 'A' international who had actually been in the 'Wegians team when I took over in the 1995/96 season, but – at the time – there was talk of him moving to Waikato and, gradually, I could sense Mervyn lose his focus. His form dipped markedly so I dropped him from the Connacht team and, eventually, Galwegians too.

Mervyn was never the confrontational type. Quite the contrary, in fact. But he had been a 'Wegians player all his life and I knew I had effectively ended his career in my short time with the club. So, when Warren proposed bringing him on board, I felt it important to mention our own history. But Mervyn made it clear that he didn't feel we had any baggage and, pretty soon, he was an invaluable member of the back-room staff.

Actually, I would go so far as to say that he became the best video analyst in world rugby.

For a time, we were dabbling in a system called 'Sportscode', buying bits and pieces. Mervyn had worked with Digital in Galway and was able to marry his computer literacy with his rugby knowledge to make the system work for us. But, as coach, I now decided we had to take our analysis to another level. This, inevitably, involved more expenditure.

I remember going to the Treasurer of the IRFU, John Lyons, and telling him that we needed to invest in an analysis system. Up to then, our facilities extended to two video recorders and a TV.

But video analysis was changing rapidly and we were still on the very first rung of the ladder. The response to anything proposing Union expenditure was always the same.

'How much is it going to cost?'

'One hundred and twenty-five thousand euros,' I said.

John's chin hit the ground. I could see he was thinking, This must be one hell of a video recorder. But, to be fair, we invested fully in the 'Sportscode' system and, over time, it became a very powerful weapon in our preparation for Test rugby. I believe it was a key catalyst in giving us consistency of performance. I once heard a saying that you can't fire a cannon out of a canoe. Well, I knew that we needed to have a strong ship in place if we were to fire that cannon and that's what I was trying to put in place here.

With 'Sportscode', we could analyse everything from opponents to our own training sessions. It was my view that you needed to identify an opponent's weaknesses and attack them. We analysed the referee too. Pretty much anything that provided valuable feedback was on the table.

I needed a strong coaching team, strong analysis and strong senior players to provide leadership and I now felt I had pretty much all of those in place. There were just eight weeks between my appointment and our opening Six Nations game, against Wales at Lansdowne Road.

I believe I used them well.

Maybe the key element to my back-room set-up was communication. There would be no point having all these different threads to it if we didn't communicate. At times this had been a major failing in the Irish set-up. It used to incense me when you'd plan a training session with fourteen backs and only twelve might show. Maybe two guys might have tight hamstrings, whatever. Fair enough, but you needed to know that before you planned the session.

The way it had been, you might bump into the doctor after breakfast and he'd happen to mention that so and so wasn't training. Or, in some instances, you'd only realise it as the session was starting. Too much information fell through the cracks of this piecemeal approach. I wanted an end to that.

Two things I learned in America were (1) You have to talk to people and (2) You had to do it properly. This was such a fundamental in America. In the NFL, there was a week between games so you had that limited time to get your points across. Our culture in Ireland is to skirt around things. We communicate in nuance rather than word. We shy away from being direct for fear the other person will take umbrage.

To me, we didn't have time for nuance. I wanted to create a culture in which, when we spoke, we said precisely what we meant. Nobody should take offence at that. It's work. It's business. You get on with it. No one's trying to piss you off. Agree or disagree. Argue, whatever. But, above all, communicate.

Maybe, to begin with, this was a bit of a culture shock for the team. I would make a point of criticising players in the team room. If one guy messes up and the other fourteen learn from it by me pointing that out . . . well isn't that the whole point of coaching? I'd do the same on the pitch. If I saw a guy making a mistake, I'd correct him. If I saw two guys make a mistake, I'd correct the whole team.

This directness shocked a lot of people because it represented a culture that had not been there until now. I was adamant that I didn't want any flip-flopping in how we dealt with one another. There would be no sugar-coating. The fundamental question every day we went to work was: 'How do we get this working?'

One of the things I initiated which, to begin with, proved a little traumatic was a staff meeting at 5 p.m. every Sunday we went into camp. Eventually we would have a staff of fourteen people and every one of them had to come to that table with a watertight schedule for the week. I wanted to do away with those sessions that might go half an hour or even an hour over. I adopted a hooter system where the specific coach might get his allotted 20 minutes and, when his time was up, the hooter sounded. I'd seen this in America.

It worked this way. I might ask Niallo what he had planned for a Tuesday morning session in Greystones. 'You've got 40 minutes Niallo, what's the plan?'

'First 20 will be scrummaging . . .'

'OK, Rala (logistics man, Paddy O'Reilly), where's the scrummaging machine?'

'Terenure.'

'You know what you have to do . . .'

Sounds simple, but it cut out the carelessness. If something came up at that Sunday meeting that affected someone's area and they let it slide, I'd be down on them like a ton of bricks. I would tear them to pieces. I couldn't have glitches on a Wednesday or Thursday because somebody hadn't spoken up on Sunday evening.

This put pressure on people and I know that some of them found it a little traumatic. You could have a fair bit of tension at those meetings. The schedule posted had to mean exactly what it said. Short of a nuclear holocaust, it wasn't going to change. People had to be on their toes from the moment we went to work that Sunday.

I would then have a breakfast meeting every morning. It might take only three minutes in a section of the dining room but I needed to know that there were no surprises coming down the pipe. The medics would then rush away to strap up people. Rala would head for the training pitch. We have this thing in Irish sport of just one voice at a time. If two people speak together, we'll look disorganised. Bullshit.

That's what I learned from my first week with the Americans

in Berkeley. Jack brought me down to watch the college football team train. They'd be practising a play and, next thing, six whistles would go off. You'd have coaches running in from all sides, feeding a traffic of information. They multi-tasked you. Think about it. If you've got 90 minutes to get your information across and only one person can speak at a time, how beneficial can that be? The key was to up-skill the players into absorbing information coming from different angles. You got limited windows of opportunity to prepare a guy to play the game of his life. You had to use them to the absolute.

Personally I felt I was good at getting a point across. To me, the best teachers are the ones who have to figure it out for themselves, not those for whom everything just comes naturally. I taught maths but, as a student, I was bad at maths. I had to really put myself through the wringer in college just to get through.

But I enjoyed teaching it. When a kid would give you that look which said, 'I haven't got a clue!' I was able to identify with him.

Under Warren, I felt we'd been playing hit–and–hope rugby for too long. Fellas going into games without any clear idea of how the game might pan out. Just worrying and wondering. There had to be more logic to what we were doing. More certainty.

I will never forget my first game as assistant to Warren and the half-time changing room at Twickenham. We were getting a hiding and the place was like Armageddon. People just shouting over one another, totally incomprehensible. There had been a story the previous year that one of the players had kicked over a table of tea and sandwiches in a half-time tirade. That kind of stuff had to stop.

I said this to Donal Lenihan after that game at Twickenham. 'I can't believe what went on at half-time.'

'Jaysus,' said Donal. 'It wasn't too bad today!'

In America we used play in Balboa Park, a municipal ground

on the south-east side of San Francisco. We changed in lockers for a swimming pool and jogged about fifty metres to the pitch. The crowd would sit in an old bleachers stand on one side, the rest of the place surrounded by trees. And, at half-time, we'd take the guys out of the sun, sit them under a tree and do the talking.

Sounds like a primitive set-up. But, in terms of communication, it was light years ahead of what I saw in that Twickenham dressing room in 2000.

I came up with a set structure for our half-time talks. The forwards with Niallo and the backs with Declan would go into conference for two minutes each. Then the full team would come together under Fordy. After that, I would say anything I had to say. The last voice would be the captain's.

I think the players realised pretty quickly that there was a logic to the way we did things. They saw that we could set targets knowing that, if we reached them, we'd probably win the game. We might have eight team-performance goals. If we achieved five of those, chances were we'd win. It wasn't bombproof, nothing is.

There were days they'd come back into the dressing room and I'd have to just say, 'Lads, no fault on anybody. Ye played ye're guts out, it just didn't work for us. These guys are good, they got on top of us!'

Equally there were games we won after which I'd give them a ferocious bollocking. You couldn't build simply on the basis of wins and losses. Performance was the key. If you allowed a winning score to paper over cracks, you were just codding yourself.

The media might have analysed us in that way and we may even have engaged with them on that level but, inside our four walls, performance was how we judged ourselves. We dealt in an environment of common sense and reality rather than just working off the euphoria of winning and the depression of losing.

As the Six Nations loomed, I felt enormous pressure building. A lot of people were clearly of the view that Warren had been badly treated and they weren't slow to make me aware of the fact.

On the Monday after my appointment, the *Irish Times* ran an article pretty much saying he had been stabbed in the back. I knew what I was getting here. There would be no honeymoon period, no gentle settling-in period.

The wigs were already on the green. It was up to me how I dealt with that.

15

SIBERIA FOR FUN

My first game as Irish coach was Graham Henry's last in charge of Wales.

We won 54–10, tore them to pieces. I should have been euphoric, but I wasn't. I just knew it was an artificial statement. Wales were in virtual disarray, Henry having lost the players in the fallout from the Lions tour. I spoke to one of their senior players after the game and he said as much. Nobody had really bought into what they were trying to do that day.

To that extent, the scoreline was a beautiful lie. Everything we tried seemed to come up trumps. I brought Keith Gleeson off the bench to win his first cap. We were just after scoring a try: Wales kicked off; Brian O'Driscoll skinned their midfield; popped it to Gleeson five yards out. And, with his first touch on his debut in international rugby, Keith dived over.

This gig was easy.

In Dublin that night, I was torn between delight and apprehension. Wales had asked nothing of our new defence system. People were clapping me on the back, telling me everything was wonderful. I knew it wasn't. Then we went to Twickenham and got butchered 11–45.

Boy was I learning to hate that place. This was my third trip in just over two years and each time the arithmetic was brutal. Prior to the 1999 World Cup, the Eagles had lost there 8–106. Then, in my first game as Irish assistant, we'd gone down 18–50. My only consolation was that the score was coming down.

Our problem was that Mike Ford's defence system was still in its infancy. When you build a new system from scratch, it's only about 20 per cent effective the first few times you use it. It's a teething process. The players are almost mechanical in how they defend. They become more obsessed with the system than actually making tackles.

Some of the media now went off on one. Predictable stuff. I knew it was coming. Walking into the banquet that evening in London, Fordy was in front of me with his wife. I could see that the guy was devastated, so I just put my hand on his shoulder and said, 'We'll sort this out, don't worry!'

I fully believed we would. I knew he'd take a terrible flaying over the coming days and that none of it would reference the fact that here was a guy, quite literally, trying to build something from scratch. I couldn't say how long it was going to take us, but I could already see that Fordy knew his stuff. That there was a definite logic to what he was trying to put in place.

Funny, two years later – after we beat England at Twickenham in their 'homecoming' as World Cup winners – Fordy would say to me how much he appreciated that gesture in 2002.

The England defeat kicked off the whole Gatland debate again, the 'Could he have done any worse than this?' chorus. It turned out too that, in a newspaper column, Malcolm O'Kelly had pretty much declared an intention to sort out Martin Johnson at Twickenham. Johnson had taken the Lions Test place Mal so coveted in Australia. It was, I didn't doubt, tongue-in-cheek stuff.

But it had taken on a life of its own and given the English

something with which to course us. Pinned up on a dressing-room wall, I knew it would have looked like a 'fuck you' message to England. And, of course, Johnson responded accordingly, taking Mal apart in the game.

There was a very important moment in our first team meeting after that defeat. Denis Hickie stood up and backed Fordy. 'This is a good system and it will work,' he said. 'We just have to learn it and trust it.' It was great leadership from Denis and I believe a big, big moment for Mike Ford. Whatever was coming down the line, he wasn't going to be made a scapegoat.

Scotland were next up and I decided to start Gary Longwell in the second row in place of O'Kelly, whose form was poor. We called Gary 'The Boat'. He was a huge man, almost as wide as he was tall. I knew Gary was overjoyed as we went training that Tuesday morning in Greystones. It would be his first start for Ireland.

But in the warm-up, he fell, stubbing his little finger in the ground. As training progressed, the finger began to throb and he went to the doctor, Mick Griffin. Mick decided an X-ray was the best option and it revealed a hairline fracture on the very tip of the finger. Driving back from the hospital, Gary was disconsolate.

'There's definitely a fracture?' he quizzed the doc.

'Definitely,' said Griffin. 'It's tiny, but no way can you play with a fracture of any sort.'

'You're sure?'

'I'm sure.'

There was a silence in the car before Gary proposed a solution. 'Could you maybe amputate the tip of my finger and cauterise it before the weekend?' he asked. Griffin almost crashed the car.

'Are you joking me?'

'No. I can live without the tip of my finger. But this is my first start for Ireland . . .'

The doc, needless to say, ruled it out immediately. But I've often thought of that story since as an example of the kind of determination that separates winners from losers. As it happened, we beat the Scots without Gary, Drico scoring a hat-trick of tries in a 43–22 victory at Lansdowne Road. Pleasing, but we had still coughed up too many points. Then we beat Italy 32–17 in Dublin. Same thing.

Our final game was against a French team chasing the Grand Slam in Paris and, despite Woody making a welcome return, we got torn to pieces. France 44, Ireland 5. One of our worst Paris hidings ever, which was saying something. Defensively, the wheels just came off. Guys panicked. The Stade de France can be an intimidating place to play and, if the French get any scent of weakness, they just devour you. And, unfortunately, we gave up. That was the brutal truth in Paris that day. We just lost the plot completely.

There was a heading in the *Irish Times* that Monday: 'Gatland not to blame for this season!' The sub-heading read, 'Far from raising the bar, the new management team has seen it lowered in this Championship.' I wasn't surprised. There was blood in the water now, especially with a two-Test tour of New Zealand looming on the horizon. We had taken two hammerings in my first five games in charge and most people assumed that the All Blacks would now make it four out of seven. Was I worried? Absolutely.

Not because I had any doubts about where we were going long-term. I hadn't. But I needed the players to hold their nerve. Not to start thinking, Hold on a minute . . . If they stopped believing in what we were trying to achieve, then we were goosed.

Before we went to New Zealand Woody rang me up and asked me to play a round of golf with him in Portumna. He brought Anthony Foley along, I brought my daughter Katie. He'd said all along that we should do this after the Six Nations.

177

Looking back, I think it was just a gesture of reassurance on his part. Nothing was really said, but I appreciated him doing it.

My problem going Down Under was that we were now without a lot of senior figures. Gaillimh and Claw were gone. Kevin Maggs and Rob Henderson were injured. I knew that, if they had half a chance, the Blacks would happily put a hundred points on us.

The first Test was in Dunedin and I took a punt. I was worried that if we played our normal drift defence, they would pick us apart. Having just won his first cap against Italy, John Kelly was going to have to play inside-centre alongside Drico. He was very inexperienced. So I suggested to Fordy that we play a blitz defence, essentially fly up man-on-man and knock the living crap out of them.

It just struck me that defending set pieces was still a tricky concept for a league graduate to get his head around because scrums and line-outs presented a different dynamic. You've eight guys in one small area, so you've got to take a different head-set to defence. That said, bottom line, I knew the guy I really had to sell it to was Drico.

So on this horrible wet Monday in Dunedin, Fordy, Drico, Woody and me met in a little coffee shop off the lobby of the hotel. I could see immediately that Drico was uneasy. His expression said, We've spent two months learning to do it a particular way and now you want to change it . . . Totally understandable.

I explained my thinking. How this wasn't a huge change, just a head-set change on one aspect of our game. It was a much simpler form of defence and I felt, if it rained (as it almost always did in Dunedin), that would play into our hands. Drico eventually saw the logic and bought into it.

That Saturday, we went after the All Blacks like mad dogs in a meat house. Maggsy was watching at home. Ordinarily, he was captain of our defence and he said that our tackling was so strong he wanted to climb through the TV set and join in. We absolutely nailed them at every opportunity. This was the Test of the famous yellow ball that neither Ronan O'Gara nor Andrew Mertens could kick.

Mertens described it afterwards as 'the lemon', which – I'm sure – royally pissed off Adidas. ROG missed four kicks at goal, we made two mistakes in defence and got fried. New Zealand 15, Ireland 6. We should have won. Everyone was shattered afterwards but, at least, the players now believed that they could defend. Psychologically, that was a massive step forward. We had gone into the so-called 'House of Pain' and fronted up to the All Blacks.

The following Saturday, we lost the second Test in Auckland 8–40. Second Tests in New Zealand are always tougher. They find your weaknesses and make you bleed. The game got away from us with twenty minutes to go. We brought on Alan Quinlan with only one score between the teams and the first ruck Quinny arrived at, he stamped on an All Black. Yellow card. By the time he got back on the field, the game was over.

We were seething. I remember leaving Eden Park that evening and Quinny coming walking towards me around the back of the bus with his hands outstretched, apologising. Niallo, who knows him better than anyone, was ready to cut him in two. So I did it for him. I tore strips off Quinny. With fifteen on the park, there was no way we'd have folded like we did.

We flew home frustrated, but – at least – we had turned a corner. Our big problem in the Six Nations games against England and France had been a failure to defend off phases. Changing to blitz on set piece was a minor adjustment that stopped people questioning the system.

The only question now was: Were we good enough?

★

Ireland's defeat in the 1999 World Cup play-off against Argentina in Lens had pitched us into the problematic territory of pre-qualifying for the 2003 tournament.

We warmed up with a nervy defeat of Romania in Limerick, the week of Gordon Wood's death. It was a really tentative, frightened performance. We beat them, but coughed up a few desperately soft tries.

After that, it was off to Siberia, crossing seven time zones to get to Krasnoyarsk for a game with Russia at the crumbling Stadium Centralny. On a map, it's pretty much on the same longitude as New Delhi. It was a nightmare journey. We chartered an old rust bucket of a jet with only cramped, economy seats. It meant the players' knees were virtually pushed into their chins for a trek that required 14 hours in the air.

The plan was to have a refuelling stopover in Moscow. This should have required maybe an hour on the tarmac, but it turned into a fiasco. They made us get off the plane and take our bags with us, putting us through customs and immigration. No one spoke English. We were delayed for five hours until, eventually, Brian O'Brien came up with a solution. Hundreds of dollars in cash.

Suddenly, the wheels began to turn. It had been that simple. We had to buy our way out of Moscow.

The delay meant us arriving into Krasnoyarsk at about three on a Friday morning. Everyone slipped away to bed and, that evening, we went to the stadium. I noticed immediately that the pitch was marked out inside an athletics track. This meant that, in order to keep within the confines of the track, the pitch had to be drastically narrowed. In other words, it was only about 50 metres wide.

There must have been 100 people at the pre-match press conference. It was a massive local event, attended even by their Minister for Sport. The Russian coach was a South African who, the moment we sat down at the dais together, leaned across and said to me, 'If there are any jobs going in Ireland, I'd be interested!'

The food in the hotel was appalling and, by kick-off time on the Saturday, the guys were still deeply jet-lagged. Then referee Joel Jutge forgot to bring his miked-up touch flags, without which he couldn't communicate readily with the touch judges. This against a big, uncompromising Russian team and on a pitch as narrow as a swimming pool. Lovely.

It was a horrible experience from start to finish. We won 35–3, but really only put them away in the last quarter. I remember thinking that we played as if we were afraid again. Nothing flowed. Everything seemed to be coming out garbled. Woody scored a try in the game, but looked utterly exhausted at the end. Then, on the flight home, he became increasingly uncomfortable. A disc in his neck had leaked.

He faced another long haul back to fitness.

The following week we beat Georgia 63–14 at Lansdowne Road in a game notable only for the fact that we had a longer journey to Dublin than they did. And then the killer. Russia ended up playing a repêchage against Spain who, after a bit of homework, discovered that two of the big South African-born forwards who had smashed us around the field in Krasnoyarsk were actually illegal. The Russians, in other words, were kicked out of the tournament. Our trip to Siberia, at a cost of €300,000 to the Union, had been for nothing.

I was concerned with how tentatively we were playing. Next up was an autumn series that seemed certain to ask awkward questions. We were playing Australia, Fiji and Argentina. I knew it would be ugly if we didn't find some form.

I am not ordinarily an emotional person, but the memory of my mother caught me momentarily off-guard the day we beat the Wallabies at Lansdowne Road in November 2002.

It was a huge win in that, basically, it called the hounds off. Ireland hadn't beaten a member of the southern hemisphere's 'Big Three' since 1979. I remember coming in under the stand at the end to meet Noreen and her sister and, for some inexplicable reason, I thought of Rena. She was always an emotional supporter and, in my mind, I imagined her watching the game.

And it just struck me how chuffed she would have been for me at that moment. I could see her face. And, for maybe 30 seconds, I was overcome with emotion.

Noreen was a bit taken aback and asked me what was wrong. I explained and quickly gathered myself again. To some degree maybe my emotion reflected the pressure that had been brewing. This was my first big scalp as Irish coach and it gave me breathing space. We had achieved something and the doomsayers would have no option but to suspend their sniping.

ROG played like someone sent down from above that day. Celestial. He kept pinning Australia in the corners and, sitting across from me in the West Stand, Wallaby coach Eddie Jones just became more and more frustrated. Ten minutes from time, I could hear him shouting, 'Run everything . . .'

The rain dumped down and you could see that this just wasn't Australia's scene. No question, we managed the conditions better. At one point, their fullback, Matt Burke, went chasing an O'Gara diagonal kick into his own 22, lumped the ball into touch and could be overheard loudly cursing the weather. ROG, needless to say, saw the funny side.

In hindsight, the rain took a little of the gloss off our victory. There was a sense that it had been a defining factor in the game. That it, somehow, suited us and dispirited the Wallabies. It fed the old stereotype of the Irish as game but limited mudlarks. I resented that. We had beaten Australia by playing smarter than they did.

They insisted on closing the roof of the Telstra Dome one year later when we played them on a miserably wet day at the World Cup. If nothing else, they had convinced themselves that we liked playing in the rain.

Next up were Fiji and we hammered them 64–17. After that, it was Argentina – another looming World Cup opponent. This was a tough, typically fractious affair out of which we carved a 16–7 win.

The Pumas were a work in progress, building from the 1999 World Cup all the way through to the tournament in 2007, at which they probably hit their peak. Games against them were always hard, full-blooded and quite often mean. They'd beaten us in our two most recent meetings and, every time you played them, you knew it would be a dogfight.

Sadly, Pauline Wood passed away on the morning of the game and, for once, it was probably as well that Woody was injured. It gave him time and space to go home to Kilaloe and grieve, not just for his mum, but Gordon too.

Beating Argentina drew a nice, neat line under the year. We had seen off the teams we were expected to beat and grabbed the bonus of a rare triumph against the Wallabies. Now all I needed was to get a healthy captain on the field.

16

OFFICER MATERIAL

The early prognosis on Keith Wood would have been a gun-and-tarpaulin job in the world of horse racing.

Anyone else probably would have been finished. His problems had been chronic and seemingly unrelenting for so long, the temptation had to be to wave the white flag. He suffered a dislocated shoulder at the 1995 World Cup and, thereafter, always seemed susceptible to problems in that area. Not good news for a front-row forward.

The reason he missed virtually all of the 2002 Six Nations was a badly torn calf. Issues with his neck then arose when he took a bang in the first game of the 2002/03 season with Harlequins. When the disc began to leak on that flight back from Siberia, I had to resign myself to losing him for another Six Nations. By now, naturally, a lot of people were beginning to wonder if we'd ever see him in an Irish jersey again.

The problem was that Woody knew just one way of playing rugby. He was an all-action commando, top class in the technical requirements of playing hooker, absolutely world class in the sheer dynamism and presence he brought to the loose. When in the best of health, he was undoubtedly the best in the world. A virtual force of nature.

At the onset of the 2003 Six Nations, I sensed he felt almost guilty at missing another championship. He knew the snipers were in the long grass for me. We talked about it and I just kept repeating the same mantra. 'The World Cup, Woody. The World Cup . . .'

Maybe the only blessing for him in being so injury prone was that he now had virtually his own private surgeon in London, Ian Bayley. Like a good mechanic familiar with a problematic car, Bayley got to know exactly what was and wasn't possible for Woody in terms of rugby time frames. That became a source of great reassurance to both the player and those of us desperate to have him back on board.

In December of 2002, Woody's neck had improved sufficiently for him to play half a game for Harlequins against Leeds. Unfortunately, as was his nature, he wasn't inclined to tiptoe back into business and soon after making a hit on the fearsome Zac Feaunati, he realised he was in trouble with his shoulder again. In the dressing room afterwards, Woody couldn't lift his arm.

Bayley scoped the shoulder and reassured him that, if nothing more went wrong in the interim, the World Cup was still possible. But neck and shoulder injuries for a guy whose job required leaning pretty heavily on both? It didn't sound good. In Woody's absence, Shane Byrne stepped up to the plate as Irish hooker and, despite coming relatively late to international rugby, proved a revelation.

I had given the interim captaincy to Mick Galwey, but Mick was gone before the end of that first Six Nations and I knew that my next choice had to be someone likely to be with us for the long haul. I got Woody to broach the subject with Brian O'Driscoll at the Glenview Hotel and he seemed a little surprised. He shouldn't have been.

I've always believed that you can't manufacture a captain. My view is that leaders are born, their qualities becoming self-evident the more you deal with them. Even with a group of strangers, you can pretty quickly identify the leaders present. They're not necessarily the people who speak most or loudest, because leadership isn't about shouting. It's about radiating natural authority.

I could see that quality in O'Driscoll from day one. There was a maturity in him beyond his years. I knew for sure there were other guys in the group who could have made decent Irish captains. And there were certainly raised eyebrows when I appointed him. He was young and relatively inexperienced. But one of the first boxes you tick with a captain is: 'Is he respected by the other players?' Drico was, unquestionably.

Maybe some people couldn't quite see it. They just looked at this kid in his early 20s with a Dublin Four accent and a background in Blackrock College. Silver spoon material. What they didn't see was the warrior behind the image. This guy *always* put his body on the line. He had all the skills, but it was his attitude that marked him down as different. He never flinched, never backed down. Routinely, he played through the pain barrier.

Some people still say to me, 'What about Paul O'Connell, was he not obvious captaincy material too?' It's a good question, because Paulie did tick all the boxes. But he was only just coming on the scene at the time; Drico had a Lions tour behind him in which he had played brilliantly on the Test side. He'd scored that hat-trick of tries for Ireland in Paris. He was just that bit further down the road than Paulie.

Two things I felt that Drico shared with Woody were (a) in an Irish shirt, he would compromise on nothing and (b) he was naturally bright. I have always believed that you need intelligence in a captain. He needs to see the bigger picture, to know the things to focus on in the throes of battle.

It already struck me that Brian had a habit of speaking at the right times. It might be in the dressing room or at training. He would take ownership of a moment and invariably say the right thing. That's not something you can teach. It's either in a guy or it isn't.

The incredible thing about Drico is that so many people have been inclined to make sarcastic jibes in his direction despite the fact that he is the most successful Irish captain ever. This has always made my blood boil. It seems to me that he has taken an inordinate amount of (largely smart-arse) criticism in his time wearing the armband for Ireland.

I did make it clear to him that he was only keeping the captaincy seat warm for Woody. The irony of course was that he ended up doing so well, there was talk that, when Woody did finally make it back, I couldn't possibly take the captaincy off Drico. Even Woody himself would eventually bring this up.

'You've a decision to make here on the captaincy,' he said one morning approaching the 2003 World Cup.

'I have,' I agreed, smiling.

'I just want it to be known that,' he said, 'if it's not me, I won't be getting in a strop. I'll be disappointed, but we won't be falling out over it.'

'Look,' I said. 'If I think you're the best guy for the captaincy, you'll be captain. If I don't, you'll be the first to know.'

Being honest, my head was clear. Drico had done a magnificent job as stand-in, but would – I knew – have been uncomfortable to be captain on a team that included Woody. Like all of us, he had massive respect for Keith. Drico's understanding was always that he was just holding the fort for his return.

Woody's road back was fraught, mind. We eventually got him in for a pre-World Cup game against Wales at Lansdowne Road, his first full game on the shoulder. He was completely new to our line-out calls that day, got totally confused and threw a few shockers. Just got mixed up. I remember the day after he could not lift his arm above his head. Now we were really in a panic. There were just two warm-up games to go.

Back in London, Bayley was reassuring. 'Perfectly natural, just give it a few days . . .'

The surgeon developed this suit for Woody which he was to wear after all heavy contact. It was essentially half a jacket, just a sleeve that could be pumped full of iced water. Like I say, the mechanic knew the car. Within a few days, Woody was good to go again.

I think it helped Keith that, no matter the discouragement, we just wouldn't give up on him. One of the first things he had said on my appointment as coach was that – as captain – he was weary of doing all the talking in the dressing room. Woody felt a support system needed to be built around the captaincy. In other words, senior players needed to be stepping up to the plate. We had put that system in place, initially with guys like Gaillimh and Claw, then people like Brian O'Driscoll, Anthony Foley, Simon Easterby, Denis Hickie and Ronan O'Gara.

And that support system was hugely important when we appointed such a young captain in Drico.

I think the interim nature of his position also helped Brian. No one was being too judgemental. There had been no big announcement when he got the job for the simple reason that, in real terms, Woody was still captain. That, of course, all changed after the World Cup. Woody's retirement meant a permanent appointment had to be made and I dealt with the matter at a training camp in the Canaries the week before Christmas. I had no doubts that this was Drico's time.

I called him up to my room and left him in no doubts about my belief in him. 'I'm asking you to captain Ireland for the foreseeable future,' I told him. 'That means probably as long as I'm going to be around.'

I told him how I wanted him to be a conduit between management and players and how, at all times, I wanted honesty. He needed, I said, to have the confidence in himself to criticise me if he felt that was what was needed. I didn't want any surreptitious stuff, leaks to the papers or whatever. My door would be open at any time and, so long as we had that rapport and trust, disagreeing on things wouldn't be an issue.

'Brian,' I said, 'I want to be ruthlessly honest here. This isn't about building a friendship. I want to be very specific about that. I don't want to be your friend. I want to be your coach. There's a big difference. If we're friends at the end of this, that's a bonus. But it's not the most important thing.'

I'm happy to say that we were still friends at the end. He wrote to me about two months after my resignation in 2008. I appreciated that hugely. It has always struck me that Brian O'Driscoll is possibly more appreciated outside of Ireland than within. He is revered around the world, yet in Ireland he endures this kind of petty negativity in the media. Maybe he hasn't always played smart with that same media. Maybe he's run with the ball of celebrity on the wrong occasions. But I would always defend him.

If you asked me to pick a moment that defined Drico in an Irish shirt I would pick Paris 2006. For 50 minutes, we played like headless chickens. In the lead-up to one of the early French tries, Brian got the most horrendous dead leg from a knee into the thigh. We went 3–43 down in that game and anyone else in his position would have left the field and been fully within his rights to do so.

I don't know how he played on, but Drico did. He knew we were in trouble that day and that he was needed as captain. People rightly raved about his performance at Croke Park against England in the 2009 Six Nations but, for me, that day in Paris was every bit as heroic.

As a team, we were in a pretty bad place. After the disappointment of the Lions tour, we'd had a really poor autumn series. The mob was out. Then we opened our Six Nations campaign with an uninspiring victory against Italy in Dublin. Now the French were putting us to the sword. It's on those kinds of days that you find your leaders.

That same afternoon, early in the second half, Paul O'Connell popped the AC joint in his shoulder while taking a horrendous knock at a ruck. Again, anyone with a shred of weakness in their make-up would have taken that as their exit clause, their 'get out of jail' card if you like. No one could possibly have pointed the finger at Paulie if he had come off the field.

But he played through the pain and, how I honestly don't know. It must have been horrendous, but I remember looking at the tape of the game after and there wasn't a visible shred of equivocation in Paul O'Connell during that second half. Of course, we almost pulled off an incredible escape that day too, scoring 28 unanswered points in the last half-hour or so.

The comeback came up short, but I firmly believe it gave us the momentum to kick on and win that year's Triple Crown.

In the Paris dressing room after that 31–43 defeat, Paulie couldn't get his jacket on because of his injured shoulder. I was standing helping him when he looked at me and said, 'The lads were playing for you today, don't be in any doubt about that!' To hear him say that meant a huge amount to me. Because, deep down, you are beginning to wonder, Jesus, am I losing these guys? Are they slipping away from me?

When the real leaders in the dressing room come through for you at those moments, you cannot put a price on it.

We had plenty of them in that Ireland team. People strong enough to confront their coach if they thought he got something wrong, resolute enough to back him if they felt he was getting a raw deal.

The autumn series of 2005 was a case in point. We struggled badly. Drico and Paulie were injured and I was trying to change the style of our play at a time, maybe, when safety first would have been a more comfortable policy with regards to my own position. I was also blooding new players like Denis Leamy, Andrew Trimble and the Bests, Simon and Rory. We got butchered by the All Blacks, then spurned a winning opportunity against Australia. I was intensely frustrated.

The Wallabies beat us 30–14, but it was a game we could have won. Afterwards, I lost it with the team. I tore strips off them in the dressing room, then stormed into the toilets, slamming the door behind me. It was absolutely the wrong thing to do. It gave the impression that I was abandoning them at that moment, washing my hands of them. This couldn't have been further from my intentions, but it was the impression given.

The reality had been that my frustration simply got the better of me and I knew I had to get out of that dressing room.

Just before Christmas, I had a good heart-to-heart over lunch with Drico. We'd had a horrible autumn and I was looking to steady the ship. In many ways, autumn was just an extension of other woes. We'd blown a real chance of a Triple Crown in Cardiff that March by playing poorly against a Grand-Slam-chasing Wales. This, again, frustrated the hell out of me.

Then some of us had endured the Lions' meltdown in New Zealand. Bad days seemed to be accumulating and maybe no one handled the pressure quite as poorly as the Irish coach.

Drico didn't spare me. He told me that the moment I stormed out of that dressing room, I had lost something with the players. 'They were upset with you for doing that,' he said. 'It was as if you were abandoning them.' I took his criticism on the chin. 'You're right,' I said. 'I shouldn't have done that.'

The defeat to Australia, of course, brought me into infamous conflict with another of the squad's strong characters. I had replaced Ronan O'Gara with David Humphreys early in the second half and, as things turned out, it was a bad decision. For one of the Australian tries, Chris Latham attacked down the short side and pretty much ran over Humps en route to the line. The try knocked the stuffing out of us and I knew that ROG was fuming after.

He felt at the time, I think, that he was always trying to shake off Humps, that he was being used as a kind of scapegoat whenever things went wrong. I would dispute this. Humphreys had a fine record. It would have been daft having him in the squad if I never took up the option of using him. But I knew that ROG was ultrasensitive. He just felt this thing was being hung endlessly around his neck.

Two days after, we were training at Terenure College and I decided not to leave ROG's frustration simmer any longer. His body language hid nothing and I could see that he was still upset, so I tackled things head-on.

We were just about to start the session and I remember thinking, I'm not going to let this thing drag into another day . . . So I called him aside. 'Look, I know you're upset,' I said. 'We have to talk this thing out. We can't just let it simmer.'

And ROG, fair play to him, let me have it between the eyes. He said that I was hanging this thing around his neck, that – against Australia – he had only been adhering to the agreed game plan, following instructions. He said that he had almost come to expect to be taken off, whether playing well or not.

'I understand all that,' I said, 'but I had to make a decision at the time.'

ROG was having none of it. He was very frustrated, very angry. The other players were at the far end of the pitch now and couldn't hear what was being said. But they could see the body language. ROG was animated. It was crystal clear we were having 'words'.

'Maybe you don't want me playing for Ireland,' he said then. 'Maybe I'd be better off just sticking with Munster.' I thought this a little childish, but it reflected where he was in his head. He felt that he had been scapegoated, end of story.

'Look, ROG,' I said, 'I made that decision based on what was in front of me. As coach, I have to be able to do that. I've got to make these decisions and can't give anyone a guarantee they're going to be left on the field. I understand your frustration but you've got to roll with the punches here.'

We talked and talked without really reaching a resolution. There was an element of agreeing to disagree at the end. We had a game coming up the following weekend against Romania and it had already been agreed that Humps would start. This wasn't an issue.

The important thing was that ROG got to vent his spleen rather than leave the thing simmering in the background. We cleared the air sufficiently to get on with the job. My point was that Humps was a top-class international out-half. He wasn't chopped liver. It was a legitimate call to put him in when I felt we needed change.

ROG didn't agree, but at least he'd got things off his chest. He needed me to know what he thought and I understood that.

Unfortunately our exchange happened in full view of the rest of the squad, albeit they were warming up 200 yards away. In retrospect it would have been better had we discussed things in the privacy of a room. And, of course, the 'story' now made the newspapers. Suddenly, O'Sullivan and O'Gara had been involved in a 'massive training bust-up'. It was spun that we had argued openly in front of the other players right in the middle of training. Nonsense.

Suddenly the camp was depicted as being in turmoil. One journalist, hilariously, likened it to Guantanamo Bay. It made good copy. Bullshit often does.

That December we were at training camp in La Santa and I went for a walk with ROG. It was a month since we'd had our disagreement and I wanted to know how he was feeling. 'You've had time to think about it,' I said. 'I've had time. You've known me a long time, both as a person and as a coach. I've always been honest with you, always tried to do the right thing. I haven't always got it right and, in retrospect, I didn't get it right against Australia. But I did what I did . . .'

ROG cut across me. 'I appreciate that now,' he said. 'But, at the time, I was very angry.'

After that, we had a great talk. He accepted that I wasn't working to any secret agenda. 'I just had to get stuff off my chest,' he said. I assured him that I hadn't been offended and that I'd always have more respect for a guy who told me exactly what he thought.

I meant that too. It takes courage to have a go at someone and I respected him for having done it. He wrote in his book that he felt the incident changed my approach to him in that he subsequently played very poorly in a game and I didn't take him off. He'd been wrong about that. Humps was retiring at the end of that season and anyway, after a while, the team wasn't under the same kind of pressure anymore.

On top of that, I could see ROG develop as a character. Over time he became one of the strongest players mentally it was my privilege to work with.

I wouldn't class the argument as a turning point in our relationship because, quite simply, I always felt that we had a healthy respect for one another. By and large, we got on well. If anything, maybe the argument strengthened our relationship. Maybe he felt that the Humphreys monkey was now finally off his back. I don't know. I'm only surmising.

But I did feel we were very comfortable dealing with one another after that. He did write in his book, too, that a lot of people were uncomfortable around me. This may well have been so. I think there's something in the Irish DNA that makes us dislike people being direct with us. As a coach, I was direct with people and, on occasion, I think that was construed as being overly aggressive.

Fair enough, that didn't bother me. I wouldn't say that the players were ever afraid of me but, sometimes, maybe they were afraid of hearing what I had to say. They are two very different things. I always adhered to the view: *You mightn't like what I'm saying, but at least you know what I'm thinking!*

People misrepresented what went on between me and ROG. He was a key player for me and I never had any issues with him arguing the toss. In fact, I remember thinking, This is what managing people is all about.

Put it this way, I'm a long time in the game and I've never dropped or taken off a player and had him congratulate me on a 'great decision'. Players will tell you themselves that they are selfish. They have to be. Any other way and they're just going to slide down the food chain. ROG believed I did him wrong that day and vented his spleen.

It was right that he did it.

There is no simple way of giving a player bad news.

Through 78 Tests with Ireland I could never become comfortable with that aspect of the job. I remember a number of Tuesday mornings seeking out Humps to tell him that he hadn't made the team. The morning in Belfast that I dropped Mick Galwey was absolutely heart-wrenching. People had different ways of dealing with disappointment.

Those two took it on the chin. Others wouldn't be so understanding. There is a saying about keeping your job as a rugby coach. You pick fifteen players to start, five of whom love you, five who hate you and five who've yet to make up their minds.

It's getting the last group on your side that is usually the key to survival.

To me, honesty is key in dealing with players. When you tell someone they're dropped, you've got to tell them why. If necessary, you go into specifics, tackles missed, poor workrate, whatever. Players invariably ask, 'If I do this, will I get back in the team?'

The only honest answer to that is: 'I don't know.' I mean the guy he's competing against might up his game too. You can't give guarantees.

Dropped players always leave the room upset and probably not liking you. That's fair enough. Bottom line, so long as they can say, 'Well at least the guy looked me in the eye and told me straight,' I don't think they can have a lasting problem. That said, it's a horrible thing telling a player you're leaving him out. Not only is he gutted to be dropped, but you're essentially damaging his market value too. It could be he will be negotiating a new contract soon after and you've just greatly compromised his bargaining power.

I've always been conscious of that. Dropping a guy can be a very public, humiliating experience for him. Because of this, I always tried to accentuate the positives of the guy taking his place at press conferences rather than get into a discussion about the one losing his place.

One of my worst experiences as Irish coach was telling Leo Cullen that he had not made the 2003 World Cup squad. I had first coached Leo at schools level with the Blackrock Junior Cup team. He's a bright, articulate guy and took the decision very badly. I had decided to include Gary Longwell instead and Leo just could not accept that Gary was a better player than him.

I could understand that. It was a tight call. In his heart of hearts, he reckoned he should have been the one chosen. Leo kept asking me over and over again, 'Why?'

It eventually got to the point where I had to say, 'Because he's a better player than you at the moment, Leo!'

'You really believe that?' he responded.

'Leo, if I didn't, I wouldn't be having this conversation with you,' I said. 'I'd be having it with Gary. I know you're upset. I also know that I might be wrong. But I'm just telling you what I think.'

He left the room angry and I couldn't blame him. I knew the floor had just fallen out of his world.

I've had huge altercations with other players on the same basis. Players who felt passionately that I was wronging them. But, on a few, rare occasions, the player being omitted saw the bullet coming and had the honesty to accept it.

A case in point was Anthony Horgan. He had been playing out of his skin for Munster when – faced with a lot of injuries – I picked him to face the All Blacks in the 2005 autumn series. Hoggy had a nightmare. He looked like a drowning man out there and I left him out of the match 22 for the following game against Australia.

I remember calling him up to my room. 'Hoggy, I've bad news for you!'

'I know what's coming,' he said.

'You know you're not in then.'

'Look,' he said, 'I'm gutted. But I can't complain. It's a fair call.'

I appreciated that. I never did like the sound of doors being slammed.

17

THE HAIRDRYER

'Eddie we've a problem here . . .' crackled the voice of Martin Murphy, our Operations Manager.

Down on the pitch, I could see Martin Johnson squaring like a schoolyard bully. He'd taken his team to the wrong side of the red carpet and wasn't for turning. Murphy radioed in a panic.

'He won't move!'

'Did you tell him he's on the wrong side?' I asked.

'Three times' said Murphy.

'And?'

'He just told me to go fuck myself!'

It was a problem that needed a diplomatic solution. Part of me wanted the Irish team to call Johnson's bluff. To stand directly in front of them and leave them staring at our backs. I had an urge to send a message down for Brian O'Driscoll to line the Irish team up in a parallel line, two yards in front of England.

But this wasn't feasible. Firstly, it would have meant us having our backs turned to President McAleese as she was introduced to the England team. Secondly, it could have kicked off a pretty unseemly row between the two teams before a ball had been kicked in anger. It was a no-win situation.

Johnson, I have no doubt, knew exactly what he was doing. There is never confusion about these preliminaries. England had been told precisely where to stand, but this was an England team determined to lay down a marker.

With hindsight, I could admire Johnson's pig-headedness. In fact, I would almost go so far as to say he was dead right. Because his England team was at a critical crossroads that March day in Dublin. They'd blown four Grand Slams already and to blow another would almost certainly kill any pretensions they had of winning that year's World Cup.

So he brought his team to Dublin on a war footing and Martin Murphy just happened to be directly in the line of fire. You could see it in their body language. They were strutting their stuff. All but inviting our lads outside.

Yes, it was ignorant. Can you imagine the hullabaloo if we behaved like that with the Queen at Twickenham? But I knew what Johnson was doing and I knew exactly why.

We decided to line up beyond them, forcing the president to walk off the carpet to meet the team. It wasn't ideal, but it was probably the best of our options. Unfortunately the scale of the defeat that followed gave some of the more predictable commentators ammunition with which to connect the two.

One former All-Ireland-winning hurling manager wrote in a newspaper column the following Monday that 'the game was lost before a ball was kicked'. I thought this pretty asinine coming from someone of his experience.

Johnson and England would beat everyone they played that year, no matter what side of the equator. They had become an awesome force. In many ways that Grand Slam showdown at Lansdowne Road was the first of a handful of days that defined their greatness.

And, at least, we were fighting for the Grand Slam on the final day of that Six Nations. We may not have been lighting up the sky just yet, but our star was definitely in the ascendant.

By the dawn of 2003 Scotland had become the great, biennial tormentors of Irish rugby.

We had not won in Edinburgh for eighteen years, coming to associate the city with habitual misery. For most serious rugby nations, Murrayfield wasn't exactly the most forbidding citadel in the world game. For Ireland, it was a kind of spiritual Alcatraz. We hated the place.

Our opening Six Nations tie of 2003 was fixed for a Sunday, but I still insisted on us travelling that Thursday. I wanted us to confront our fear. We always stayed in the Balmoral Hotel, right at the bottom of Princes Street, and I actively encouraged the players to go out and walk the city, embrace the atmosphere.

'I don't want anyone locking themselves in their room for two days,' I said.

Too many of the players associated Edinburgh with some kind of lion's den. Most of them had no memory of Ireland's last win in the city, the 'give it a lash' triumph of Mick Doyle's Triple Crown winning team in 1985. Since then a succession of defeats had infected the Irish mindset with irrational negativity.

Funny, we never feared Scotland at Lansdowne Road. At Murrayfield we treated them like the All Blacks.

This was ridiculous. We'd beaten the world champions in a successful autumn series, yet now there was a great sense of trepidation across the country as we prepared to play the Scots. I decided that we needed to change the communal head-set. But, before that, we needed to sell a dummy.

I knew that, eighteen months previously, we'd been scouted

by the Scottish management for the 'Foot and Mouth' game. Given the miraculous ease with which they read our set plays that day, it wasn't difficult to work out. Two years before that, Donal Lenihan discovered two Scottish Development Officers wearing workmens' overalls over their tracksuits, watching an Irish training session from a nearby prefab.

This time I decided to set a trap.

We had been offered Watsonians as a training venue and accepted without hesitation, though I hadn't the slightest intention of going there. Through a contact in the bank, we found a nice training ground by a school maybe ten miles outside the city, and so Watsonians went unused.

But Scotland in early February was in the grip of a big freeze and, eventually, we were reduced to hiring a gym in which to get in some line-out practice. At the time Scotland had a very good line-out and Niallo and I were on a mission to make sure that we were able to protect our own ball against them.

The line-outs had gone badly for us in the 2002 Six Nations, chiefly because we hadn't enough time to change from the previous regime. We were, essentially, working with old line-outs that our opponents had figured out. It was only during the summer tour to New Zealand that Niallo had been able to put his own stamp on things.

After a session in this Edinburgh gym that Friday, we now deliberately left a set of old line-out calls on a dustbin.

When we returned for another session the following day, we asked the caretaker if perhaps he'd seen a few sheets of paper left behind on the bin?

'Och no,' he said. 'I found nothing at all!'

So we were pretty confident that Scotland now had a set of our line-out calls, albeit a set of obsolete ones.

It made for some hilarious images the following day. They were like the *Keystone Cops* trying to defend against our throws, myself and Niallo chuckling in the stand. We didn't lose a single line-out that day in Scotland. In time, they became so confused they effectively stopped contesting our throw.

I'm not sure if Scottish coach Ian McGeechan ever quite understood our dominance out of touch that day. But it gave us a good platform and, scoring some cracking tries, we broke our Murrayfield hoodoo with an emphatic 36-6 win. With about 20 minutes to go, I put on David Humphreys, effectively to close out the game. It was a nice feeling, sitting there, knowing the points were in the bag.

I'd been quite animated in my team talk at the hotel beforehand. I'd pointed out how great players like Fergus Slattery, Willie Duggan and Moss Keane had all tasted defeat at Murrayfield in pretty ignominious circumstances. I said it was time we confronted our history there once and for all. Because no one believed we could win there. Everyone assumed we'd be leaving with our tails between our legs again.

And why?

'Look at us and look at them,' I finished up. 'Name me one player on the Scottish team that you're afraid of, one guy that we should worry about if we play to our potential. Ye can't because you know something? THERE ISN'T ONE . . .'

Some days you know you pitch your team talk just about right and, for me, that was one of them. Mervyn Murphy was never one for hyperbole, but he said he was cleaning up the room afterwards, the team already gone on the bus, and he could feel a strange residue of electricity in the place. A presence almost. Mervyn said he'd never got such a sense of certainty about a team heading into a game.

Next up, we beat Italy 37–13 in Rome. As ever, the Italians were physical and undisciplined. Their scrum half, Troncon, was sent off for punching Peter Stringer and, afterwards, the Italy coach – Brad Johnstone – came into our dressing room to congratulate us. Brad was an old-style New Zealander who wasn't inclined to conceal his temper.

He was absolutely fuming now. 'Good on you guys . . .' he began before launching into a tirade about the Italians' lack of discipline. 'They won't listen,' he said. 'And while they won't listen they'll never bloody learn!' Johnstone was exasperated and would, by season's end, be replaced by another New Zealander, John Kirwan.

I have a vivid memory of the next morning, our bus absolutely bombing to the airport, four *caribinieri* outriders for company. We were running late, the committee people already fifteen minutes ahead of us. The driver was young, wore shades and seemed oblivious to the personal safety of anyone inside or outside the bus.

It was the most incredible white-knuckle ride imaginable. I particularly remember us hurtling down one side street at what must have been 70 mph, the wing mirrors practically clipping railings on both sides, the policemen speeding along in front. The bus was absolutely full with players and their wives and girlfriends.

We came around this corner onto a cobble-stoned piazza and you could feel the bus sliding. I was sitting in the shotgun seat. Maybe I should have been worried, but all I felt was a strange exhilaration. The sun was shining, the sirens were blaring and all of Rome seemed to be taking notice of this bus speeding its important cargo to the airport.

And I remember thinking, I have this job by the scruff of the neck now. I have it exactly where I want it.

Next up, we beat France 15–12 at Lansdowne Road, a game that would sadly mark my only victory over *Les Bleus* as Irish coach.

When I think of the impact the French had on my time with Ireland, it's a little hard not to feel regretful. Three times in four seasons they alone stood between us and a Grand Slam. People often ask me why I didn't have more success against them. The answer is brutally simple. They were invariably the best team in Europe. Beating them just happened to be a bigger challenge than beating any other Six Nations opponent.

I remember the 2003 game particularly for two extraordinary tackles. The first was by Brian O'Driscoll at the Havelock Square end approaching half-time. We were pinned under our posts and the giant French back-row Olivier Magne made a charge for the line. Drico buried him. The tackle should not have been possible by a centre on such an imposing number seven, but then Drico was no ordinary centre.

The tackle represented one of those moments where both teams realise that a line has been drawn in the sand. For the French, that realisation pretty much told them they would not be crossing the Irish line. For Ireland, it was a declaration of no surrender.

Much later in the game, Kevin Maggs hit French centre, Xavier Gabajosa like a dumper truck. They were trying to break out of defence and, classic Maggsy, he just lined the guy up in his sights and smashed him. Gabajosa's nose virtually exploded across his face on impact and Drico told me that night that he'd actually heard the sound of it cracking.

It was, of course, the captain's controversial try that won the game and I remember talking to him at the banquet of the calmness that now seemed to envelop the whole unit. We looked like a team that was simply getting business done. Doing the right things. Picking our way serenely through history.

Or so we thought . . .

It's quite uncanny the similarities between our subsequent trip to Cardiff and the one in March 2009 that confirmed Ireland as Grand Slam champions. Because, in 2003, the game was also on a knife-edge when Stephen Jones nailed a late drop goal for Wales to seemingly secure victory.

People talk of the calmness that brought the team back from the brink this year but I would suggest that same calmness was in evidence six years earlier. ROG restarted the game, put it on a sixpence for Malcolm O'Kelly, we set up a ruck, ROG slipped into the pocket and, from Peter Stringer's pass, nailed an epic drop goal.

Paul O'Connell branded this year's winning kick as 'manky'. The description would have flattered the kick of 2003. Of course, seconds later, Denis Hickie made a wonderful block on another attempted drop goal by Jones and then, as last March, we quite literally fell over the line.

I had been furious with the team at half-time. They were playing so far below their potential I could see the Championship go up in smoke before our eyes. And, in the dressing room, I had made my feelings known. As my anger reached a crescendo, I swung my fist at an open ice cooler and the lid flew across the dressing room, glancing off Keith Gleeson's head. Just a few weeks earlier, an enraged Sir Alex Ferguson had lashed out in the Manchester United dressing room after their FA Cup exit at the hands of Arsenal, kicking an errant boot that cut David Beckham in the eyebrow.

Coming away from Cardiff that evening, Anthony Foley – typically – saw the funny side. He said they'd decided that my new name was 'The Hairdryer'.

The Cardiff victory meant that we were four from four and now facing England in a winner-take-all Grand Slam shoot-out at Lansdowne Road. This was thrilling and worrying in equal measure. England were a serious team, destined to win the World Cup a few months later. I knew, too, that they'd be on a mission to make up for their loss in Dublin two years earlier.

In only my second game as Irish coach they'd filleted us at Twickenham. Briano had encouraged me to go into their dressing room after that game and congratulate them. I was sorry that I listened to him. I knew the England players hadn't a clue who I was and could almost hear them mumbling under their breaths, 'Who the fuck's yer man?' I felt an idiot.

But one thing did catch my eye that day in their dressing room. A big notice on the wall with two words in giant lettering. 'REMEMBER DUBLIN' it read.

England were at the height of their powers in 2003. They were about to go to the southern hemisphere and beat New Zealand (twice) and Australia. The World Cup had their name on it. It was the best England team of all time and they were looking to avoid the ignominy of falling at the last Grand Slam fence for the fourth year in succession.

I had a game plan for them but, looking back, we just didn't have the polish at the time to execute it. They tended to have a soft defence out wide so, ideally, you've got to throw long passes and attack them in the corners. It takes cojones to carry it through and I believed we had those in plentiful supply.

The game was nip and tuck for an hour. They'd got a lucky first-half try through Matt Dawson, the ball squirting from a scrum into Lawrence Dallaglio's hands. Then Kevin Maggs got past Jonny Wilkinson only for Dallaglio and Neil Back to scramble a desperate rescue on the line. On another occasion, only a bad bounce prevented Denis Hickie going in under the posts.

Deep down, I knew we needed at least one of those scores. With 20 minutes remaining, England led 13–6. Then they cut us to ribbons. I often think that would have been a very interesting game if the seven-point England lead entering the final quarter had actually been a deficit. Because they were under enormous pressure that day in Dublin.

But they won pulling up in the end, the 42–6 scoreline a bit of a travesty. Still, I could feel happy for Clive Woodward. I'd sat directly opposite him at the post-game banquet two years earlier and watched the English Union's CEO burn his ear over another spurned Grand Slam. For all the stress of his situation, he'd been generous and gracious about Ireland's win. Now I had no difficulty reciprocating.

We sat together at dinner this time and I told him, 'Listen, I'm gutted we didn't win a Grand Slam today but, if we couldn't have it, I certainly can't begrudge it to you guys.'

I meant every word too. England had, undeniably, been the best team in the Championship. But I felt we were now coming up fast on their shoulders.

18

STARVE THE DOUBT!

Sir Ranulph Fiennes holds out his disfigured left hand like it's a comedic prop and tells the story of tidying the finger stumps with a micro blade in his garden shed.

Guffaws rattle around the room as if we're watching Tommy Cooper pull rabbits from a hat. We're rolling in the aisles as this man guides us through his history with pain. Every grisly mishap comes with the accompaniment of a punchline. He's got us utterly spellbound.

'Tried a fretsaw, but it didn't ruddy work,' he grumbles, 'so went into the village and got a Black and Decker . . .'

We are in a room in the Citywest Hotel, counting down the days to the World Cup. The squeamish among us are invited to blame Woody. Knowing my voracious appetite for books about the great explorers, he'd given me Fiennes' book *Fit for Life* and waited for a response. Within days he had me where he wanted me.

'Astonishing,' I said one morning. 'I've never read anything . . .'

Woody cut across me. 'OK, how about getting him in to talk to the boys.'

I looked at him as if he was proposing an audience with Elvis. And maybe dinner to follow with Lord Lucan. 'Fuck sake, Woody . . .'

He cut to the quick. 'Seriously,' he said. 'We could get him.'

I can say today that Fiennes is my greatest living hero. The privilege of having him talk to us in 2003 was, for me, only surpassed by him mentioning the visit in his subsequent autobiography. Four months earlier, he had undergone a double bypass after suffering a heart attack. Yet, within days of that gathering in Dublin, he ran seven marathons in seven days on seven different continents to raise money for the British Heart Foundation.

All this while closing in on 60.

My fascination with explorers came from reading Jon Krakeur's *Into Thin Air,* the story of the tragic day on Everest when eight people died and so many others were stranded by a 'rogue' storm. In America in the late 90s so much of my time was spent alone in airports and hotels, I had come to devour books. Fiction never appealed. To me, the stories and characters had to be real.

I went from Krakeur to Jim Wickwire's *Addicted to Danger,* a book that opens with the story of falling into a crevasse on Mount McKinley, scrambling out with a dislocated shoulder, then listening helplessly as his best friend, trapped and face down, literally died underneath him.

Wickwire vowed never to climb another mountain, but the book charts the story of how he proceeded to break that vow over and over again. One day, climbing Everest, a female friend fell 2,000 feet to her death without him even noticing. She was behind him, they were chatting. Then she didn't answer.

The physical courage of these people fascinated me. I got into Hillary and Shackleton and Crean, wondering why people would voluntarily place themselves in the face of such overwhelming danger. You think of the pressure on Ronan O'Gara slipping into the pocket for a last-minute drop goal in Cardiff. His life isn't on the line. His reputation maybe. Not his life.

So to have Fiennes with us that evening in the Citywest was absolutely compelling. Not many of the players would have known his story beforehand. Actually, I'm damn sure if we had announced his visit in advance, a lot of them might even have been underwhelmed.

But the guy had every one of us in the palm of his (slightly battle-scarred) hand that night.

One week later, I walked into the team room and announced that we had arranged another speaker. Without dropping any names, I left the players in little doubt that this was another 'A-lister'. That evening, there was an expectant hush as I grandiosely announced, 'Lads, it gives me great pleasure tonight to introduce to you . . . Jim Neilly!'

The groans could almost be heard in Belfast. Jim is a BBC commentator who most of the players would have known personally and the plunge from Sir Ranulph Fiennes to a bloke they saw every second day in camp was too stark for some to conceal their disdain. I had encouraged Kevin Maggs, a devoted boxing fan, to sit in the front row, assuring him that I knew he'd 'enjoy this guy . . .'

Now Maggsy was staring daggers. Everyone was. I could almost read what David Humphreys (a good friend of Neilly's) was thinking. *'For cryin' out loud, Eddie . . .'*

Jim played along brilliantly, telling the story of an old fight he'd covered in Las Vegas. The fight was between Thomas 'Hit Man' Hearns and Marvelous Marvin Hagler and looked set to be stopped early in the third round as Hagler bled profusely from a bad gash on the forehead. The referee leaned in, had a look and said to Hagler's corner, 'Think it's all over, guys.'

Neilly, knowing how to unspool a story, had their attention now.

'And Hagler says to the ref, "If you stop this fight, you won't get out of the ring alive!" The ref is ashen. He says to Marvin, "You've one round, buddy, then it's over!' And what does Hagler do? He goes out and just takes Hearns apart. Ends the fight to order. One round. Job done. Marvin. Bloody Marvellous.

'That fight to me,' says Neilly now, 'was the one that proved Hagler to be maybe the greatest fighter of all time. All the celebs were in the crowd. Sharon Stone. Jack Nicholson. Half of Hollywood. No one gave a damn. Nicholson was climbing over chairs just to shake his hand. Gentlemen, to me, Hagler defined greatness that night.

'And tonight it gives me great pleasure . . .'

Hagler walked into the room and Maggs fell off his chair. Everyone was dumbfounded. Contrary to what many presumed, he lived in Italy, not America. So Neilly and Briano had managed to organise it, Marvelous Marvin with the boys in green.

You see, we were plucking every emotional string we could to get the team right for Australia. Where Fiennes was very educated and articulate, telling his story with great humour, Hagler was impressively straight and honest. He talked about the doubt that creeps into a boxer's mind before a fight.

He kept reciting his favourite saying: '*Starve the doubt; feed the faith.*' That was his mantra.

Technically everything was in place for our World Cup bid. Our captain was healthy, the team was in form. We were in a good place and just determined to keep it that way. Fiennes and Hagler in the Citywest kept us moving in that direction. Now all we needed was a rub of the green . . .

We took a tired group to Perth that June for a World Cup dress rehearsal against the Wallabies that proved little more than a charade.

Virtually on touchdown in Australia, we heard that Frankie

Sheahan had failed a drugs test. Frankie was in the air now, having just taken off from Singapore, and we had to send him straight home on arrival. Frankie, an asthmatic, used a Ventolin inhaler and – to begin with – we understood the problem to be a mere paperwork issue. But, unfortunately, the levels of salbutamol in Frankie's system would lead to a two-year ban, subsequently reduced – on appeal – to three months. Australia thumped us 45–16 in that Test, a game that, to be frank, signified nothing. The Irish performance was stamped with end-of-season torpor.

Encouragingly, I felt I was able to pinpoint areas where we had the Wallabies in trouble, but the general tiredness fed a lack of on-field awareness. Our failure to execute let them off the hook and, in the end, they slipped away from us.

We had started our strongest team in Perth and most of them went home immediately after. That was always the plan. There was nothing to be gained by bringing them on to Tonga and Samoa, where essentially the emphasis would be on nailing down World Cup squad places.

It was pretty much the same procedure I would follow for the 2007 tournament, going on a two-Test summer tour of Argentina with a group of largely fringe players.

In Tonga, we stayed in the International Dateline Hotel, which to put it mildly wasn't the most salubrious of bases. The joke among the players was that, when it was Saturday in the restaurant, it was only Friday in the kitchen. The food started out reasonably, but went sharply downhill as the week progressed.

Girvan Dempsey actually went down with food poisoning, giving Mark McHugh a (distinctly traumatic) first cap at fullback.

There was a funny incident during training when I was trying to get across my game plan for beating the islanders. This amounted simply to kicking the ball into space and defending it on our own terms. But the message wasn't reaching its intended target. The players were running about like dervishes.

I stopped the session. 'Everyone stop and stay exactly where you are,' I shouted. 'Look down to the right corner of the pitch. How much space is down there?'

'Acres,' someone answered.

'Acres?' I replied. 'You could napalm that corner and nobody would even get their shorts singed, there's so much space down there. That's where I want the ball.'

The whole squad dissolved in laughter. Not quite the reaction I had sought, but at least it broke the mood of hardship.

We played badly against the Tongans in dreadful heat and on a Teufavia Stadium pitch as hard as a footpath actually trailed 0–11 after 22 minutes. The experience was surreal. New Zealand referee Steve Walsh blew up five minutes early for half-time and, when Mike McGurn, our fitness adviser, pointed out his error as the teams ran in, Walsh just shrugged impassively.

'Oh fuck. Sorry, mate, you're right!' And out we all lumbered again to conclude the half.

As it happened, we scored two tries in those five minutes to lead 20–14 at the break against fearsomely physical hosts. Eric Miller would have his face stamped on in the second half (breaking his nose and splitting an eyebrow) and Walsh, enduring a bad day all-round, sent off the wrong player. We won 40–19 in the end, but I tore into the players afterwards.

Much of what we'd produced had been sloppy and unprofessional and I knew the upcoming game with Samoa would provide us with a much stiffer test.

Yet the players were furious. They'd just played in 90-degree heat on a car park of a pitch and were covered in cuts and bruises. Though the Tongans were doing their best as hosts, conditions all round were basic. So the whole vibe of the tour was low on enjoyment and, whatever the players might have needed that evening, it wasn't a rant from their coach. It was the wrong place and the wrong time. You might say the right message delivered the wrong way. I just felt the performance was way beneath the standards we had set for ourselves. But I also felt the need to apologise straight away afterwards.

I got them into the team room and did just that. Woody disagreed with me doing it. Briano thought it was 'the right thing'. The truth probably lay somewhere in between.

We stayed an extra day in Tonga and took the players for a day of rest and recuperation on a nearby island. It was exactly what they needed. A lot of stress ebbed away over the barbecue and a few beers and, while I came back early, a lot of them came back on a local's open boat, something I wasn't too happy to hear.

In Samoa, we stayed at Aggie Grey's Hotel, in beautiful, individual huts named after famous actors. It was nice to have a decent base again because weather conditions were horrendous. In 90-degree heat and with 95 per cent humidity, I knew that the Samoans saw this as a huge opportunity to take a scalp before the World Cup.

They were coached by John Bowe and former All Black legend Michael Jones, and wanted desperately to send a message around the world.

The night before the game, Woody took me out for a pizza. He was getting closer and closer to the point where we could confidently say that he was winning the battle with injury. That day, he had settled into his first scrum and emerged with no ill-effects. I could detect a spring in his step now.

We went into this slightly seedy pizzeria/bar and my abiding memory of the place is of this transvestite in a leopardskin miniskirt sitting down next to us. Can't remember much about the pizza.

As it happened, we didn't give Samoa a sniff the following day. I sensed the players reacted positively to my apology in Tonga and, despite Anthony Horgan and Jonny Bell both going down with heatstroke during the game, we won 40–14.

Again conditions were extraordinary. The temperature in the locker rooms soared way beyond 100 degrees, so we spent as little time in there as possible. Outside, referee Paul Honiss was being a stickler for the IRB's new ruling, aimed at restricting the number of water carriers coming on a pitch. All fine and dandy on a grey Six Nations Saturday. But fellas were dying out there now.

I had a huge row with him about it at half-time and he pretty much told me where to go. To be fair, Honiss didn't want to mess up his World Cup prospects. I understood that. All I asked was that he be cognisant of the extraordinary heat and, thereafter, he was.

Even the anthems took it out of us. Ordinarily, only one verse of 'Ireland's Call' is played before a rugby international. In Samoa that day, all six got an airing from a kid standing on what looked like an orange crate. Worse, he sang it at funereal pace.

I'd warned Briano about this beforehand. I said, 'Whatever happens, make sure we're not left standing in that heat for any more than a short anthem.' Six verses. Fucking hell.

Then the ball was kicked off, their fullback put up a bomb and Girvan, rock solid as ever, made the catch. Only trouble was he got ball and man (imitating dumper truck) all at once. The ball popped out and, two passes later, they were in under the posts. 0–7. Heat. Ireland's Call. Fuck.

If I had learnt anything in the US though, it was how to beat the Islanders. And, in fairness, the guys stuck to our game plan. Samoa eventually did what they always do, they tried to run. And we nailed them. Ronan O'Gara gave one of his masterclasses with the boot, pinning them into places they didn't want to be and scoring a wonderful, individual try from a grubber kick.

The Samoans were devastated. Jones told me afterwards that they really fancied their chances of beating us. Given the difficult circumstances, I took great satisfaction from that victory. We were down to the bare bones by the end, David Wallace having to fill in as an auxilary centre when Bell was sidelined. That move completely baffled Simon Easterby.

When he saw Wally on the field, he presumed he'd come on for Eric Miller. Then, packing down at a scrum, he noticed both Eric and Wally together. 'Thought I was hallucinating!' said Easterby.

One of the key decisions I had to make on that tour concerned Gordon D'Arcy. I left him out of the 22 for the Samoa game which, naturally, was a pretty strong signal that he wouldn't be making the World Cup squad. 'Darce' came to me at a complete loss as to why he wasn't getting a run.

For me, it was simple. Talented as he was, Gordon had no consistency in his game. He could do things that took your breath away, then follow them up with something completely asinine. Or, sometimes, he'd make a mistake and overcompensate by attempting the spectacular which, often, just made things worse.

I tried to explain to him that playing Test rugby wasn't a balance sheet. It wasn't like six good things and two bad meant you were at a score of plus four. On the contrary, the two bad things could cost you the game.

I felt that he was making too many mistakes for me to be able to trust him in a crunch Test situation. I also knew that by saying what I was saying, I was crushing the guy. But I just couldn't pretend. I couldn't lead him up the garden path, then drop a bombshell with the squad announcement. So I told him straight out, 'Gordon, short of a nuclear holocaust at a training session, you won't be in the 30 going to Australia.'

I was being brutal about it, I know. But the penny had to drop with Darce and I felt this would either make or break him. He says himself that he went home and literally cried on his mother's shoulder. But, while we were at the World Cup, he got an opportunity to play centre for Leinster coach Gary Ella.

I knew I had broken his heart, but his career was at a crossroads. At the time, I felt he was going in the wrong direction. In many ways Ella moving him to the centre resurrected Gordon as a rugby player. And he would, in time, become a phenomenal inter-national player for Ireland. I'm not sure that would have happened had he gone to the 2003 World Cup.

Sometimes cruelty has its place in the game.

We carried serious form into the tournament, winning our warm-up games against Wales by 23 points, Italy by 56 points and Scotland by 19 points.

There was a great sense of optimism about but, deep down, I felt apprehensive. Our whole World Cup would hinge on the game with Argentina in Adelaide. The games against Romania and Namibia were mere appetisers for the raw meat of a collision with the Pumas. Everything revolved around how we coped in that collision.

Win it and we were in the quarter-finals with a 'free' shot against the Wallabies in our final pool game. Lose and we'd be playing the hosts just to stay in the tournament.

To get dumped out of the World Cup at the pool stage was unthinkable. I knew the sense of outrage Warren Gatland had encountered after our exit in Lens four years earlier and I didn't want a reprise. Warren still had his supporters in the media. If we didn't escape the group, they could argue that we'd made no progress on my watch. And I'd have struggled to contradict them.

That would have been hard to digest given that, prior to the Grand Slam defeat at Lansdowne Road, we'd actually won an unprecedented ten games in a row.

I will never forget the atmosphere in Adelaide that morning. After giving my team talk in the hotel, Woody and I got into a lift to head down to the lobby. We were chatting away quietly when the doors slid open and, suddenly, we were hit by this extraordinary wall of noise.

Just a huge throng of people, everyone in Irish gear. They spotted Woody and I thought the roof was going to come off the hotel with the roar. The two of us just looked at one another. 'Holy fuck!'

It's history now that Alan Quinlan's try helped us beat the Pumas by a single point (16–15). Personally, I cannot remember a more stressful game in my rugby career. ROG came off the bench to nail a crucial penalty in the end, but those last minutes were excruciating.

Argentina were throwing the kitchen sink at us, attacking up our right flank, when we managed to scramble the ball to touch. Through my earphones I could hear the TMO advise referee Andre Watson that time was up.

'Andre, that's it. Game over. Call it!'

And Watson replied, 'I'll decide when this game is over. We're taking the line-out!'

My blood ran cold. Our fate now hung by a thread. Everyone knew the deal. There was nothing more to be said. Nerve just had to hold. The Pumas won the line-out and ran the ball, putting a winger around the corner. I could hear my heart thumping.

Then Girvan Dempsey appeared like a one-man cavalry, burying him in over advertising hoardings. Hallelujah. We had avoided the curse of 'another Lens'.

The sense of relief was seismic. We now faced Australia in the Telstra Dome, the loser likely to face France in the quarter-finals, the winner getting a favourite's shot at Scotland. Needless to say, we wanted the Scots in Brisbane.

Should have got them too. With a huge weight lifted from their shoulders, the boys played out of their skins, going after the Wallabies like there was no tomorrow. But a few key decisions went against us. Keith Gleeson was wrongly penalised for offside in front of our posts, then – late in the game – Australia blatantly collapsed a scrum on our feed in their own 22.

At the very least, the referee should have reset the scrum. Inexplicably, he penalised Marcus Horan, allowing them to clear their lines. Two big calls that went against us. Possibly a six-point swing. We lost the game 16–17.

Drico had scored, arguably, the try of the tournament and, near the end, I brought on Humps to try and get us a drop goal. Not, mind you, that I imagined ROG couldn't do it. He had in Wales after all. I just felt we needed a bit of freshness in the pocket, a bit of zip. ROG had played his guts out.

We got Humps in position and he seemed to connect beautifully. He told me afterwords that, at the moment of contact, he would have put his house on it going over. But, just at the death, it curved. Wide by a matter of inches.

Then, in the last play of the game, we got Shane Horgan away around the corner. Shaggy wouldn't be an out and out speedster and, realising he was going to get caught, should ideally have cut back inside to keep the ball alive. He didn't. The tackle tossed him out of bounds, Australia winning the line-out and running the clock down. Heart-wrenching.

I was shattered, but I could hardly play the 'Mother of Jesus' card. We'd just played wonderfully against the hosts, lost by the smallest margin and now faced a winnable quarter-final against France. Scotland would have felt like a comfortable ticket to the semi-finals. France felt like a 50/50 bet.

Sadly it took only a matter of minutes for that bet to blow up in our faces.

What do I remember? I remember that we were 0–17 down in a matter of minutes without having missed a tackle. An intercept, a cross-kick, a penalty. As a team, we had a lot of things going for us so this was pretty gut-wrenching to watch. Before we'd got a proper sweat up, we were left with a mountain to climb.

This, as we've so often found to our cost, is one of the difficulties against the French. If they get a quick start on you, they can put you away in a flurry of scores. Before you know it, you're playing catch-up. Just chasing your dignity. If you don't steady the ship, they'll put 50 on you no problem. We steadied it right enough. We scored three tries in the second half, but eventually ran out of time. France 43, Ireland 21.

If only there was a third half . . .

The game was always going to signal the final international appearance of a rugby great. It would be either Woody bowing out or the wonderful French scrum half, Fabien Galthie. Sadly the distinction fell to Woody and only the coldest of hearts could have been left unmoved by the sight of these two warriors embracing so emotionally at the end.

I'm not one for getting emotional after a game, but this was different. Woody had never actually said to me that he was retiring after the World Cup. He didn't have to. I knew what he'd gone through just to get his body on the paddock this time. And the wonderful thing was that he'd played in the tournament like there was no tomorrow, which – in a sense – there wasn't.

He played the rugby of his life in Australia and, for me, one of the great international careers was now over. He was quite emotional in the changing room afterwards and, seeing that, made me quite emotional too.

I couldn't stop thinking of the utterly horrendous year he'd been through, the personal losses suffered, the injuries, the seemingly endless emotional setbacks endured. In my view, 99.9 per cent of players would have walked away. But Woody didn't.

I was so glad now that I had backed him all the way. So glad that his extraordinary efforts had carried him to a really dignified farewell.

At the press conference, he was asked about his future.

'That's it,' he sighed. 'I'm finished now.'

Just the sound of those words triggered something in me. I welled up. The finality of it was now hitting home. And maybe that emotion slightly got the better of me. Because I made a mistake at the conference, for which I was subsequently pilloried by sections of the media. Someone asked me what I thought 'overall' of Ireland's World Cup.

And I responded that I thought we'd had 'a very very very good World Cup'.

This was maybe two 'verys' too many. It was subsequently argued that we were just a single point from 'disaster' (against Argentina); that we should have beaten Australia, but didn't; that France had given us a good spanking. The hounds were loose again. Fair enough, I half expected it.

Sometimes I feel that supporters and media exist in two entirely separate worlds.

That night, the hotel was swamped with people. There must have been a thousand supporters in the lobby, cheering at every sighting of a player. And I couldn't help think what the scenes would have been like had we just made the semi-finals. The whole thing would have kicked on to a different level. So there was a sadness there. A frustration too.

We had a few low-key drinks down in the basement team room. Sonia O'Sullivan dropped in, just to offer her support. And John Quilligan, the IRFU President, presented Woody with a bottle of champagne, thanking him for his contribution to Irish rugby. Quilligan is a Garryowen man and I got great mileage subsequently out of slagging Niallo and Briano – two Shannon stalwarts – of Garryowen's central influence (Woody, Quilligan and yours truly) in official pictures of that World Cup party.

I knew we could have done better and, maybe more pertinently, I understood the fundamentals that we lacked. The 2003 World Cup would be a watershed for Irish rugby. We needed our players to be bigger, fitter, stronger and fresher. Our whole approach to physical preparation needed to be smarter.

When we got home, I would give my debriefing to the Union. The group had been together a long time and, now, everyone just needed breathing space. It was time to step out of the bubble and back into reality. What do you do with your disappointment?

I remember the question being asked in a US dressing room some years ago just after Canada had put 50 points on the Eagles in a Pacific Rim game. And Tom Billups, the Eagles captain, pretty much nailed it in a sentence. 'You pick up your shit and you walk on!' he said.

That's what you do. You don't wallow in grief, you don't take refuge in self-pity. You do, I suppose, what the great explorers, always did. You move on. You just take yourself to the next challenge.

There is always another mountain.

19

DECLAN AND ME

Declan Kidney and I parted company after the 2004 Six Nations.

In the history of sports partnerships, I don't suppose we were ever going to be remembered in the same breath as Clough and Taylor or Redgrave and Pinsent. Ours had been an arranged marriage that, in hindsight, was fundamentally flawed. It was born of the IRFU's desire to have us both on the one management ticket without any great forethought for the likely working dynamic that would develop between us.

I can say now that it was probably unfair on us both. Had either refused to work with the other, it's a pretty moot point what implications that refusal would have had for our future job prospects in Irish rugby.

When I was asked in late 2001 if I would have 'any problem' working with Declan, it sounded less a question than a condition. Likewise, I'm sure, for him when he was asked about working with me. It wasn't, I might add, that there had ever been any profound differences between us. There hadn't.

The evolution of the professional game simply led to certain tensions between provincial coaches and those involved with the

223

Irish team. I think it suited the Union to step back from those tensions and allow us to resolve (or not) them between us. This led to the provinces almost habitually butting heads with the national team. A 'them and us' mentality ensued.

So, for two seasons, I – as assistant Ireland coach – and Declan – as Munster coach – were operating on opposite sides of that fence. Beyond this, I don't believe we had any great philosophical differences about the way forward for Irish rugby. We were, essentially, just chasing different targets.

In terms of personality we wouldn't have had a great deal in common, I admit. Declan is quite forensic in discussion, teasing arguments out exhaustively, weighing up every option no matter the impatience of others to move on.

Let me say that Declan is a very bright guy and brilliantly well organised. And his record now stands comparison with just about anyone in the professional game. Two Heineken Cups with Munster and a Grand Slam in his first season with Ireland identify him as an absolutely top-rank coach. Bear in mind too, that he coached Ireland to the under-19 World Cup in 1998.

But the point I would make about our time working together is that he simply wasn't cut out to be a number two. When he became my assistant, he'd already guided Munster to a European final. Assistant is a difficult role to fulfil if, on instinct, you are a head coach.

The problems between us were never overt. Just a nagging tension that, over time, I imagine became more palpable to everyone concerned. Maybe his role was a little too ambiguous. He was coaching the backline but, in reality, coaching backlines was my forte.

So maybe Declan found himself in a bit of a no-man's land. He would put an arm around a disappointed player after team announcements, often taking complex, left-field angles into selection meetings and rehashing old arguments as if, eventually, different conclusions might be drawn.

Over time, his presence in the management set-up became a little strained. He was uncomfortable, I was uncomfortable. Once we got through the 2003 World Cup, I decided to bring it to a head. I went to the Union and told them that the relationship between Declan and me just wasn't working on any level.

We didn't socialise together. Or, if we did, it tended to feel contrived and awkward. If anything, I found his presence draining. Niallo had been his number two with Munster and now had a pivotal role on my team with the forwards. Declan, in contrast, was peripheral. I knew this made Niallo uncomfortable.

Deep down, I think the Union had known for some time that pairing Declan and I together was a mistake. In any event, I wanted to be more hands-on with the coaching myself. Letting him go made sense.

There was never any question of not appreciating his talent. I eventually got criticised for letting him go, but assistant coach just wasn't the place for him.

Approaching the 2004 Six Nations, I made my views known to Declan. He was contracted as assistant until July but, that February, the Union offered him the job of 'Performance Manager, Age Grade Rugby'. A desk job, essentially. It was a contrived position – looking after Ireland's elite talent – they created it in an effort to ensure he wouldn't be lost to Irish rugby. Declan, as a front-line coach, was unimpressed. He declined the IRFU offer, meaning that – technically – he would remain my assistant for that Six Nations. The working dynamic was now pretty wretched.

He joined Newport Gwent Dragons that summer as head coach but, three months later, he left Wales, coming home to take charge of Leinster. Less than a year after that, he was back at the helm with Munster.

In a perverse way, maybe the fact it didn't work out between us worked to his advantage long-term. After all, within a year of returning to Munster, he was a European Cup winning coach. Going back to his roots in 2005 gave Declan a fresh impetus in his career that he might never have got had he stayed as my assistant all the way to the spring of 2008.

Press conferences were repetitively uncomfortable during our time together. Declan would sit almost invisibly by my side until, eventually, some member of the media might direct a sympathetic question his way. It became embarrassing, to him – I suspect – more than anyone.

There was no concealing the fact that things weren't working out between us and, long before his departure, I was aware of rumours circulating about us not getting on. Some of my critics suggested subsequently that I felt threatened by his presence, that maybe I feared he might be after my job. I can categorically deny this.

When you are a head coach, the one certainty in your life is that someone else will get your job one day. Who that someone is hardly matters. Unfortunately, throughout my coaching career, great play has been put on a nickname I picked up during my college days in Limerick.

At Thomond, I was known as 'Dagger'. It originated, quite harmlessly, from the games of five-a-side we played but was subsequently hijacked by certain people to depict me as some kind of back-stabber. This was especially so when Warren Gatland didn't get his contract renewal in 2001 and was now recycled again when Declan was let go.

In my heart of hearts, I'm not sure I was ever convinced that things would work between us. Even going all the way back to that day at Lansdowne Road when we first shook hands as coach and assistant, I suspect I knew that we weren't really compatible.

After the 2004 Six Nations, Declan asked for a meeting with me. I met himself and Pa Whelan (representing the IRFU) in Limerick and I can't say that the experience was pleasant.

Declan was clearly upset. I had to go through the process of explaining my thinking again, though I'd already done this with both him and the Union. Some of what I said was diplomatic now, some wasn't. But, bottom line, I told him, 'Look, I want to get back into coaching. I miss being hands-on . . .'

Declan then said to me, 'Is it because you think I'm not up to the job?'

'No, that's not it,' I answered.

Leaving that meeting, I knew that Declan felt hard done by. I knew, too, that I would never be on his Christmas card list. So I can only admire his graciousness, after guiding Ireland to that long-awaited Grand Slam in Cardiff in 2009. Because in mentioning those of us who, maybe, managed to put down some of the foundations, he showed an immense dignity in his finest hour.

Declan and I will never be best of buddies. But I would like to think we can, at least, look one another in the eye with mutual respect. We just weren't meant to be a team.

20

DID HE REALLY SAY ...

The day before the launch of the 2004 Six Nations, I was interviewed for the job of Lions coach to tour New Zealand.

It was, in some respects, an exercise in diplomacy. I knew the
job was Clive Woodward's and, as a World Cup winner, he was
clearly the stand-out candidate. Both of us went before the Lions
committee in a hotel at Heathrow Airport and I was given the
impression afterwards that my interview had gone well.

The Lions budget was £5.5 million, the interview focusing on
selection matters and, generally, how the ship would be run. I got
unofficial word that evening while having a drink with Wales
coach Steve Hansen that the gig was Clive's. I had no issues.

All the indications were that I would have a role in the tour
and I was happy with that. I was also pleased for Woodward. In
my dealings with him, I always found him decent and sincere. It
actually bothered me that, in Ireland, there was a kind of glib
consensus during the 2003 World Cup that an England triumph
would be a cause for national gloom.

I made a point of leaving a message on his phone before the
final, expressing the hope that they would bring the Webb Ellis

Cup back to the northern hemisphere. Clive mentioned getting the message on *Sky News* and told me later how much he appreciated it.

People like to have cheap shots at him and I can see how, sometimes, he seems to radiate a vague arrogance. But I've always liked the guy. He's pleasant, interesting company and, from my experience, he has a graciousness that maybe isn't easily reconciled with the popular media depiction.

That summer of 2004, Clive came to Dublin for Conor O'Shea's wedding and we had a breakfast meeting in the Shelbourne Hotel, where he formally asked me to be one of his assistants. He had a plan for the 2005 Lions that could probably be synopsised into the phrase 'super-sizing'.

Graham Henry had been desperately unlucky not to win the previous Test series in Australia, Justin Harrison's famous line-out steal effectively changing the whole profile of that tour. Those Lions thus came home defeated and the perception of 'failure' was further contaminated by the outpourings of people like Austin Healey and Matt Dawson.

Clive rightly believed that the twin-pronged nature of a Lions tour was problematic. Striking a happy balance between the Test and midweek teams has proved, historically, difficult. It is, after all, the only rugby environment in which you are asked to prepare for two games in one week. Clive's solution was to bring 44 players instead of the traditional 35 and have them served by two entirely separate staffs. It seemed an obvious solution to an obvious problem. Maybe that was the rock he perished on.

A Lions tour moves on complex energies. It starts out, not just as a very diverse group who have never played together, but as one populated by people who are accustomed to kicking lumps out of one another. The key to success is weaving the various threads into a coherent pattern. That never happened with the 2005 Lions.

The tour failed in a number of ways but maybe the most fundamental was in the matter of focus. In bringing 44 players and 28 staff, this vast entity of 70-plus personnel was created and, over time, it took on the feel of a three-ringed circus.

For me, the alarm bells were ringing from the moment we assembled in the Vale of Glamorgan. The group immediately felt unwieldy. Everything was a slow, tortured grind. Just getting to and from training sessions seemed to be a bit of a logistical nightmare. There was such a sense of vastness, I couldn't help wondering how on earth it was ever going to be pulled together.

Clive's decision to bring separate staffs came from a desire to keep the midweek 'Dirt Trackers' happy, something they patently hadn't been under Henry. So he put Ian McGeechan in charge of the Wednesday team and, over time, they would acquire the somewhat juvenile identity of 'The Midweek Massive'. This name became a symbol almost. A badge of honour. Bullshit.

They were beating teams that amounted to little more than a Kathy Barry XV and trying to hold it up as some kind of higher calling than being part of a Test side. To me, this became more toxic as the tour went on. I said it to people. The Wednesday side would beat the likes of Manawatu by 103 points and celebrate it as some kind of Herculean deed.

My view was that 'Geechs', as a former Lions coach, should have recognised that this thing was getting out of control and reined it in. It didn't happen. I have to admit that it did cross my mind during our time in New Zealand that, perhaps, he had already set his sights on the 2009 gig in South Africa. At the end of the tour, T-shirts were presented to anyone who had played on the Wednesday team celebrating the fact that they'd won all their games.

Now, given that all but a handful of the touring party had some involvement in at least one Wednesday game, this was the ultimate exercise in posturing. There was, effectively, no Wednesday team. 'The Midweek Massive' was a myth.

But maybe Clive's biggest mistake was to believe that he could just pick a first-choice fifteen the week before the first Test and imagine they'd be ready to take on the All Blacks. To me, you've got to pick your Test team early in the tour and get them onto the paddock. Injuries and form can, obviously, alter things thereafter. But you need to have the spine in place.

Clive didn't do this. Worse, he then decided to throw a curve ball by picking two out-halves – Jonny Wilkinson and Stephen Jones – for the first Test, the Englishman starting at twelve. I had had a feeling that he was going to do this, but he only said as much the week of the first Test. To me, it left us worryingly vulnerable in the midfield area. It gave us kicking options, no question. But, attack-wise, it restricted us.

I shared coaching duties on the Test team with Andy Robinson and Phil Larder; McGeechan, Mike Ford and Gareth Jenkins taking charge of the 'Massives'. Approaching that first Test, there was no real enunciation of a game plan. It was as if we were all trading on that old theatre hall maxim of it being 'alright on the night'.

Which, of course, it wouldn't be.

Technically, there were eleven people on the selection committee, which didn't make for the cleanest lines of planning. Clive basically walked into the room, put his side on the board and invited contributions. 'Right, there's the team I'd like to put out, what are your thoughts?'

Bottom line, if you had a problem with a position, you needed to get sufficient backing around the table to have any hope of getting a change. There was, in fairness, a fundamental honesty about Clive's approach. Nothing was nuanced or disingenuous. People just shot from the hip and got on with it.

But say you had six positions you weren't happy with, you knew you were never going to win six arguments. So you cut your cloth to measure. You prioritised. Better to go to battle on two of those six positions with a reasonable chance, than to try getting your way on all six.

The trouble was there were people in the room who, in my view, shouldn't have had any say in picking a Lions Test team. The fitness advisor, the kicking coach, the refereeing consultant all had a voice in selection. Absurd. Another little wrinkle in the 'super-sizing' plan.

In terms of logistics, the tour was wonderfully well organised.

We were an army on the move and the sense of military order was constant. You couldn't escape the impression of privilege involved, from the personalised folders and iPods presented to everyone, to the way your bags would magically materialise in each new hotel room without any reference to check-in desks or baggage carousels. The tour bus would arrive at an airport, drive straight onto the tarmac and pull up beside the plane.

All the little worries then were concealed beneath a polished, confident skin. We had a bonding session in the Vale of Glamorgan, the squad broken into small teams, each one painting a section of what turned out to be this giant mosaic honouring the Lions. Within hours of completion, the jigsaw was completed and everyone had their picture taken beside this great mosaic in the indoor hall. Mine is now framed in an office at home, 72 signatures across the bottom!

There was a sense of the Lions doing it the England way and, though no one ever articulated it, I could sense a little unease from the outset among the Irish, Scots and Welsh. Alistair Campbell's appointment as Press Officer was a case in point. I really liked Alistair, but he was the wrong guy for the job.

Firstly, the media were immediately hostile towards him. Secondly, he knew nothing about rugby.

This made for a constant undercurrent of tension and Alistair himself made one rank bad call after we'd lost the first Test in

Christchurch. With the second Test looming in Wellington, we were all in the team room one day when he took it upon himself to deliver a speech about passion and pride and what a successful Lions tour meant to people back home.

At one point, he pretty much suggested that maybe defeat didn't hurt the players as much as it should. You could have heard a pin drop.

The speech was lunacy. Here was this guy essentially challenging the players' commitment, questioning their integrity almost. At a time when they needed picking up, this guy was kicking them down. On any level, that was bad judgement. But factoring in that it was coming from the media guy, not the coach, it was daft.

People were sitting there, literally in shock. You could almost read their minds. '*Did he really say what I think that he just said?*'

Clive had been sitting beside Alistair as he spoke and I couldn't help but wonder if, like the rest of us, he got a slightly sinking feeling as the room went quiet. It was a big room, the acoustics weren't great and Alistair wasn't miked up. So people were literally straining to hear what he had to say.

A bad, bad decision.

One of the rituals of the tour was for players to be formally presented with their Lions jersey by a member of the party before every game. This sense of ceremony has its appeal in one-off situations. I never used it with Ireland, but I have done in America. I just feel that it can be overdone and, as such, ends up reduced to the realm of cliché.

In an eleven-game tour, that certainly proved the case. There was a repetition to the whole thing: tired, old speeches about past tours being recycled to bleary-eyed players. Again, you could almost read a few minds going… '*Give us a fucking break here!*'

The whole thing becomes a little tired and lazy after a while. It ends up antagonising rather than inspiring.

The scale of the party also created this surreal dimension whereby it became physically impossible for everyone to make a meaningful connection. People on the Wednesday rota might not necessarily have much to do with the Saturday group for days at a time. We were like two independent states.

To some degree, there was a certain amount of superficiality about our preparation too. I remember training for weeks in Takapuna, over on the North Harbour side of Auckland. The pitch was completely sealed off from public view. You couldn't have squeezed a razor blade through any gaps in the tarpaulin, the idea obviously being that we could prepare away from prying eyes.

But then we we went to Christchurch for the first Test and trained on the fields of Cathedral Grammar School, the place completely open. To me, that was a contradiction. Anyway, I'm pretty sure that if Graham Henry really wanted to know what we were doing at any given time, he could have organised a tape of it at pretty short notice.

Then there was the decision, à la England, to put the players in single rooms. I felt this gave them the option of retreating into their shells a little. Their rooms became bunkers almost. They could cut themselves off from one another when, if anything, they needed to be communicating more.

With Ireland, the only player who got a single room was the captain. After a time, I even allowed the players to draw up their own rooming lists because I sensed the energy was right in the group. And that, I knew, wasn't something you could always presume upon.

I remember my first training camp in Limerick as Irish coach came immediately after a Celtic Cup final in which Eric Miller had been sent off for kicking Anthony Foley. I put them rooming together. My attitude was: 'You'll be playing together in a month's time for Ireland, so get over it!'

I presume, at some point, Eric apologised. That was their business. I left it to them to sort out between themselves.

With the Lions, wives and girlfriends were encouraged to come up to the team hotel. I've always felt you've got to be sensible here. These guys are going into battle. There's a real gladiatorial dimension to rugby and you've got to be ready for the physical confrontation. The fight, in other words.

And it *is* a fight. I know that no one's going to get shot or blown up, but there simply has to be an edge to a player going into a Test match. There must be an adrenalin flow. It's like boxers being cut off from their families for the couple of weeks leading up to a big fight. It makes them mean and angry. They are ready to hit and be hit.

I've no problem with wives coming in on the morning of a game maybe to drop their bags in. But, basically, a player's entire focus on game-day should be on the 80 minutes ahead.

I remember coming out of a lift about four hours before one of the Tests on that tour and seeing Julian White, a wonderful prop and a really quiet, decent guy, playing with his little daughter in the corridor. It struck me that, for someone about to go to war in the scrum with the All Blacks, this mightn't have been the ideal head-set with kick-off looming.

The physicality coming down the line was huge and, to me, the players should have been in a virtual tunnel beforehand. There should be nothing else that matters at that moment beyond those two acres of ground and winning the war. Because, if you're in the wrong frame of mind in that environment, you're going to get blown away.

Which, of course, is pretty much what happened.

I haven't a single pleasant memory of that first Test in Christchurch.

The infamous spear tackle on Brian O'Driscoll pretty much set the template for a series of unrelenting strife that, by the second Test, would even spill over into the coaches' box. I didn't see the tackle initially as, like most people, my attention was on the ball. Out of the corner of my eye, I just saw a body on the ground and then the word crackled through on the radio.

'Drico's down, it looks bad . . .'

When I saw the tackle afterwards, I could hardly believe my eyes. It was disgraceful. Tana Umaga took most of the heat afterwards but, for me, Keven Mealamu was equally complicit. There surely had to be repercussions.

Personally, I would question if the haka has any place on a rugby field. We all cherish strands of our own, individual culture, but we don't inflict them on opposing teams. I can see all the arguments they make about heritage and tradition and the special place it holds in Maori hearts. But how you face the haka has always been a problem for teams playing against the All Blacks. Any number of responses can be interpreted as an insult.

There were issues in 1989 when they came to Ireland. The Leinster team slipped off to the far end of Lansdowne Road and completely ignored it. The Irish team, with Willie Anderson to the fore, did the complete opposite, fronting up, going almost nose to nose with Buck Shelford's team.

Anderson and Leinster coach Roly Meates both got heavily criticised. It seemed neither way was acceptable to the All Blacks. To me, it's grossly unfair that a team is obliged to try to untangle the correct protocol for facing what is, essentially, a war dance.

Clive, to be fair, tried to do the right thing. He went to a Maori elder and asked what was the most respectful way to meet the haka challenge.

It was explained to him that you needed to front up to it. Not in the Willie Anderson way, mind. You had to give them space, he explained. Make sure to show your bravery by not wearing the 'protection' of tracksuits. Don't link arms, because that showed weakness. And get the youngest warrior to go to the front as a symbol of how ready you are for the fight.

They gave us a Maori welcome the day we went to Rotorua, throwing what looked like a little arrowhead on the ground. Bill Beaumont picked it up, symbolically accepting the challenge. This was, essentially, the punchline. Your acceptance of the fight.

It was explained to Clive that when the Blacks jumped in the air at the conclusion of their haka in Christchurch, Drico should pick up a blade of grass and throw it in the air. That, he was assured, would not ruffle any feathers.

How galling then, in the days after that Test, when we were told that Brian throwing the grass had been interpreted as some grievous insult by the Maori people. This, it seemed to me, was no-win territory. Of all the coaches to face the haka, Woodward had gone to more trouble than anyone to establish the most appropriate response. And his reward was to have his captain quite brutally removed from the tour.

No question, Drico's injury infected the mood of the whole team. It was as if people slipped into a mild state of shock and we just never got out of the blocks during the course of a 3–21 defeat.

Back in the hotel afterwards, I met Alistair Campbell in a lift. It was after midnight and the air of gloom in the place was palpable. The lifts were glass-fronted and you could see the traffic going up and down, everyone wearing funereal expressions.

'Any idea what Umaga's suspension is going to be?' I asked Campbell.

'He's got off!' said Alistair.

'What?'

'Scot free!'

'He can't have, that's ridiculous.'

'They said there was no case to answer.'

Incredulous, I walked into the team room and sat for a while chatting to Drico and his parents, Frank and Geraldine. The sense of being thousands of miles from home now weighed pretty heavily on everyone. Over the coming days it was as if an entire nation would slip into denial mode. Either the spear tackle had not happened or 'It was an accident, stop whining and get on with it.'

The New Zealand media, historically, has never been inclined to turn on its own and this time was no different. I gave a press conference the following Wednesday and there was a distinct atmosphere of bloodletting in the room. Danny Grewcock had been suspended for biting Mealamu's finger and local media were more interested in discussing Grewcock than Umaga.

I cut loose. Maybe, deep down, I was thinking to myself, I'm going to be without a captain in the autumn now... I was seething. It just seemed to me that O'Driscoll had been brutally taken out of the tour and no one had the remotest interest in taking responsibility or accepting blame.

I was asked if Umaga had phoned to apologise. Maybe my response wasn't the most diplomatic. I said that he had phoned to enquire after Drico's well-being, but there had been no apology. 'To me, that's like kicking a ladder from under someone, then asking if they're alright,' I said.

The facts to me were pretty stark. Brian O'Driscoll was the Lions captain and, probably, the Lions' most dangerous player. And, within 90 seconds of the start of the first Test, he'd been cynically (and potentially lethally) removed from the tour.

I couldn't understand how our own media settled so quickly on a consensus that the Lions were now whining. They took the view that Clive was playing this card too much and, effectively, turned on the Lions management. Alistair was depicted as a kind of puppeteer in the background, pulling the strings of outrage. This was nonsense.

But there was blood in the water and, like hungry sharks, they were upon it now. Our captain was gone. We'd got a good pounding in the first Test. If we lost the second in Wellington, the tour was over. A disaster. So they were lining people up in their sights and our press officer was the number-one target.

If they didn't like Alistair Campbell to begin with . . .

We went into the second test in Wellington with eleven changes from the side beaten so comprehensively in Christchurch.

Some of the changes were forced upon Clive by injuries, others I felt were the product of media pressure. There was certainly a degree of lobbying in the press for the inclusion of more members of Wales' Grand-Slam-winning team, so the call-ups of Gavin Henson and Shane Williams were universally welcomed.

The 'Massives', meanwhile, kept up their perfect midweek record with a facile 109–6 destruction of Manawatu in Palmerston North, scoring 71 unanswered points in the second half. It was a meaningless contest, Williams alone scudding in with five tries. Yet I could sense Clive attach more credence to the performance than it merited.

Gareth Thomas had taken over from O'Driscoll as tour captain and we made a wonderful start to that second Test, Thomas scoring under the posts. The defiance was illusory though and, hard though the team undoubtedly tried, that evening we would ship the biggest points haul ever conceded by a Lions team in an 18–48 defeat.

It was absolute annihilation that certainly made for uncomfortable viewing. During the game I was the only Lions coach wired up to the touchline, where Mike Ford was operating as runner. At one point, Ryan Jones came out of his line defensively and New Zealand almost picked us off. It was a basic error, one that others were threatening to commit too. When this happens the whole house of cards is in danger of coming down.

Instinctively, I said down the line, 'Fordy, tell Ryan not to come out of his line!'

Phil Larder, our defence coach, immediately erupted. Just ripped into me. 'How dare you put in messages on defence,' he roared. 'I'm in charge of defence, don't you ever . . .'

My gut reaction there and then was to thump him. You don't speak to a fellow professional like that in front of others. Clive, Andy Robinson and Dave Alred were in the box with us, Tony Biscombe – the video analyst – too. But I took a deep breath and managed to hold my calm. I just turned to Larder and said, 'So are you telling me you have no message for Ryan Jones?'

He said, 'No!'

Down in the dressing room after the game, I tore into him. 'Don't you ever in your longest day even think of talking to me like that again,' I said. And, basically, he started fucking me out of it again. So we had this big set-to, a really nasty exchange that might easily have come to blows. In my mind's eye, I can see Gordon D'Arcy walking in on it, turning on his heels and walking straight back out again.

The following day, Clive came to me, wondering if we'd 'kissed and and made up.'

I knew a row on the coaching staff was the last thing that he needed now, but I told him that we hadn't. 'Listen, Clive, maybe I crossed a line by putting in a defensive call,' I said. 'It was a gut reaction. I was the only guy on the radio and I could see the defensive line unravel. But I wouldn't speak to a dog the way he spoke to me.'

Clive agreed that Larder had been out of order and said he'd have a word. And the following Tuesday at a coaches' meeting, Larder finally apologised. So we parked our differences without ever quite resolving them.

At this stage of the tour, people just wanted to get home. I remember Clive saying at a press conference that he was intent upon enjoying his last week in New Zealand. The truth was that we all just wanted to get the hell out of Dodge.

The Test series had been lost and, while I personally tried to put a spin on the final Test in Auckland – saying that 1–2 would look a hell of a lot better than 0–3 – the truth was we were running on empty. You had to say something at press conferences, but the tour was already a disaster. In my heart I knew it was going to be desperately difficult to thieve the momentum now from a rampant All Blacks team. We all did. Our chances of winning that third Test were never anything better than slim.

The build-up was also notable for the distraction of a story that blew up, implying friction between Clive and Gavin Henson. It focused upon a photograph taken of the two chatting on the Wednesday before our first Test in Christchurch. The photograph was, reputedly, taken through a long lens without Henson's knowledge.

Henson had, naturally, been disappointed not to make the Test team. The idea of the photograph was to imply that, whatever his level of disappointment, it had not affected his respect for the Lions coach.

It was accepted afterwards that the photograph was a set-up, supposedly to generate 'good PR'. Who was responsible? I honestly don't know. Did Henson know it was being taken? I haven't that answer either.

We got thumped 19–38 in the final Test as it happened and I have to say it was an education for me to see how wretchedly Clive was treated.

Maybe it's a part of human nature that when someone reaches an incredible height (as Clive did at the 2003 World Cup) people take great delight in giving them a good kicking when things go wrong. Suddenly World Cups and Grand Slams seemed to mean nothing now. It intrigued me how the British media almost took a delight at his failure. I thought that was horribly unfair.

No question, the whole tour had unravelled pretty spectacularly, spinning out of control. Instead of the tour party becoming more focused the longer we were together, it went the other way.

Clive was showing signs of the pressure. I remember sitting with him at the final press conference and sensing incredulity in the room as he declared the tour 'successful'. By now, I suspect, he was just jammed in defensive mode. A lot of the media stuff had stung and he pretty much said that he wouldn't forget some of the things that had been written about him.

Sitting there, all I could think was: 'Don't do this, Clive . . .'

We were all going to get a flaying anyway and I sensed Clive was just fuelling the fire. He was mentally and physically drained. We had been in New Zealand for over eight weeks now and I don't think any of us wanted to spend another minute beyond what was absolutely necessary there.

I don't blame Alistair for the bottom falling out of the tour. He was asked to do a job and probably thought, PR is just PR, I'll do it! He was impervious to the criticisms of the sports media. At times, I think he thrives on that kind of hostility.

Yet I felt sorry for Clive. No question, he deserved criticism. But what he got was vicious ridicule. Sadly, that's just where the media is gone now. They see a victim and they go for the jugular.

There is a surreal dimension to the ending of a Lions tour, any tour maybe. It's strange the way people just disperse in different directions. Quite a few of us flew back to Heathrow but you literally touched down in the airport and headed straight to transfers. You didn't really get a chance for goodbyes.

I've always likened it to a spinning top that's slowing and slowing until eventually it topples and stops. That's how the end

of a tour feels. You've been together for weeks and, suddenly –
in a matter of minutes – you are all gone your separate ways
again.

And it's not as if you make phone calls to one another when
you get home. You don't. It's just a chapter in your life that's
over. I didn't ring Clive, he didn't ring me. And that didn't feel
in any way strange.

A few months later, when I was taking a bit of a media kicking
for Ireland's poor performances in our autumn series, he did send
a text. 'Hang in there, don't listen to the crap . . .' it read.

Coming from a man who had put up with more than his share
of media vitriol, I could appreciate the sincerity.

21

THE ROSE AND CROWN

A season that was to bring Ireland's first Triple Crown in nineteen years began with more bad news than you'd see jotted down in an undertaker's order book.

Eight days after our elimination from the World Cup, our fitness coach – Mike McGurn – gave an interview to the *Belfast Telegraph* in which he outlined the need for a 'fitness revolution' in Irish rugby. The interview was like an incendiary going off within the game. Intentional or not, he was seen to be critical of just about every strand of rugby in Ireland, from the provincial coaches right down to his own boss, Dr Liam Hennessy.

Mike said there were too many 'roadblocks' obstructing his desire to get the players into the best physical condition possible. He suggested that they were operating at no more than 'sixty to seventy per cent of their capacity', implying that their time with the provinces was non-productive. I had a high regard for Mike, as did the players. But he was, essentially, criticising the Union here, so I felt compelled to step away from the controversy. It was an employer/employee issue and, as such, I couldn't interfere.

In any event, I wasn't Mike's direct boss. He was answerable to Liam Hennessy.

Mike felt passionately that a three-week pre-season for international players was pitifully inadequate. He was coming from a rugby league background, where pre-season averaged 14–16 weeks. There was no doubting the logic to his argument, yet the provinces already felt hard done by with the existing schedule.

In fact, tensions were already at an all-time high when I took the players to a training camp in Lanzarote after the first two rounds of the Heineken Cup. I then had them in for a mini-camp in Dublin in January. Munster and Leinster, I knew, were furious. There was palpable friction between us and, being honest, it was nobody's fault.

I had a ten-Test schedule ahead of me and I needed all the time with the players I could get. The provinces were fighting their own corner, I was just fighting mine.

McGurn was called back from holiday in Australia to explain his interview amidst speculation that he might be sacked. As it happened, he was suspended by the Union, ruling him out of most of our Six Nations campaign. It wasn't ideal, but worse would follow.

On our final night in Lanzarote, we ran a tab in the bar to allow the players to unwind with a few Christmas drinks. It wasn't, as some portrayed it, an invitation for a session. We had training scheduled for the following morning and everyone was expected to attend. Unfortunately Malcolm O'Kelly and Anthony Horgan, who were sharing a room, didn't show. I immediately suspended them from the upcoming mini-camp and made the suspension public rather than have the news leak out at a later stage.

This was grist to the mill of my critics, some now choosing to depict the Lanzarote trip as little more than a piss-up in the sun.

There was a lot of sniping coming our way now. Tony

D'Arcy, our Australian scrum coach, had been let go after the World Cup and, with Declan Kidney's departure imminent and McGurn now suspended, I was portrayed as a troubled, isolated figure at the helm.

The snipers had other targets too. Brian O'Driscoll had a new hairstyle and, given his relationship with a fashion model, was supposedly leading a 'celebrity lifestyle'. When *Social and Personal* magazine named him 'Ireland's Sexiest Man', the heat from the media just intensified.

Drico's contract with the Union was up for renegotiation and he was snapped attending a Biarrittz game in France. Two and two suddenly added up to six, some of the media believing he was trying to provoke an auction for his services.

I sensed the critics smelt blood and I knew exactly why. Drico had picked up a hamstring injury playing for Leinster and there was a growing belief that we could lose our first three games in the Championship, given they were against France in Paris, Wales in Dublin and World Cup winners England at Twickenham. Three losses, I knew, would place serious pressure on the Union to present me with my P45.

The portents weren't exactly reassuring either. The day before our game in Paris, we were returning from training at the D'Orsay club and had to evacuate the team bus because of a strong smell of burning rubber. Then *L'Equipe* captured the sense of impending gloom the morning of the game by branding us *'Les Irlandais Orphelins'*, the Irish orphans missing their 'parents', Wood and O'Driscoll.

I had appointed Anthony Foley, David Humphreys, Ronan O'Gara, Reggie Corrigan and Paul O'Connell as vice-captains and, on the Tuesday, chose O'Connell to take over the captaincy against France. People seemed a little shocked that Paulie, the youngest of the five, was my choice. To begin with, he was a little surprised himself.

When I called him to my room, he thought – initially – I was going to give him a bollocking over some messing on the training ground with Donnacha O'Callaghan. Paulie was just 24, but he already had a presence in the group that defied his youth. I had little doubt he was a natural leader.

If we were without Drico, Geordan Murphy and Denis Hickie, one key inclusion in the team now was Gordon D'Arcy. I knew I'd broken his heart by leaving him out of my World Cup squad, but 'Darce' had been reinvigorated at Leinster by Gary Ella's decision to play him as a centre. His form was sensational and I gave him the number thirteen shirt.

On the day, sadly, the game pretty much passed us by. We lost 17–35 and afterwards the media criticised me for what they saw as our lack of ambition. Personally, I wasn't as down as the coverage suggested I should be. No question, I was niggled by the fact that we'd effectively lost the game in five second-half minutes. But the defeat didn't sicken me like others would in Paris. Just a few basic errors had caught us out.

And basic errors were, generally, fixable.

That said, the general climate led to an edginess in the squad after France. On the Monday before the Wales game, we had an extremely physical training session in Naas during which a fight erupted. Part of me was delighted. The aggression, if controlled, wouldn't do us any harm. And, at least, it told me that the players cared.

I paired a returning O'Driscoll with D'Arcy in the centre for the first time and targeted Wales with one particular trap. Steve Hansen, a good friend of mine, had taken over as coach and we chatted beforehand in the middle of the pitch. I knew exactly what his game plan would be.

Wales would try running at us from the off and get on the board early. They knew our confidence was brittle and that a few quick scores might trigger panic. Ball in hand, they were always dangerous. Yet I reckoned they had fundamental weaknesses too. We just needed to release the hounds early and get into them physically.

Firstly, I knew their backs were very poor at going to rucks. Secondly, I reckoned if we got to Stephen Jones quick enough, we could block down a few of his kicks. Bottom line, we just had to be out of the blocks quickly, get on them like a rash. 'Here's the deal,' I said in the dressing room. 'Put the ball down into the corner and force them to kick it out.'

You see, I knew they wouldn't risk running out of their own 22 and, from the line-out, we could railroad them into the in-goal. 'When they kick out the ball, do the exact same thing again,' I said. 'And you keep doing that for 40 minutes!'

It sounds brutally simple, I know, but it worked to perfection. From the very first kick-off, we won the line-out and 'Munch' (Shane Byrne) rumbled in unopposed from the back of a maul. There was absolutely nobody at home. Minutes later, we repeated the trick, same result, same scorer. Then ROG blocked down a Jones clearance and, suddenly, we were 20 points clear.

We won 36–15, two late Welsh tries giving them a trace of respectability in the end. But, having wiped the floor with Scotland in their opening game, Wales were now well and truly humbled. They had come to Dublin believing their own publicity and we'd proceeded to pick massive holes in the hype.

After the game I had a pint with Hansen. He's a decent guy who doesn't get precious on good days or bad. We talked about our respective game plans. 'Steve, your backs won't go into rucks,' I told him.

'I know,' he said. 'They're breaking my heart.'

Keith Wood 'honoured' Shane Byrne's two tries by wearing a mullet wig on *Rugby Special* that Sunday night. We'd strangled the life out of Wales, mauled them into oblivion. I could sense a mix of relief and renewed confidence in the squad.

But everyone knew there was a much bigger storm now rolling our way.

England's World Cup homecoming was to be, essentially, a show without a supporting cast.

The build-up to Twickenham didn't really tap into the normal energies of a Six Nations contest. Clive Woodward and his team had come back from Australia as rugby royalty and to be Irish that week in London was pretty much to be invisible. England had the Webb Ellis Trophy. This was, essentially, their victory parade.

They had already hammered Scotland at Murrayfield and been antagonised by the welcome afforded them in Edinburgh, a marathon jamboree of pipers and Highland dancers they seemed to suspect was intended as a distraction. There was all manner of rumour as to the kind of innovation Clive was now bringing to the English dressing room.

He was said to have an aromatherapist releasing scents like basil and peppermint to sharpen the alertness of his players. There was, supposedly, a visual awareness specialist too working on their peripheral vision. The impression being given was of England stretching the boundaries of preparation while the rest of us gaped in awe.

It suited us perfectly.

Drico maybe captured our mindset best with his infamous pre-match observation that Ireland hoped to make the Twickenham crowd 'choke on their prawn sandwiches'. He said it tongue in cheek but, deep down, I think it reflected the sense of determination within the group not to keel over meekly for England's titillation.

Woodward's response identified a chink in their armour. He was disdainful rather than dismissive. He could have laughed it off but, instead, found himself drawn into a slightly condescending retort.

'It's best to keep quiet,' he said. 'I'm surprised teams haven't learnt that lesson when it comes to playing England. We had it from the Scots in Edinburgh and I'm sure we'll get it again when we play Wales. I think you'll see a big display from us in this game.'

Much as I liked Clive, I sensed he was disregarding us as a threat.

The day before the game, while training at Bracknell, I proposed applauding England onto the pitch. It was a kind of reverse psychology. Applaud them on, then kick them off it. I just felt it might add to their complacency. Initially, the players agreed but – back at the hotel – a few reservations began to gather steam.

I had to meet some IRFU officials on a budgetary matter and returned to base about 9 p.m. Drico came to me while I was having dinner.

'You know you were talking about clapping them on the field tomorrow, then kicking them off it?'

'Yeah.'

'Well fuck the clapping bit!'

It turned out that the players, generally, were not comfortable with the idea. I had no problem with that. I knew it would stick in some of their throats to do it. 'Anyone in particular speak out against it?' I asked Drico, already knowing the answer.

'Maggsy,' he answered smiling. 'He nearly went fucking crazy!'

Complacent or not, I genuinely believed England to be vulnerable. Had we a little more polish to our game the year before, I felt we could have beaten them in that Grand Slam showdown at Lansdowne Road. Now we were 11 months older and wiser as a team. They were without Martin Johnson (retired) and Jonny Wilkinson (injured), unequivocally their two most important players in 2003.

They were also without Danny Grewcock and Simon Shaw. Iain Balshaw was still at fullback, Jason Robinson in the centre.

Take away the aura of being world champions and I saw plenty for us to target.

That aura, mind, was everywhere. One of the first things we noticed was a line of 22 plaques arranged around the frame of the dressing room door, signifying each of England's consecutive victories at Twickenham. They hadn't lost a championship game at home since 1997. No doubt the engraver was already somewhere in the stadium now, poised to put the finishing touches to a 23rd.

There was a really heavy shower before kick-off and, chatting to Clive on the pitch, we were joking about how the wind and rain didn't suit either of us. In the old days, it was almost a cliché that Irish rugby teams thrived on mud and mayhem. Not now. We were a decent rugby team, looking to do a hell of a lot more than spoil. I felt that if we could find an early rhythm and just stay in the game we could really cause them problems.

And that's pretty much what happened. We targeted England's set piece, their line-out in particular, and got 6–0 up through two Ronan O'Gara penalties. The stats showed we'd had 75 per cent of the first-quarter possession, but then they got a try, almost a replica of one they got the year before in Dublin, just a ball squirting out of a scrum and Matt Dawson getting the touch-down. They quickly added a penalty, but two more O'Gara kicks had us 12–10 clear at halfway. So far, so good.

I knew England would come back with a vengeance and they did, Peter Stringer and Gordon D'Arcy just forcing Ben Cohen into a double-movement touchdown picked up by the TMO.

One of the things I'd said to the players beforehand was to back themselves if an opportunity presented itself. And that they certainly did for Girvan Dempsey's try. It was a score straight off the training field and ROG's nerveless conversion gave us the vital nine–point buffer. Thereafter, England came at us with the kitchen sink and, true, we were hanging on for dear life at the end.

But Fordy's defence system held up brilliantly. England 13, Ireland 19. The homecoming had been ruined.

There were extraordinary scenes afterwards as we came out of the stadium, maybe 700 people waiting to applaud the players onto the bus. It took us an hour and a half to get back through awful traffic to the Chelsea Harbour Hotel and we were then an hour late for the post-match banquet at the Intercontinental,

None of it mattered. I'd left my phone in my briefcase and it practically exploded with messages when I switched it on. In a sense, it was only then that the magnitude of what we'd done began to sink in. When we got to the banquet, the Webb Ellis Trophy was on display, there was a string quartet, a brass band . . . everything you'd expect for a glorious coronation.

We'd pooped the England party here. Actually, we'd even messed things up for the Six Nations' organisers whose scheduling of an anticipated Grand Slam finale between England and France for the final weekend now looked a presumptuous folly.

The following morning, I left the team behind me, taking a red-eye fight back to Dublin so I could get to Moylough in time for Barry's confirmation. A newspaper photographer showed up in the church to get a picture and that really bugged me. It was a private occasion that I felt should not have been thrown into the media glare.

I felt like telling him where to stick his camera, but decided against it. It was an otherwise enjoyable day. Why spoil what felt like a perfect weekend?

All the talk, inevitably, was now of a Triple Crown. Yet, before Scotland came to Dublin, we had to take care of Italy. I brought Geordan Murphy back for his first game since breaking a leg in the pre-World Cup game at Murrayfield. This, I knew, was harsh on Tyrone Howe, who'd been one of the heroes at Twickenham. But a fit Murphy just couldn't be overlooked

McGurn returned as fitness coach too, his suspension now served. There was a real sense of rehabilitation in the squad.

Yet shocking weather turned the game into a farce. A vicious gale came howling through Lansdowne, the goalposts swaying like reeds on a lake. On such days, the oldest rugby ground in the world offered scant protection from the elements. It became almost impossible to play.

We wore them down in the end, conceding only a Roland de Marigny penalty in a 19–3 win. But it was ugly, unfriendly stuff, the Italians taking a few cheap shots and Drico actually being sin-binned for a high tackle on Paul Griffen. I was relieved to get it out of the way.

Scotland alone now stood between us and a place in history. We fancied our chances, no question. But Ireland had won just six Triple Crowns in the previous 103 years. And the Scots, now led by former Leinster coach Matt Williams, were desperate to avoid their first Championship whitewash in almost two decades. We could rest assured they wouldn't roll over.

Nor did they. Early in the second half, when Alistair Hogg dived over from the side of a ruck after a long sequence of phases, the score was tied at 16–16. We'd dominated the game territorially, yet here they were now in our faces. You could have cut the tension with a knife.

In the stand, I remember thinking, How we react now is going to tell me what's really in this team.

The response came in a David Wallace try that only David Wallace could have scored. Wally is one of the most powerful ball carriers I've ever come across. He could have made a running back in the NFL with his ability to get through the tiniest of gaps and, with just under half an hour remaining, he put us back in front.

After that, Gordon D'Arcy pretty much took over, setting up a Peter Stringer try, then scoring one himself (his second of the day) to seal a fine personal Six Nations that would see him voted 'Player of the Championship' on the BBC website.

I found it immensely satisfying to sit in the stand for the last ten minutes of that game knowing the Triple Crown was ours. Maybe the biggest test for me that week had been to convince the Irish players that this was going to be no garden party, that if we got it wrong we'd lose.

The key had been to get rid of all the nonsense about how we were going to hockey them. Now I could relax and savour a job well done. We'd scored five cracking tries and played some scintillating rugby. The players did a lap of honour at the end, much to the enjoyment of the Lansdowne crowd. Yet, coming in off the pitch, I could sense something wasn't right. People were talking in strangely hushed tones. Faces seemed oddly drawn.

Just after giving my post-match TV interview, I was taken aside and told the reason. John McCall, a 19-year-old from Armagh playing for Ireland in the Under-19 World Championship opener against New Zealand, had died on the field in Durban. The celebrations literally ground to a standstill there and then.

By the time I got to the dressing room, the players had already heard. There was an eerie kind of silence. Bottles of champagne were left unopened. A terrible fatigue set in and, that night, there was a minute's silence before the banquet. France, meanwhile, were Grand Slam champions after a narrow win over England at Stade de France.

Drained physically and emotionally, I took myself off to bed reasonably early. And slipped away into the deepest sleep.

22

TAMING THE 'BOKS

Before becoming the Irish coach I had only ever been to Lansdowne Road once as a spectator.

Crowds never appealed to me. Maybe it's the analytical side of my personality, but I've always preferred watching games in a relatively quiet, restrained environment. I've always been drawn more to the mechanics than the emotion. Winning the Triple Crown now brought a level of attention on me that I wasn't altogether comfortable with.

As best I could, I went with the flow, appearing on RTE's *Late Late Show* just a few weeks after the Scotland game. Not long after this, I went on another TV programme, *Buried Alive* – a kind of Irish-style *This is Your Life*, again with a live studio audience. This sudden elevation to the status of celebrity put me in a place I didn't really want to be.

Pretty soon I found myself retreating from the scrutiny and was glad to be heading to South Africa that June for a two-Test tour. At least it took the focus off trivia and put it back on rugby.

That said, the tour was probably a bridge too far for us. It didn't get off to an auspicious start with the squad threatening to strike over tour fees. Then we lost both Tests in Bloemfontein and Cape Town, 17–31 and 17–26 respectively. Not disgraced by any means. Just worn down by hugely intimidating and physical hosts.

Before we even arrived in South Africa, their coach – Jake White – made what I considered a pretty inflammatory statement about Irish rugby. He said that we had no tradition of achievement in the game and that, at best, maybe two of our players would make it into a Springbok squad. I could have jumped on the comments there and then, but I decided to keep my powder dry. We were, after all, in their backyard. They were coming to ours in November.

We played our guts out in both Tests but the players were tired. I couldn't fault their effort and told them as much in the Cape Town dressing room. 'Trust me, we'll do a number on them when they come to Dublin,' I said. I genuinely believed it.

We'd organised tickets to the second Test for Irish actor Colin Farrell, and he asked me afterwards if he could go in the dressing room. Farrell was in town, shooting a movie, *Ask the Dust,* with Salma Hayek. That night was John Hayes's stag and, once the players had time to gather their thoughts, they began to warm to Farrell's presence.

Back at the hotel, they involved him in the customary 'Court Session' and 'Red Ass' (don't ask), before heading out on the town, where, at or around midnight, a slightly under-the-weather Farrell was poured into a cab and despatched to the safety of his bed.

Ask the Dust was produced by an Irishman, Redmond Morris, the son of Lord Killanin. As I was staying on after the tour – Noreen and the kids coming over for a holiday – Redmond invited me out to the set one night. It was based in a forest and the scene they were trying to record involved Colin and Salma having a row. Between takes, they just chatted to me as if we were all sitting around in a coffee bar.

Later that night, Reggie Corrigan, Victor Costello and Eric Miller all pitched up on set and we retired to Farrell's trailer for a few beers. He struck me as a really decent guy, no airs, graces or Hollywood bullshit. Actually, the following week, I brought Noreen and the kids out there and he couldn't have been more welcoming to Katie and Barry.

I never did get to watch the movie though I did notice it crop up on the pay-per-view a few years later while we were based in Killiney. It wasn't, I suspect, Oscar-winning material.

Leaving South Africa, I had stored Jake White's comments for future reference. Before our arrival, the 'Boks had won the Tri-Nations on points difference and I suspected that had made him a little cocky. If I could just get someone to ask the right question when he came to Dublin, I reckoned he'd play right into my hands.

The 'Boks were good, no question. Just not as good as White wanted everyone to believe.

Sure enough, that November, he stumbled right into my line of fire. Repeating his dismissive view of our players, he suggested that few if any would make the Springboks' squad, never mind their team. I was driving to an IRFU reception in Portmarnock when I got the phone call I wanted.

It came from the *Irish Independent*. 'Eddie, do you have any response to make to Jake White's observation that . . .' Bingo.

I chose my words extremely carefully, making no predictions or declarations about the game looming. I described his words as 'an affront to Irish rugby', pointing out how they flew in the face of the respect traditionally shared between our two countries. And I said, 'Even if we lose on Saturday, it doesn't give him the right to say what he has said.' I knew that was just about enough fuel in the furnace. The players were all but frothing at the mouth by game-time. It made my team talk simple.

Deep down, I knew White just didn't see us as a threat. In my opinion, he probably reckoned he was just in town to jump all over a bunch of Paddys. I told the players, 'This guy pissed all over us last June and we had to take it on the chin. We could have won a Test down there, but didn't.

'Well, we've a chance now. And he's just stuck his size twelves in to make that chance even bigger. Let's make it count this time!'

You could detect an edge to the atmosphere even on the bus, swinging around by Beggars' Bush, people pouring out of the pubs and gesturing with clenched fists. Lansdowne was almost full as the players finished their warm-up and, walking back in, the crowd began to cheer. You could feel the tension in the air, the sense of people desperate for us to right a wrong.

And right it we did.

The South Africans were completely undone by ROG's quick thinking for our try and finished the game pounding our line. I can vividly recall the referee's voice say, 'Last play!' There must have been eight rucks in a row, the decibels rising ever higher with each one. Eventually, John Smit took up a ball, got hit and spilled possession. Anthony Foley snaffled it, went to ground and, when the ball came back to Peter Stringer, he launched it into the East Upper. Ireland 17, South Africa 12. The roof almost blew off the stand.

Ordinarily, the opposing coaches shake hands after a game, but White literally bolted down the steps and away. That night, he sat opposite me at the meal, yet never lifted his head to even make eye contact. Briano actually started to feel sorry for him and went across to make conversation.

It turned out that White's dismissive comments about Irish rugby had actually offended a lot of South Africans back home. Having lost the Test, he was now getting it in the ear from his Union. And he was feeling sorry for himself. The following week, they played England at Twickenham and Clive Woodward told me he had a good chuckle at White's expense.

Jake was going on about how his comments in Dublin had been completely misrepresented. And he saw Clive laughing.

'What's so funny?' he asked.

'Eddie set you up,' said Clive.

'You think so?'

'Chalk it down, you walked right into it!'

In fairness, White had been rather pointedly asked by a journalist after the game in Dublin how many of the Irish players he now reckoned would make the Springbok squad. 'Probably most of them,' he said. It had been a fair cop.

You can take it that Jake and I were never destined to be bosom buddies. I was actually the opposition coach for his last game in charge of the 'Boks, just six weeks after their World Cup win in 2007. It was, in fact, one of the great privileges of my career to coach a star-studded Barbarians team to a 22–5 defeat of the World Champions at Twickenham.

Almost 60,000 attended and, in the best Baa-Baas tradition, one of our tries was a virtual length-of-pitch spectacular after Joe Rokocoko's wonderful cover tackle forced a turnover and Ma'a Nonu, Conrad Smith and Matt Giteau contrived a stunning counter-attack, the latter getting the touchdown.

The experience was hugely enjoyable for me, coming, as it did, so soon after our own World Cup meltdown.

Anyway, having seen off South Africa in that 2004 autumn series, we beat the US Eagles 55–6. There had been a fairly dramatic changing of the guard since my time in America and I knew few of their players now. Yet, at a reception under the stand afterwards, their manager – Chris Lippert – gave a speech in which he said how much I was appreciated in US rugby.

I was really touched by that. To some degree, I suppose I was delighted for people within the IRFU to know that my time in America had meant something. That I hadn't been just swinging the lead, waiting for the call to bring me home.

We completed our autumn series with a 21–19 victory over Argentina in a really mean-spirited game. Six of our players were gouged in that match, eyes and mouth. The gouging left a really bitter aftertaste that would boil over into bitter correspondence between myself and their coach, Marcelo Loffreda.

Argentina had scored an early try and we spent the whole game trying to reel them in. Eventually we managed it right at the death, ROG dropping a goal from 40 metres in the rain. There was a photograph taken of him jumping up and seeming to click his heels in celebration at one of the Pumas' props and it emerged subsequently that they felt he was trying to rub their noses in it.

Yet the gouging was the main bone of contention. Anyone wired up to the 'ref link' would have heard Drico complaining to Tony Spreadbury during the course of the game. The Pumas had history here. Both Reggie Corrigan and Keith Wood had been gouged during our World Cup meeting the year before, leading to suspensions for Mauricio Reggiardo and Roberto Grau. It's a despicable practice that should have no place on the rugby field.

That said, I had no intention of bringing it up at the post-match press conference. It was, I felt, a matter for the citing commissioner.

The Argentine captain, Agustin Pichot, was coming out of the conference as I arrived though and completely blanked me. I knew something was up. Then I was asked if I had any response to the allegation that Ireland had been 'unsporting' in the game. It turned out that Pichot had accused Drico of trying to get some of the Pumas binned. This, he reckoned, violated some fundamental moral code.

I cut loose. 'Firstly,' I said, 'I think you'll find that Brian didn't ask for anyone to be sin-binned. But if you want unsporting, here's unsporting. I've six players in the changing room who've been gouged . . .'

That kicked it off. We had taken photographs of the injuries and I said my piece now. That night, I sat with Loffreda and Les Cusworth at the meal. The gouging wasn't mentioned. It wasn't the time or the place. Our wives were with us and we enjoyed a thoroughly pleasant evening. I wasn't going to lean across and say, 'By the way, Marcelo, you're in charge of a bunch of thugs!'

The story was all over the papers the following morning and, while Loffreda tried to defend his players, there was no great indignation in his tone. How could there be? We had the photographs to back up the accusation.

Imagine my surprise then to get an email from Marcelo just before Christmas.

Loffreda wrote of his 'surprise and disappointment' at my post-match comments and, incredibly, wondered what I was trying to achieve by drawing attention to 'things that did not happen at all'. He said that my comments had caused outrage in Argentina and, as such, reflected badly on him as a coach.

They gave, he wrote, 'the wrong idea about Argentinian rugby'.

I wrote back, pointing out – firstly – that I hadn't introduced the issue to the media, but that six Irish players had reported to our medical staff that they'd been gouged. Photographs taken of those players, at the insistence of the Chief Medical Officer, substantiated medical opinion that these reports were valid.

In reference to his concern about people getting the 'wrong idea' about Argentinian rugby, I did point out that two of his players, Reggiardo and Grau, had both been formally suspended for gouging after our World Cup pool match in 2003.

And I suggested to Lofreda that, maybe, some of his players simply needed to 'mend their ways'.

I never heard another word about it. It had been a real 'Hear no evil, see no evil' defence that I considered beneath contempt. Malcolm O'Kelly had got two stitches inside his eye. Inside!

Simon Easterby had a really dirty gash inside his mouth, where nails had scraped him. Other players had marks on their faces around the eye area.

It's not something you ever raise with much enthusiasm but, sometimes, you simply have to take a stand. In Adelaide the year before, we had been at the airport on the Monday when I got a phone call from the citing commissioner. He had seen the evidence and he wanted to investigate it. Would we support that investigation?

Of course we would.

Yet the inquisition the players had to then undergo in Melbourne was outrageous. It was done by a video link to Sydney and our doctor, Gary O'Driscoll, was absolutely grilled by their solicitors. Right down to: 'Where did you qualify as a doctor?' It was absolutely appalling.

I know for a fact that Woody said to Syd Millar that if this was the kind of inquisition inflicted on players trying to assist in the disciplinary process, they could kiss that process goodbye. The victims were, essentially, being treated like dirt.

It was a real eye-opener for us as to where the game was going.

23

THINK I'M HAVING THE SAME NIGHTMARE

A telephone rings in a hotel room in Bracknell and I know it's trouble before I answer.

'Eddie,' begins Gary O'Driscoll. Now if there's a list of voices I don't want to hear early this Friday morning on the outskirts of London, our team doctor's is written in neon at the top of it. 'It's Drico,' he says. 'He's done his groin.'

'How bad?'

'Bad.'

Brian O'Driscoll has just ripped a muscle stepping into the shower. Our captain thrives in a world of physical attrition, yet he's just gone and crocked himself by stepping over a two-inch ridge on the bathroom floor.

'I don't fucking believe this, Gary.'

Tomorrow we play Andy Robinson's England at Twickenham. Victory will bring us our second Triple Crown in three seasons, defeat leave us with three wins out of five and some blood on the wall. The English are on a mission to avoid losing three on the bounce against us.

We need all hands on deck.

Gary gets to work and, in the meantime, I go in search of cover. I phone Michael Cheika, telling him that I need Denis Hickie on a plane to London. 'Oh, and Michael,' I add, 'this has to be kept under wraps. I don't want anyone to know that Drico is a doubt.'

Cheika is as good as his word. Hickie flies into Heathrow that lunchtime, a baseball cap pulled low over his face, unseen and completely under the radar. He'd been out of favour for a while now, missing the autumn series with a leg fracture and unable since to unseat Andrew Trimble from our starting fifteen.

If Drico doesn't make it, I have already decided I will play Denis on the wing, Shane Horgan moving to centre.

The media gain access for just the closing minutes of our Friday workout. Gary is walking our captain around the pitch, his groin tightly strapped. Yet no one asks a question. It turns out that Drico had collected a bruise on the hip the previous week against Scotland. The bruise bled internally. Scar tissue formed and, stepping into the shower, Drico essentially ripped the scar tissue. Cue intense pain for the captain, fevered worry for the coach.

By the next morning, he's moving a lot more freely and Gary eventually clears him to start. Hickie is handed a ticket for a seat in the stand, the media utterly oblivious to the fact that he's been so close to starting. We go on to win the game and the Triple Crown in hugely dramatic circumstances.

And poor Denis is the invisible man. A guy who missed our first Triple Crown win because of an Achilles tendon injury sustained at the 2003 World Cup. And who's now just missed our second by the skin of his teeth.

Few people even notice that he's in London.

The 2005 season had uncorked a degree of negativity that was, at times, breathtaking. We won our first three games in the Six

Nations, Italy (28–17) and Scotland (40–13) away, England (19-13) at home. Drico got a smashing try in the England game, literally tiptoeing down the touchline by the West Stand. It was our second successive victory over the world champions, yet it felt as if we encountered sarcasm at every turn.

A day or two after the game, it was suggested to me that the RTE television coverage had been particularly snide. I got a tape of it and, sure enough, the prevailing tone was unpleasant. George Hook tore Drico apart in his analysis and then, while Brian was waiting to do a post-match interview, Tom McGurk said rather crassly, 'Now we have Golden Balls . . .'

This was how they introduced the captain of the Ireland rugby team! The lack of any semblance of respect was nauseating and, personally, I'd just had enough. It seemed to me that we just couldn't win with these people.

Two really bad calls by referee Tony Spreadbury then cost us dear when France came to Lansdowne. We lost the game (19–26) and I subsequently raised the issue of Spreadbury's performance in my end-of-season report to the IRB. He had penalised Malcolm O'Kelly for coming in the side of a ruck when he clearly came in the back (three points to Yachvilli). Then – late in the game – we were running the ball from our own 22 and Serge Betsen – from an offside position – tackled Peter Stringer without the ball, France thieved possession and scored a try.

The IRB agreed with me that Spreadbury was wrong on both counts. I'm not just saying that, I actually have it in writing.

Had we won, we'd have been facing into a Grand Slam showdown in Cardiff for our final game, so the loss was devastating. We subsequently played poorly at the Millennium Stadium and got turned over (20–32) by Wales. The knives were back out.

That night, Mike Ford came to me in the Hilton Hotel to say he was leaving. Basically, he wanted to be more than just a defence coach and I couldn't really accommodate him. I think he was a little concerned too that the IRFU wouldn't release him to be part of the Lions' management that summer in New Zealand. If so, that concern was misplaced.

It was subsequently spun into a story of me having 'sacked' Fordy. I hadn't. To this day we're still good mates. I actually tried to talk him out of leaving (he went to Saracens). He was still relatively new to the union game and it was my belief that he wasn't quite ready to be a head coach.

By the time I came back from the Lions tour I knew I needed new faces. Both Drico and Paul O'Connell were out of the autumn series, a series which – unfortunately – pitched us into battle with Australia and New Zealand.

We lost against both, getting torn to shreds by the Blacks (7–45). They were the wrong opposition at the wrong time. We were in the process of trying to bed in our new defence coach, Graham Steadman, and I suppose it was his misfortune that his first game up happened to be against the best side on the planet. I also felt sorry for Simon Easterby, who captained us through the series. To me, he is one of the great, unsung heroes of Irish rugby, but one who never seemed to get a fair acknowledgement in the press.

The defeats to New Zealand and Australia meant that we had now lost four games on the bounce. The flaying from the media was extraordinary, so much so that I genuinely began to worry about the impact it was having on the players. It was around this time my argument with ROG had become the subject of such intense media speculation. There was a mood brewing. We rounded off the autumn series with an unimpressive 43–12 win against Romania.

It had been a bit of an *annus horribilis* then, a bad end to the Six Nations, a bad Lions tour, a bad autumn series. The only way was up.

★

I've been accused of being a slave to American Football-style coaching, prescribing every play, bringing an almost mechanical dimension to the business of setting up a team.

That accusation gathered real impetus after events at the Stade de France in February of 2006. We'd already scrambled our way to a 26–16 victory against a typically physical and aggressive Italy in Dublin. The game was tied 10–10 at half-time and, frankly, I was happy just to see the back of it.

We went to Paris with that typical sense of spring foreboding, especially given the French were coming off a rather chastening opening-day defeat at Murrayfield. I knew that their coach, Bernard Laporte, was under intense pressure and desperate for a victory. Yet nothing could have prepared me for what followed. The game blew up in our faces virtually from the kick-off, France scoring four first-half tries, each one the product of a fundamental Irish error. It felt like a living nightmare.

For the first try, Tommy Bowe slipped and Geordan Murphy missed a tackle on Aurelian Rougerie. For the second, Geordan and Denis Leamy made a bit of a hash of a quick 22 between them. For the third, ROG had a kick blocked down. For the fourth, Geordan threw a bit of a Hail Mary pass to no one in particular and it was intercepted.

Approaching half-time, I turned to Niall O'Donovan and said, 'Niallo, I sincerely hope I'm going to wake up from this nightmare in a minute and find myself still in the hotel bed!'

Niallo responded, 'Well, if you do, wake me as well because I'm having the same fucking nightmare!'

France led 29–3 at the break and, hand on heart, we had gifted them every single point. I remember making my way down this big, wide tunnel towards the dressing room and feeling ridiculously calm. We were facing possibly the hiding of our lives, yet the first half had been all about our error count, not France's creativity. In other words, the stuff going wrong was fixable.

It subsequently became a bit of an urban myth that the players took control in that dressing room. That they supposedly ditched my prescribed game plan for a more spontaneous, attacking option. Nothing could have been further from the truth.

Inside, I sat everyone down. It was important we held our heads. 'Look, lads,' I said, 'we are playing like lemmings at the moment. Hang onto the ball. Calm down. We've got to back ourselves here. We're not doing a lot wrong, we just have to stop making silly plays.'

There was no shouting, no roaring, no panic. We knew we'd been stretching France. We'd just been coming undone by our own silly errors. I have to admit, there was a faint voice in my head whispering, 'This can go either way now . . .'

Seven minutes into the second half, France had crossed for their fifth and sixth tries to leave us trailing by a humiliating 3–43. And now I certainly did find myself wondering if everything said at half-time was redundant. The thought struck that we could be headed for a 60–point defeat.

But the players, critically, held their nerve. They kept playing. They kept doing the right things when the easy option would have been to curl up into a ball and become France's plaything. We scored four unanswered tries in the half-hour that followed, through ROG, Gordon D'Arcy, Donncha O'Callaghan and Andrew Trimble. Started ripping the French to pieces but, essentially, just ran out of time. The game ended France 43, Ireland 31. Afterwards, Joe Maso – the French manager – embraced me and said, 'You were better than us in the end. We were so happy to hear that whistle!'

In the dressing room, the feeling was that France had been out on their feet. That, if we'd had another five minutes, we might actually have won.

I felt intensely proud of the team and how they had kept their heads up. Drico had picked up that dead leg in the build-up to their second try, yet resisted any invitation to step out of what had looked like a looming humiliation. Paul O'Connell popped the AC joint in his shoulder early in the second half. I'd already put on O'Callaghan for Malcolm O'Kelly, so Paulie stayed on, played through the pain. Excruciating pain.

To me, these guys were absolute warriors. And it was in that dressing room, as I helped him put on his blazer, that Paulie made the comment about the players playing for me. I deeply appreciated that.

No question, I would have been run out of town had France put sixty points on us. Yet, the knives were still out. At the following Tuesday's press conference in Killiney, I stupidly got involved in an argument with a journalist. He had written that I publicly criticised the players after the game.

I hadn't. The accusation needled me. It was used as a tool to imply that my management of the team was beginning to unravel.

'By the way,' I said, unsolicited, 'contrary to what some have written, I haven't criticised any players publicly.' An argument ensued. The journalist was claiming that I had criticised Tommy Bowe. What I actually said was that Tommy had 'slipped' for France's first try. A statement of fact.

'Anyone can slip,' I said. 'It's hardly a criticism of somebody to say that they slipped.'

He then suggested that I had criticised Geordan Murphy for missing a tackle. I hadn't. The exchanges became quite asinine and I was a bigger fool for engaging in it. Afterwards, he wrote a predictably negative story. It was illustrative of the mood.

Wales were next up in Dublin and they prepared for the game by parting company with their Grand Slam coach Mike Ruddock. It was an extraordinary mid-season eruption that worried me. Ruddock was replaced by Scott Johnstone and I feared that the Welsh players, having essentially squeezed their coach out, would come to Lansdowne Road with a point to prove. I sensed they'd come at us like rabid dogs.

They did too, scoring an early try. But they then lost Stephen Jones to injury, bringing on Gavin Henson. We devoured them, running at Wales from all angles when the temptation might have been there to stick the ball up our shirts and hope for a lucky break. In the end, they just couldn't live with us. The final score was 31–5, yet I felt the team never got credit for the quality of the performance.

There was one moment in that game which, I felt, typified the innovation of the performance. Ronan O'Gara moved as if to find a touch, but aborted at the last second, dinking a little kick to John Hayes, who almost made it over. Had 'Bull' scored, the move would probably have been acclaimed by pundits. After all, whoever heard of kicking to your tighthead as an attacking strategy?

But no try, it seemed, translated into no interest. It never got a mention.

Two weeks later, we beat Scotland 15–9. They came to Dublin on the back of victories over England and France, yet our confidence was flowing. But for the fact that it poured with rain all day, I honestly believe we would have beaten them far more emphatically. The game just degenerated into trench warfare, which suited them more than us.

We edged the second half 3–0, a statistic that tells you every-thing you need to know about the game. It was an eyesore. We won by five penalties to three but I didn't care about the aesthetics. Three from three in our home games meant that we were headed for Twickenham now with a shot at the Triple Crown.

To hell with the begrudgers.

★

London on St Patrick's weekend was always likely to be a city dusted in green. The Irish poured down out of the West Country buoyed by a remarkable haul of ten winners at the Cheltenham Festival. English rugby was in trauma after defeats to Scotland and France.

Seldom has there ever been a greater sense of the old empire hanging frail and vulnerable.

All of which worried me. Maybe it's part of my make-up to become suspicious when all the planets seem aligned. But I knew England were desperate for a victory. I knew, too, that we were taking a calculated gamble on Drico's fitness though, mercifully, no word of that particular drama had seeped out to the press.

What transpired was an extraordinary game. I won't recycle the detail because, in many ways, the entire script can really be condensed into what happened in the dying seconds. Suffice to say, England attacked us ferociously and, on more than a few occasions, had victory in their nostrils. It was real, edge-of-the-seat business. An emotional roller-coaster ride.

Little things made the difference. We were leading 14–11 in the second half when Niallo and I decided it was time for fresh legs in the pack. We made the call to replace Malcolm O'Kelly but, in the time it took to get a replacement organised, Mal lost concentration, came out of his defensive line and Ian Borthwick got in under the posts for an English try. Those were the margins. That was the intensity.

Nearing the end, Simon Easterby was wrongly yellow-carded. A terrible decision. He came back on with two minutes to go and, by now, we were trailing 21–24. The drama was only beginning.

Entering injury time, we got a scrum inside our own 22 and England sensed we had to run. They pulled their wingers up flat, leaving the fullback deep and isolated. What did we do? We didn't run. ROG played a sublime little chip-kick, Drico got on the end of it and put Shaggy (Shane Horgan) away.

Now Shaggy had previous in this kind of position. When we played Australia at the 2003 World Cup, he had a similar opportunity in the dying seconds, went for the outside and Wendell Sailor buried him in touch. Trying to outrun a flyer had been the wrong option. The great players know when they have the fuel to make it home and when it's best just to keep the ball alive.

This time Shaggy had the presence of mind – with Lewis Moody tracking him – to straighten up and come back infield. He knew he couldn't make the line. Moody made the tackle, a ruck formed and ROG – like most out-halves not a man famed for cleaning out – arrived at the ruck like a dumper truck. The ball came back and Drico went left, taking the ruck infield, opening up the short side.

And that's when Peter Stringer threw this most sublime pass over the top to Shaggy, who needed every last inch of his six-foot-five frame to get the ball down in the corner. A wonderful, wonderful team try. What followed is still so fresh in the memory it could have happened yesterday.

The match clock said there was one minute eighteen seconds remaining. I sent word down to Mike McGurn to tell ROG to milk every second he could while lining up the conversion. If he took a minute, we'd have only eighteen seconds to survive.

The kick, mind you, was absolutely critical. We now led 26–24. If he missed, a drop-goal or penalty could still win the game for England. If ROG scored, only a try would save them. I didn't doubt for a second what was coming.

'We could do with this one,' said Niallo.

'Don't you worry,' I replied. 'I guarantee he'll nail it.'

I knew Ronan O'Gara well enough by now to understand what made him tick. The more chips on the table, the more likely he was to get it. The guy has ice flowing through his veins when others are hyperventilating. So ROG lined up the kick.

Took his full minute to do so. Checked the wind. His studs. The result of the 3.15 at Wincanton. Nailed it.

Eighteen seconds to the Crown . . .

Hallelujah, we claimed the restart, mauled for the requisite few seconds and Stringer thumped the ball out of play. The referee called a line-out. I couldn't believe it. I looked at the clock and, inexplicably, he'd forgotten to say 'time on' as ROG prepared to line up the conversion. It meant the minute killed had just come back from the grave. FUCK.

We managed to steal the line-out, pile forward and kick the ball dead again. 'Line-out,' he repeated. What? I've never felt more helpless in my life. I could see the body language of the players. It was like someone was having a laugh at their expense. Surely this couldn't go belly-up?

Finally, England, having won the second line-out, turned the ball over. We kicked it dead again and, after another pause, a long shriek of the whistle. Twickenham erupted.

I was absolutely elated. In a single year we had reinvented ourselves and still managed to win four out of five Championship games. The official statistics would show that, having kicked more and passed less than any other team in the 2005 Six Nations, we had now passed more and kicked less than any of our opponents one year later. It was an extraordinary transformation.

For the first time, too, there was an actual trophy to represent the Triple Crown. We were only too happy to have something to wave to the hordes of Irish supporters now. The players had been extraordinary. I felt so pleased that they'd got a tangible reward from what had been a difficult season.

Afterwards I was very mindful of the added stress our victory had placed on Andy Robinson. I'd been with him on the Lions trip the previous summer and liked him. It strikes me that there's nothing worse when you lose a game than the opposing coach coming to you full of the joys of spring.

There has to be an empathy there. I can honestly say that losing Test games has led to some of the worst days of my life and now I could see how much defeat was hurting Andy. We had a good chat. I knew how close they'd come to beating us and, by extension, how close I was to being back on the media skillet.

It's funny how utterly wasted you can feel at the post-match banquet. The meal is always lovely, but you can hardly taste it. You drink a beer and you feel the energy leaking out of you like grain from a sack. There are so many people you have to engage with. Opponents, supporters, committee members. All are entitled to your time until eventually, at maybe two or three in the morning, you get back to your hotel and slump into bed with exhaustion.

That's how it was that night in London. But at least we were back in a good place. The carping had gone silent. We were headed for a summer tour to New Zealand, touted by some as a team good enough to beat the All Blacks.

This, just seven months after they'd fleeced us so badly in Dublin. Something told me to remember that old adage about a slap on the back being just six inches above a kick in the arse.

24

BUNGEE BOYS

Funny how, sometimes, a rugby life pitches you into two parallel worlds.

The most enjoyable tour of my career was, unquestionably, New Zealand and Australia in the summer of 2006. It was a revelation. We played some wonderful rugby against the giants of the southern hemisphere and, as a group, had incredible fun. Yet we lost the three Tests.

The frustration felt at those defeats was pretty intense as, in all three cases, we had opportunities to win.

Yet the surreal dimension to that tour was the feedback coming from home. The sense of incidentals being freighted with a significance in the media coverage that simply didn't tally with our experience. Sometimes you'd ring home and get the impression that the tour being reported on bore little if any similarity to the one we were experiencing.

We played really well in the first Test in Hamilton but, essentially, panicked from a position of strength. The All Blacks kicked their way back into the game and, eventually, a late try sealed their 34–23 win. We were sickened. Our indiscipline had offered them a fire escape and they took it.

This was especially galling because, at the time, we were the most disciplined team in world rugby. Most teams might concede ten or twelve penalties in a match, fifteen on a bad day. A bad day for us would have been the concession of eight.

So the errors that brought us down in Hamilton were uncharacteristic and we were determined not to repeat them.

There is always a sense in a two-Test series against the Blacks that the first Test is the one to catch them in. That, second time round, they come to business forewarned. But we travelled back to Auckland absolutely bullish about our chances the following weekend. I articulated that mood in the dressing room: 'Lads, these guys are worried,' I said. 'Make no mistake, they'd rather be playing someone else next Saturday.

'Let's keep our discipline and have a real crack at them. They're there for the taking!'

The week that followed was incredibly positive. We were going out to dinner one night when Jerry Flannery got his timing wrong. Everyone was sitting on the bus, but no sign of Jerry. 'Where's Flannery?' someone asked.

'Gone to get a haircut!'

So we drove downtown, pulled up outside the Toni and Guy hair salon, and a few of the lads went in and literally carried him outside, his hair half-cut. The next day, the players had an afternoon off. One of our liaison officers made up a placard with a picture of a clock, surrounded by the words, *My hair is more important than Timekeeping*!

And we made Flannery march back down to the salon, dressed in lycra bottoms and a pink T-shirt with the slogan *Daddy's Girl* on the front, carrying the placard above his head. Behind him, the entire squad followed, letting off air-horns to ensure an attentive audience.

He had to walk into the salon and announce in front of the customers, 'I was late for a team meeting last night, because my hair is more important than timekeeping.' It was hilarious.

The whole vibe of that tour was really enjoyable and a good deal of credit for that had to go to our two liaison officers in New Zealand, John Sturgeon and Pete White. They were the same guys we'd had on our last visit in 2002 and Sturgeon, who came out of retirement to do it, was a particularly good mate of Briano's.

One of the first functions we attended in New Zealand was a sponsors' lunch at a racecourse on the edge of Auckland. Darce (Gordon D'Arcy) had shown the catastrophic judgement to bring a guitar on tour, with a view to learning how to play.

After this particular lunch, Drico said a few words on our behalf and finished by announcing that there'd been a special request.

'Gordon's been working very hard on his guitar-playing,' he said. 'And we'd like him to come up now and honour us with his very first live performance.' The guitar promptly materialised like a rabbit from a hat and a mortified Darce stepped forward. I think, by now, he had mastered maybe a chord and a half.

He played 'My Lovely Horse' from *Father Ted*. Brought the house down.

On tour, laughter keeps people sane. Players have a lot of recreation time and a tour without fun is, frankly, a tour doomed to fail. So we kept things light as much as we possibly could. One afternoon in Auckland, I did a bit of shopping, bought myself a few tops.

That night, I decided to wear one of the tops to dinner. The moment I walked into the team room, a huge roar erupted. Out of the corner of my eye, I spotted ROG spinning out the door like a scalded cat. He'd been down the town too and purchased exactly the same top.

There was no escape now. Some players followed him to his room (where he had already changed) and forced him to put the new purchase back on. So ROG and I had to go to dinner wearing the same top. On the bus, the squad sang the Cat Stevens song 'Father and Son' all the way to the restaurant. When we got there, they insisted on a table being made up for two, with candles.

So ROG and I sat there for the night, wearing identical tops, looking sheepishly at one another in the candlelight. The two of us done up like a pair of kippers.

The day of Flannery's march of shame, a group of us went down to Auckland Bridge. I've always been terrified of heights and wanted to do a bungee jump to challenge that fear. So myself, ROG, Flannery, Peter Stringer, Mick O'Driscoll and Jeremy Staunton took up the invitation to plunge 150 feet towards the harbour waters on the end of a cord. To say there were a few sweaty palms would be a bit of an understatement.

The city seems to have this masochistic effect on me. In January 2004, I'd gone there to speak at an IRB conference and Steve Hansen, the Welsh coach at the time, talked me into jumping off Auckland Tower. It's not quite a bungee jump. You don't actually free-fall as there's always a bit of tension on the cable. They put a harness on you, you walk to the end of a ramp and, with the street directly underneath, jump.

The day I did it, a six-year-old was in the line ahead of me. He took off without as much as a second's hesitation. Whatever noise the coward in me was making, I couldn't be seen to baulk at something this kid just took in his stride.

Walking down Queen Street now, Micko turned to me. 'Fuck, I don't know about this, Eddie'.

'Calm down, Micko,' I scoffed, my own stomach beginning to churn like a cement mixer.

'Yerra, I signed up for this,' he said, 'but I don't know if I can do it.'

'You'll be grand.'

While we were lining up for the jump, some of the other players passed underneath in an America's Cup Grand Prix yacht. I'm damn sure every last one of us suddenly wished we were on board with them. You get weighed before the jump and that weight is scribbled on your hand, so that they can adjust the bungee to suit.

Micko, being the heaviest, was told he would be first. Next thing, he's standing on the ledge, peering down in a lather of sweat. At that moment, every single nerve in your body is screaming, 'DON'T DO THIS!' The guy in charge is trying to get Micko to jump, but he's like a racehorse that won't go into the stalls.

'Just lean forward, mate . . .'

'Give me a second . . .'

'Look, just . . .'

He makes the mistake of touching Micko. 'I'll tell you one thing,' says O'Driscoll, 'if you push me off this bridge, I'll climb back up and fucking rip your head off.'

Message received, loud and clear. No one's going to push Mick O'Driscoll off the Auckland Bridge today. He gets his few moments, takes a deep breath. He mutters something to himself. And, next thing, seventeen stone of prime Munster beef is plummeting towards the water. 'Holy fuck,' we all shout in unison. A few sick bags would be handy here.

Jeremy is directly in front of me now. He's hesitating, and the more Jeremy hesitates, the longer my own ordeal. I decide to pare his options down to two. 'Jeremy, you either fucking jump or I'll throw you off myself . . .'

Jeremy jumps.

Now I'm absolutely terrified. On our first week in Auckland, a few of us had done a reverse bungee where three people are strapped into a cage and catapulted skyward. The funniest one was when Gary O'Driscoll went up with John Hayes and Rala. There was a camera in the cage and Gary, being a doctor, was reassuring the others that they had nothing to worry about.

But, just before the cage released, the dynamic between them changed. We could see Gary absolutely losing it. He went into a complete panic.

The following morning in the team room, just before we went training, I announced that there was something I wanted the players to look at. The room went quiet in expectation of something technical. I started talking about the importance to the group of our team doctor, of his reserve under pressure. His utter professionalism.

'Today I want to show you what a team doctor is all about. How he looks after people in times of trauma and . . .'

The video suddenly went on of Gary in the cage with Rala and Bull. He was flailing and flapping like a harpooned fish. And the room completely dissolved in laughter. Fellas were on their knees, practically crying. It took a good five minutes for some kind of order to be restored. And I'm thinking just how happy this group is in each other's company . . .

Suddenly, a voice interrupts.

'Don't mean to rush ya, mate . . .'

I peer down at the grey water. What I wouldn't give for a cage around me now. Or a get-out clause. But I can't back out of this. I'll be annihilated if I do. I swallow hard and say a little prayer. And, against every single impulse in my body, I let myself topple head-first towards the harbour. 'Whhhoooooaaaaaaa . . .'

I knew the players were riled over reports they were getting of some of the coverage from home.

They were particularly disgusted with an article in the *Irish Independent* which they felt depicted them as losers. Here was a team that had just pushed the All Blacks right to the wire in their own backyard now, essentially, being ridiculed by their own media. The players had had enough.

All season they'd felt that the writer of the article, David Kelly, had been taking potshots at different people. They decided that they wouldn't engage with him any further. In other words, that they wouldn't accommodate him with one-to-one interviews. Karl Richardson, our media officer, informed him of the decision at that Tuesday's press conference.

He also indicated that the players would not welcome his tape recorder being left to record other journalists' one-to-ones.

Next thing, the story blew up at home that he had been thrown out of the press conference. He hadn't. That our sponsors, O2, had called for an emergency meeting to discuss the issue. They hadn't.

It became utterly surreal. At home, this seemed to be the only aspect to the tour now getting any attention. Yet, within the group, it was an absolute irrelevance. We couldn't believe what was happening. Because of the 12-hour time difference, everything was coming to us second-hand. It seemed to drag on interminably.

The so-called 'furore' was also used by some to feed the argument that I needed a strong manager at my side. After Brian O'Brien's departure, Ger Carmody came in essentially as logistics manager and was doing the job brilliantly. The players could see exactly what was happening. The last thing they wanted was some ex-international parachuted in now to start patrolling the corridors.

Hand on heart, I can honestly say we didn't break stride. It was irritating only in the way of a fly in the room. We had another Test looming against the All Blacks and nothing was going to distract us from it.

Bottom line, our hosts knew that we could play rugby now. They were cagey. I knew from talking to Hansen that Ireland was one of the teams they were wary of playing. They had that respect for us that comes from knowing if they weren't on their game, we were capable of turning them over.

In the first Test, we had targeted Ma'a Nonu in the centre. We scored a peach of a try off a line-out by running a short line through Andrew Trimble, making Nonu check when he was supposed to push out. Gordon D'Arcy then threw a perfect pass across him, Drico hitting it and getting in under the sticks.

It was a move right off the training ground. Denis Hickie has a great rugby brain and, because he wasn't making the Test fifteen, he had to defend against the move in training. One day, he said to myself and Drico, 'That's the one that's hardest to figure out.'

So we knew how to get at the All Blacks and were absolutely determined to make the second Test count.

There was big pressure from Sky that week to allow cameras in the changing room. I wouldn't hear of it. This, apparently, is quite common practice in the southern hemisphere but, to me, it violates the last remnant of privacy for a player. A changing room at half-time isn't exactly a pretty place. Anything goes. I've seen guys throw up on the floor they're under so much pressure. Why expose them to a camera lens?

We were in no mood to be pushed around by people on or off the field, so the Sky team stayed outside.

Saturday dawned sodden and charcoal grey in Auckland. All day, the rain just bucketed down. We scored two terrific tries in the first half, but a couple of shocking refereeing decisions by Jonathan Kaplan cost us dear. Kaplan's a guy I've a lot of time for. He actually texted me when I resigned from the Irish job. But he dropped two clangers here.

Firstly, there was a blatant New Zealand knock-on near our line, Chris Jack losing the ball in contact, but diving on it again and recycling through his legs. The ball squirted out and a prop picked up and dived over. Secondly, Denis Leamy made a fantastic steal right in front of our posts and was wrongly penalised. A ten-point turnaround.

In both cases video evidence would back our protests. Then, in another second-half incident, Shaggy tackled someone out on the wing and held him down. The All Black lashed out with his boot, leaving a gash over Shaggy's eye that would require five stitches. The touch judge missed it.

We lost 17–27 in the end and I was incandescent with anger. In the dressing room afterwards my frustration got the better of me. I made a speech about guys having to take opportunities when they came. 'If this team is ever going to fulfil its potential,' I said, 'those fucking chances have to be fucking buried!'

My speech went down like a lead balloon with the players. They were emotional, I was emotional. They had just left their guts out on the pitch and it came across as if I was having a go at them. That had never been my intention, but we'd just blown two Tests and the atmosphere was pretty charged.

Within 24 hours, it was made clear to me that I had pissed them off pretty royally. I knew I had fucked up. One of the first things I would do when we got to Perth was sit them down in the team room, explain myself and apologise for any offence caused.

The night of that second Test, just about everything seemed designed to exacerbate my frustration. We were determined to pursue the matter of that kick on Shaggy and took it up with the match commissioner. Ordinarily he should be supplied with every available camera angle so that he can investigate this kind of incident. But Sky gave him a single, inconclusive tape.

I couldn't help but feel this was some kind of payback for my refusal to let them in the changing room.

Then I walk into the post-match function and the first thing I notice is this giant Irish tricolour on the wall. It's the biggest flag I've seen in my life and it flies in the face of accepted protocol. We have issues with flags in Irish rugby. Everybody knows this.

The deal is that, whenever the Irish team plays away from home, the tricolour can fly if it's accompanied by the Ulster flag. If both cannot be accommodated then the IRFU is the only flag flown. This is out of consideration for our Ulster players, just as is the singing of 'Ireland's Call' after 'Amhran na bhFiann'. The IRFU sends letter after letter to impending hosts to make sure all sensitivities are considered.

And now I'm standing in downtown Auckland, we've just lost the second Test, one of my players has been kicked in the head, but nobody gives a damn. And there's this tricolour the size of a football pitch staring down on me. It's like somebody's having a laugh at our expense here.

And, just at that moment, a voice asks, 'Eddie, what are you drinking?'

It's Wayne Smith, the All Blacks' backs' coach. One of nature's gentlemen. The night before I'd been down at the Blacks' hotel for a meeting with referee Kaplan. A routine engagement. And, afterwards, I'd had a drink with Hansen, Joe Stanley and Wayne. Now he's just got me at the wrong moment.

'Nothing, thanks very much,' I respond to his offer of a drink. Essentially, I blank him.

Wayne walks away and I can see, clearly, that he's upset. To this day, I haven't spoken to him. I regret that. The speeches end around midnight and, on cue, I walk straight out and head back up the hill to our hotel. I go straight to bed.

At 1 a.m. my phone rings. It's Ger Carmody. The match commissioner says he can't take the kick on Shaggy any further. Thus the matter is closed. I turn the light off, resigning myself to a night of broken sleep.

One of the first things I had to address on arrival in Perth, apart from a chastened dressing room, was a delegation from the Irish Rugby Writers.

They were, it seemed, unhappy with how they were being treated by the Irish team. Above all, they felt entitled to more access to people, not least the back-room staff of people like Niall O'Donovan, Mark Tainton, Graham Steadman and Brian McLoughlin. Trouble was, the back-room staff weren't particularly interested in attending press conferences and I didn't see any reason to make their attendance mandatory.

The journalists came up to my suite and we had a decent meeting. One of their delegation, Brendan Fanning of the

Sunday Independent, I would have a lot of time for. We agreed to a few modifications and I made my views known about the hullabaloo that had erupted after the first Test.

Again I couldn't escape the sense of us existing in parallel worlds. Once I had explained my dressing-room outburst in Auckland, the players were absolutely first class. I'm not, for a second, pretending that everything was sweetness and light. The day it is, you can rest assured the competitive instinct is gone from your dressing room.

I decided to drop Geordan Murphy and he let it be known that he was unhappy. I could respect that. There is an image of Geordan and I being at loggerheads for much of my time as Ireland coach. We weren't. I did come to the conclusion over time that he had a tendency, for whatever reason, to play poorly against France.

Geordan is a beautifully gifted athlete but he has missed a few tackles for Ireland that proved costly. In that second Test against the All Blacks, I felt he had simply missed too many. I dropped him. It wasn't personal.

Denis Hickie, too, was frustrated that he couldn't get in the team. Again, I would have been worried if he wasn't. But, as I explained to Denis, Andrew Trimble was now playing too well to be unseated.

The media, though, had another stick to beat us with. For whatever reason, we had to travel to Australia in two groups. Most of the players had gone straight to bed after the second Test, so Sunday was declared a 'down day'. Some of us travelled, some didn't. Those travelling on Monday had permission to relax with a few beers.

At some point, a photograph was taken of Drico, looking a little under the weather. He was in a club, surfing on peoples' shoulders, his hair wet. The guy had been working his socks off for three weeks but, now, it was spun that he represented a team 'celebrating' two near misses against New Zealand. The photo-graph would appear in an Irish tabloid two days before the Test in Perth.

Some journalists jumped on it as further proof of the need for 'a strong management figure' to oversee the team. Lovely.

Team-wise, I knew I had a big call to make. I sat down with Drico on the Monday night to discuss it. A few guys on tour had yet to see any game-time. We could make changes for the sake of making changes now but, deep down, I felt we owed it to ourselves to have a real crack at the Wallabies. Drico agreed.

'Absolutely,' he said. 'We deserve to take home a win from the southern hemisphere.'

The game, unfortunately, proved just a bridge too far. We did score a phenomenal try from our own 22 involving about six off-loads and Neil Best, wearing one boot, getting the touchdown. Having trailed early, that put us back in the game. But they then scored a try from 80 yards and eventually ran out comfortable 37–15 winners. At the end of a long season, we had simply hit the wall.

I was criticised afterwards for sticking, largely, with the same players. One journalist asked me at the post-match press con-ference if, in hindsight, I considered this a mistake. My response was to ask, 'Well, what changes would you have made?'

This was portrayed as me 'bristling'. Maybe I was foolish and should have been more diplomatic. But the same journalist had written positively in his preview of our 'golden opportunity' to beat the Wallabies. He knew the team I'd picked when he wrote those words. Now a convenient revisionism seemed to have kicked in.

I couldn't understand this negativity. I couldn't equate it with either the rugby we had played or with the harmony in the squad. People back home must have felt we were in a pretty miserable place at the end of that tour. True, we'd lost the three

Tests, but we'd terrified the All Blacks in their own backyard and played some fantastic rugby.

If people wanted to see the tour as some form of catastrophe, that was their business. But, flying home, I couldn't help wonder if – as a country – we'd maybe lost the run of ourselves.

Had I just been given a glimpse into the future?

25

CROKER

When I think of Vincent Clerc, I find it hard not to see a kind of cartoon image with horns, a tail and cloven hooves.

There was a time when Clerc seemed to consider it his life's work to inflict misery on the Irish rugby team. In my spell as national coach, he played in five internationals against us, scoring seven tries. Six of those came in my last thirteen months in the job. He became the Grim Reaper as far as I was concerned. I hated the very sight of him.

Clerc is, of course, a wonderful rugby player, a beautifully graceful runner and consummate finisher. But two of his tries sank us in the World Cup game at Stade de France in September of 2007 and, five months later at the same venue, he crossed for a hat-trick in the Six Nations.

On reflection, I could just about have lived with those had he only kept his powder dry at Croke Park on 11 February 2007. Sadly, he didn't.

Hindsight will forever haunt me with the realisation that Clerc's last-minute try in Dublin that day, essentially, cost us a Grand Slam. It was like watching a nightmare unfold. I would liken it to an out-of-body experience almost, that split second when you notice a terrible mismatch. The game hanging in the balance and Clerc, this phenomenally elusive runner, materialising in a gap between Neil Best and John Hayes.

I pretty much saw the try in slow motion, a voice inside my head screaming 'Nooooooo!' And, as he touched the ball down, I wheeled away thinking that I might just vomit on the spot.

If anything, the historical significance of rugby being played in Croke Park obscured the sense of opportunity we carried into that Six Nations.

We had played the rugby of our lives in the autumn series, beating South Africa 32–15 and Australia 21–6, lifting our IRB ranking to number three in the world. These were statistics that Irish rugby just wasn't accustomed to.

True, the Springboks were experimenting. Jake White picked Brian Habana in the centre and I remember being delighted in the team room when I heard that. Habana is one of the world's best wingers, but he's no centre. We just picked them off that day at Lansdowne Road, running dummy lines through Drico and Darce, Andrew Trimble flying slingshot off ROG's shoulder.

The move brought an early try and, in the stand, I said to Niallo, 'We can get these fellas big time today.'

The margins of victory in both games were deeply satisfying, but it was the quality of our performance that made the most compelling statement. We were playing high-risk rugby and playing it beautifully. After the Australia game I made nine changes for the last international game ever to be played at the old Lansdowne Road,

Guys like Jamie Heaslip, Stephen Ferris and Luke Fitzgerald came in for their first caps against the Pacific Islands. We butchered them 61–17 and finished the day with a lap of honour. I knew that we could look any team in the eye now and have a real crack at them. The Six Nations couldn't come soon enough.

We would go into that tournament as favourites and understandably so. It was a unique position for an Irish team. People were talking us up and, so long as we had the benefit of a little luck, I felt the Grand Slam was achievable.

That expectation was palpable in Cardiff during our opening game. We didn't play particularly well, yet won the game 19–9, scoring three tries. I wasn't entirely happy and told the players that I felt there was a hell of a lot more in the tank. We needed to bring that out because, now, we were headed for Croker and a game against opponents we consistently struggled to beat. France always worried me. They were pretty much our nemesis.

And, unknown to the public, there was an unsettling little backdrop to the game.

It would be refereed by Steve Walsh, who ran one of the lines in Cardiff. That night, at the function, Niallo and I noticed him in pretty animated conversation with some of the Welsh coaching staff. Alarm bells immediately began ringing. It wasn't uncommon for referees to be in the company of coaches, but the body language just seemed unusually intense. I knew there was something up, so invited myself into the company and started up a rather pointed conversation.

'What did you think of today, Steve?'

'I was very unhappy with Ireland.'

'You were?'

'Ye were killing a lot of ruck ball and if ye do that next week . . .'

'What do you mean?'

'Ye were off ye're feet, playing the ball after the tackle. Just giving you a pointer for next week, mate.'

'Well, if you're unhappy with us I'd like to know specifics and see exactly where we were making mistakes.'

'Yeah, well, I intend to have a good look at it.'

'Well we'll be happy to supply you with a tape.'

'Nah, it's OK. I'm getting one from the Welsh Union!'

I was horrified. If the Welsh were supplying him with the tape, it was specifically to highlight their complaint about Ireland's play. It seemed to me that he'd already begun refereeing our game with France. I also felt it was totally indiscreet of him to be even having this conversation with the Welsh, yet worse was to follow. The following day, it was up on the website *Planet Rugby* that he was 'unhappy with Ireland'.

I got straight on the phone to the IRFU Head of Referee Development, Owen Doyle, expressing my disgust. To me, we now had good grounds for insisting that Walsh be pulled from the game. It would have been a massive story had it happened and, deep down, I didn't really want to do that to the guy. There was a bit of history there. During the 2005 Lions tour, he'd been reported for verbal abuse of Shane Horgan while running the line. While no action was taken against him, he had to apologise for the incident. Walsh, I knew, had issues. He was a good referee but, sometimes, he didn't help himself.

Next thing, I got a call from Paddy O'Brien (Head of the IRB's Referee Board), who was at the San Diego 7s tournament in the US. It was agreed that Walsh should meet with me and be given the opportunity to explain himself.

So he flew in early and came to our Killiney Castle base that Tuesday night. It was a tense meeting. I knew his career would have been on the line had we insisted on him being pulled from the game. He knew it too. I asked him for specifics of where we'd been transgressing the law in Cardiff. He hadn't been able to pin any examples down.

'Steve,' I said, 'we play the referee and you weren't referee on Saturday. Now if you want to call things differently next weekend, we will play to your recommendations.'

'I agree, I agree,' he said. 'Looking at the tape, you did what the referee asked you to do. I couldn't see anything wrong.'

'So there's no issue here?'

'None!'

'How can I be sure of that for Saturday?'

'Look, I take back what I said in Cardiff. I don't have any issues with Ireland. I might be a little stricter at the breakdown, but I'll call it.'

'Well, you call it, we'll play it, Steve.'

We'd actually gone through the tape with him in that room and, on reflection, there was nothing he could take issue on with us.

I rang O'Brien in San Diego to confirm that I was now agreeable to Walsh taking charge of the game. But it was a close thing. I'd been affronted by the things he'd said about us because, over the years, we'd worked really hard on ridding Ireland of the reputation for being a spoiling side.

As it happened, that day in Croke Park, Walsh would call a pretty good game. In 80 minutes, we gave up a paltry total of three penalties. Our discipline was exemplary. But, of course, a certain Monsieur Clerc was also on the premises. And that, ultimately, would be the story.

Croke Park is a special place. It is the headquarters of the Gaelic Athletic Association, the largest amateur sports organisation in the world. It is also a repository of rich history.

You cannot really be of rural Ireland and feel ambivalence towards the GAA. Its volunteerism is everywhere. The bulk of Irish towns and villages find identity in the hurling and Gaelic football teams that wear their colours. In a country utterly besotted with sport, the GAA has a natural draw on the community that has long been envied by rugby and soccer.

I played a bit of Gaelic football myself, lining out for

Moylough-Mountbellew in the 1982 Galway senior county final. Though rugby became my life, I – like just about every other sporting enthusiast in the country – had distinct flecks of the Association in my DNA.

For rugby and soccer to gain access to Croke Park required a massive leap of faith on behalf of the GAA. It upset many people. Quite apart from what some saw as the great gamble of renting their premises to professional bodies they competed against for the hearts of the nation's children, there was the decidedly vexed question of England. Or, maybe more specifically, the singing of 'God Save the Queen'.

This would have been conspicuous in the minds of delegates to the 2005 congress that agreed to the opening of Croke Park for the duration of Lansdowne Road's redevelopment on the other side of Dublin. To do away with their Rule 42 (which precluded the use of Croke Park or other GAA facilities for so-called 'foreign' games), the Association was, essentially, throwing open its doors to an historic enemy.

Croke Park was the scene of an appalling massacre during the Irish War of Independence, fourteen innocent people losing their lives to 'Black and Tan' bullets at a Gaelic football match between Dublin and Tipperary on 21 November 1920. The shootings were in reprisal for the assassination of fourteen British intelligence officers earlier that same day by a Michael Collins hit squad.

Thirteen spectators and the Tipperary captain, Michael Hogan, died in an event that became known as Ireland's first 'Bloody Sunday'.

Given that context, the thought of the British national anthem being sung in Croke Park was always going to be deeply offensive to a great raft of GAA people. So it took courage and a remarkable generosity of spirit for that hand of friendship to be extended to rugby and soccer.

It was important, I think, that France were the first 'foreign' team to play in Croker. The England game was always going to bristle with such unique energies, it probably felt more palatable that we faced 'neutral' opposition on the historic day. More often than not, the French might have beaten us, but our history with them had no darkness.

The build-up to the game was surreal. It was all about this magnificent stadium and I spent a good deal of the week trying to rinse the sense of occasion from players' minds. We had a difficult game to play. Not a ceremony to attend.

We had to play that game without Brian O'Driscoll and Peter Stringer too and, even now, I find it hard to escape the feeling that the Grand Slam would have been ours had Drico, especially, been available. France eventually nailed us in the midfield area where our captain's defensive prowess is so revered.

When Vincent Clerc dipped his shoulder, sadly our most important player was sitting in the stand. I'd always said that our chances as a team would be defined by our ability to keep our key players fit. This was precisely what I meant by that.

To begin with, the occasion definitely took a toll. Geordan Murphy missed an early tackle to let Rafael Ibanez in for an easy French try and they led 10–0 almost before we had a sweat up. Actually, for twenty minutes, France were completely on top. We were playing like rabbits caught in headlights.

But we clawed our way back and ROG's touchdown late in the first half put us right back in the ball game. Gradually, the history of the occasion was overtaken by the energy of the contest. It was finely balanced and two key calls would go against us. First, Geordan exploded onto an intercept and had a clear route to the French line only for play to be called back, Walsh immediately apologising for not playing an advantage. Then Marcus Horan was blatantly obstructed after putting through a grubber kick, but no penalty.

Still, I felt we had things under control. Leading by a point going into the last few minutes, we got a line-out in our own half and mauled France 40 yards up the pitch, forcing them into the error of pulling down the maul. It was textbook stuff. They gave away a penalty and ROG nailed it. France now needed a try. Up in the coaches' box, I sensed we were almost there.

But France won the restart with what I can best describe as a tennis serve from one of their forwards, the ball spilling infield and, suddenly, they had a line-break. Now here's the killer. A ruck formed and ROG said to me afterwards that he had considered deliberately killing the ball at the likely expense of a yellow card. It might have played to preconceived notions about us as a team, but if it averted danger . . .

ROG, though, stayed on his feet. To be fair, if he hadn't, France would have had a penalty five metres from our line and we'd have been down to fourteen men. Had they scored from that position, he'd have been castigated.

The moment Clerc materialised under our posts was indescribable. It was clear there was no way back. I left my seat immediately after the conversion because I wanted to be in the changing room when the players came in. The place was silent as a morgue. It was, literally, like sitting at somebody's wake and I knew I had to say something. Clive Woodward came into my head. All the times his England team had been kicked in the teeth chasing a Grand Slam and, ultimately, drew strength from the experience.

'Listen,' I said, 'this is horrible. It's probably the sickest feeling you'll ever have in your life. But this will make you a better team. Because it's times like this you have to bounce back.'

Paul O'Connell, captain in Drico's absence, reminded everyone that there was still a championship to play for. He was right, of course. But bellies were on the ground here.

Hand on heart, I wanted to go home, climb into bed, turn the lights off and pull the covers over my head. Everyone did. You want to find a dark hole and lock yourself in. But you can't indulge in that kind of self-absorption. Where does it get you? It may be the worst kick in the stomach you'll ever get, but fellas are looking to you for a lead. They're looking at you as if to say, 'What the fuck do we do now?'

And if the coach just gives a blank stare back, then you're absolutely rudderless.

I was invited in a TV interview afterwards to lambast the referee, but that didn't interest me. To jump on his back would have been too convenient an excuse, albeit the Murphy and Horan calls had clearly cost us. And I'll always give the team credit for that. Excuses didn't interest them. When they lost, they got angry with themselves.

People would ask about the difficulty of 'picking them off the floor now'. There was no difficulty. Getting them to train in St Gerards' the following Monday morning was easy. People have this misguided idea that, after a defeat, players are motivated to prove other people wrong. It's not about anybody else. It's about the group and a feeling of having let themselves down.

They were so angry after that game, they could have trained within an hour. If anything the job was to restrain them. Because that anger fires them up so much in training, a session can easily boil over.

The historic first rugby game in Croke Park had been lost then, but England would be next through the door. Now if ever there was pressure on a team to win one game in their lives, we were about to feel it. It was time to park our sorrow.

Because this thing was already slipping off the Richter scale.

When I look back at the build-up, I suspect our survival instincts shut out the bulk of it.

I requested the media not to question the players about the

historical significance. After all, what could they say? I didn't want them sidetracked by talk of flags, anthems or potential protests by republican groups. They were rugby players facing a game that could make or break their season. That had to be the beginning and the end of their focus.

Through the two-week lead-in, I made a point of never discussing the game in anything but rugby terms. You could call it a form of denial, but I didn't have a choice. I didn't want the players debilitated by the occasion. In the end, I suspect they were aware of no more than 60 per cent of the build-up. Anything more would have been too heavy a burden to carry.

Even I couldn't buy into the history 100 per cent. I was in a tricky position. The big talking point was how the crowd was going to react to 'God Save the Queen' and it was inevitable that I would be asked about this. I planned my response carefully. I couldn't disregard the fact that a lot of Irish people would be unhappy about it nor, frankly, that it was entirely within their rights to express that unhappiness.

So, when the question came, I said, 'Ireland is an open-minded country where people hold many different opinions and it's fantastic that they are free to express those opinions. My belief is that, when it comes to a sporting event, there's nobody better than an Irish crowd to embrace it and turn it into a spectacular occasion.'

The following day, President Mary McAleese said something similar. I was relieved. In a sense, it was as if we were all walking on eggshells here.

Within the squad, I could detect a kind of subliminal understanding that this was a game we could not, under any circumstances, afford to lose. Actually, losing was unthinkable. That awareness began to heighten the closer we came to kick-off. On a personal level, it almost became unbearable.

On the coach journey to Croke Park, I remember seeing a fella on a bike, cycling in the opposite direction, fresh baguettes under his arm. It struck me how he seemed so oblivious to what was building around him. Would he even watch the game on TV? I felt envious.

Like everyone, I was concerned that 'God Save the Queen' would not be respected. Can't say it was exactly number one on my list of priorities, but the thought did strike that it would only take three or four gob-shites in a crowd of 82,000 to create a problem. As it happened, everyone behaved impeccably and, when their anthem finished, England back-row Martin Corry applauded the crowd.

It was a wonderful gesture from one of the game's great warriors.

Then 'Amhran na bhFiann' and emotions just started spilling over. Some of the players were sobbing. People in the crowd too. 'Ireland's Call' followed and, though it doesn't carry the same weight, it has its own resonance for the Ulster players. I didn't cry but I will admit that I felt pretty close to it.

This was Ireland. Everything that defined us, that made us proud of our mixed-up little country, seemed palpable in those moments. But I remember watching them roll up the red carpet and thinking, 'Holy fuck, our job is only starting now!'

My worry was that the emotion might drain the players. Would their heads be clear for the fundamentals? The first line-out call? It seems asinine to recall, but that's what I was thinking now. The coach had put the patriot to bed.

I needn't have worried. In a Test match, there are maybe ten boxes you ask your team to tick through the course of 80 minutes. Ordinarily, they might tick only six and still win the game. That day against England, we ticked all the boxes.

It was a complete performance. We were all but out of sight by half-time (23–3), yet the dressing room was remarkably calm when the players came in. Drico and Paulie were wonderful, challenging people to sustain the performance. 'We've been good, I'll give you that,' said Drico. 'But we can be fucking great . . .'

Early in the second half, as the packs bound down in a scrum, someone in the crowd stood up directly in front of the coaches' box, obstructing my view. I jumped to my feet, thumping the glass angrily. The guy, to be fair, obliged immediately and made the point later of seeking out John Baker to apologise.

His face had been vaguely familiar but, in the heat of battle, I was pretty much in another zone. It was only when John mentioned it that I realised the guy I had told to 'sit the fuck down' had been U2 drummer Larry Mullen.

One of our tries in the second half had a particular poignancy. It had Gaelic football written all over it, ROG'S perfect diagonal kick fielded, Gaelic style, above his head by Shane Horgan. It came directly off the flip chart in the team room too. You see, we knew if we could suck Jonny Wilkinson close to the ruck (and his bravery always offered opportunity), that there'd be a big hole in the corner.

That said, the kick would have to be absolutely on the money. And that's where ROG put it.

We won 43–13 in the end, putting us right back in the Championship reckoning. A phenomenal job. There was a huge sense of euphoria in the stadium, a feeling that the script couldn't have been written better. We'd destroyed one of the biggest teams in world rugby and, as a nation, shown real dignity.

It was, in truth, a perfect day.

England coach Brian Ashton was extremely magnanimous afterwards, suggesting that we'd given his team 'a lesson'. Likewise my good friend, Mike Ford, who was now their defence coach.

The following afternoon I was back in a hotel room in Killiney when my mobile rang. I didn't recognise the number and toyed with the idea of not answering. That would have been a mistake.

'Eddie, it's Martin McAleese here,' said a voice I recognised from Aras an Uachtarain. 'Mary wants a word with you.'

And the President of Ireland came on the line to tell me how it had been one of the best days of her life. 'Just a fantastic day to be Irish,' she said. I couldn't have put it any better.

The euphoria became a flooded river now, sweeping all reason before it.

We went to Edinburgh, a city we hadn't won in for 19 years up to 2003, as ludicrously hot favourites. I went up to the referee's hotel that Friday afternoon and was intercepted by a group of supporters on the piss. The talk out of them was obnoxious. As far as they were concerned, we'd put fifty points on Scotland.

'Lads, this game is going to be a dogfight,' I argued, but they were having none of it. I remember going back to the team hotel in a taxi, thinking, 'Fucking hell, have we lost the run of ourselves?'

The dogfight duly materialised. It was a nasty game, punctuated by cheap shots and furious physicality. We won 19–18, ROG getting all our scores. Afterwards, Drico held up the Triple Crown with one hand, some people in the Murrayfield crowd interpreting this as ambivalence to the prize. It wasn't. He'd hurt his shoulder in a late collision, almost dislocating it just as he had done on the Lions tour and, literally, couldn't lift both hands above his head.

Our achievement was overshadowed by a late incident in which ROG, pinned down at the bottom of a ruck, could have been very seriously injured. Some of the players were seething in the dressing room after. I was asked about the incident at the press conference and reported, essentially, what I had been told. ROG had almost choked on the field.

That night, I got a distinct vibe from some committee members that it might have been better had I said nothing. The attitude was that we'd secured our third Triple Crown in four seasons. Better, maybe, to brush any negativity under the carpet.

I know it didn't win me any friends in Scotland and ultimately the Six Nations crown eluded us, an injury-time try in Paris against the Scots, no less, edging the French to the title on points difference.

We played some phenomenal rugby in Rome that same day to trounce Italy 51–24, but our destiny was always in French hands. We'd turned over a ball late in the game after taking a 'tap' penalty, allowing Italy to score a try. In the dressing room after, I told the players I couldn't have asked more of them. 'Bottom line, never fucking die wondering, lads,' I said.

I remember Shane Horgan sitting in his playing gear, looking dejected.

'C'mon, Shaggy, get up,' I said.

'I've just a bad feeling,' he replied, 'that we've just left something special behind us here.'

Most of the team gathered around a big screen back in the hotel lobby to watch the last few minutes from Paris. I went to my room. And I sat there on the end of my bed, watching France kick us in the teeth for the second time in a month with a last-minute try to take the Championship.

I could have been miserable, but I wasn't. Actually, I felt quite sanguine. We'd come within a bounce of a ball of winning the Grand Slam. We'd demolished two southern hemisphere giants in the autumn series. We were in a good place. The team was humming.

Now all I had to do was re-create this energy in the World Cup . . .

26

HOME THOUGHTS . . .

Santa Clara, California, my first game back in America.

I meet Declan Kidney in the middle of Buck Shaw Stadium and we greet one another with a handshake. Two photographers come running towards us, snapping frantically for what one of my back-room staff suggests later must have been 'the money shot'.

Declan and I stand chatting and, except for the photographers, we could be old acquaintances meeting on a street corner. We talk about family, exams, everyday issues of home. It feels easy and natural.

Except, deep down, we both know that it's probably best to keep smiling for the duration. Because everything is open to interpretation here. In three days' time, I begin my career as US Eagles coach with a Test match against, of all teams, Ireland. The Gods have a prankster in their midst.

I've been following some of the build-up at home on the Internet and this, apparently, is a 'grudge match'. So, standing in the middle of this university stadium now, every facial expression potentially that money shot, we could be Gerry Adams and Ian Paisley shuffling side by side on the steps of Stormont Castle.

It feels ridiculous.

Declan has come to America with a second-string squad, the bulk of his Grand Slam team now in South Africa on Lions duty. I'm still trying to cobble together a coherent fifteen from a depleted and almost entirely amateur group I've essentially had a week to get to know.

Outside, America isn't exactly holding its breath for the outcome.

The sports pages are full of the NBA and NHL play-offs. Rugby? A few paragraphs appeared today on the back of the *Wall Street Journal*, flagging an observation from US Rugby chief executive Nigel Melville that I know Ireland's players 'better than he knows ours'.

He's right. I do.

Game day arrives and I do what I've always done as the team boards the bus. I stand by the steps, making sure everyone is marked present. Beside me, the bus driver starts up a conversation.

'So you're going to the game?' he says.

'Yeah, well suppose we'd better show up anyway.' I grin sheepishly.

'Where all you guys from?'

It dawns on me that he thinks we're just a group of schmucks on a day out. The tracksuits mean nothing to him. US Eagles could be an ice-hockey team for all he knows. Maybe he imagines we're all on the piss.

'Well, all over America really,' I answer. 'We're the national rugby team.'

'Hey that's cool!' he says, utterly underwhelmed.

Ireland beat us 27–10. I can't fault the American players. By the time we're playing our World Cup qualifiers, maybe half these guys won't be in my first fifteen. They know that, I know it. I've picked six new caps, put two more on the bench. Yet, for 80 minutes, they've given everything. The mistakes that cost us are fundamentals. We've been killed in the line-out, smashed by the Irish rolling maul. We've missed four kickable penalties.

It's funny, when I first worked here in the late 90s, Ronan O'Gara was maybe third in line of Ireland's out-halves. And I remembered that conversation I'd had with him flying home from the under-21 game in Edinburgh. About how he'd been born in San Diego.

ROG happened to be in America on a holiday that summer and Jack Clark and I met up with him for a meal in Perry's on Union Street, San Francisco. There was a World Cup looming and it didn't look like he'd be needed by Ireland. I knew he'd have been some addition to the Eagles squad.

We didn't exactly proposition ROG in the restaurant, but we did lob the idea into the ether. I made a point of emphasising that, while he'd be guaranteed international rugby, he'd be closing the door on Ireland for good. Can't say I was especially comfortable. ROG listened to us without ever, I suspect, seriously considering the idea.

And I'd be thankful for that fact many times as Irish coach. The guy has an ice-cool temperament and the ability to land high-pressure kicks for fun. You can't put a price on that.

Back in Santa Clara now, I knew we should have been maybe 9–13 down at half-time, not 0–13. I knew, too, that we'd let Ireland off the hook at 10–20 by dropping a ball in our own 22. Basic errors beat us, but I consoled myself with the thought that basic errors could be fixed.

It felt strange and it felt good to see so many familiar faces. I took some of my new back-room staff for a beer with Ger Carmody, Karl Richardson and Mervyn Murphy on the Friday night.

Then, when the band played 'Ireland's Call' in the match preliminaries, I had to stop myself singing. The stadium was full to its 10,000 capacity, yet the sounds of lawn mowers and passing trains and jets taking off and landing from the nearby airport filled the air.

It's another world to Landsowne Road or Croke Park and it's wonderful. I often think back to the day I coached Connacht to beat Fiji at the Sportsground in 1995. Running one of the lines that day was English referee Ed Morrison. Two months earlier he'd been in charge of the World Cup final between South Africa and New Zealand.

We shared a taxi to the airport the following morning and he seemed just as happy to talk about being up to his ankles in Galway mud as he was to reminisce about being in charge of the biggest game on the planet at Ellis Park. I liked him for that. His enthusiasm reaffirmed my love for rugby as a truly international game.

In Santa Clara, we all poured into an inflatable marquee for a cursory exchange of plaques. There was no meal, just a quick few words and the Irish boys slipped away to pack. Next stop for the Eagles was Chicago. Plenty more work to be done.

The wheel would keep turning.

27

LAST WORD

Jack Clark: 'Eddie is an extraordinary coach. He's a thinker about the game who has the ability to teach, to instil tactical awareness. To be fair, I hadn't seen that in a lot of foreign coaches. A lot of guys who have been around high-level rugby for a long time almost speak in code.

'Eddie's teaching background probably doesn't hurt. But it's a great compliment to him that he could coach all fifteen players on the field. To be perfectly honest, it shattered me when he went back to Ireland to be assistant to Warren Gatland. Of course, I knew it was the right decision for him, but I had planned that Eddie would succeed me as US national coach.

'I wanted American rugby to be pushed forward and I knew that Eddie was the right guy to do that. In my dealings with the IRB, I sometimes came in contact with Dr Syd Millar and I could detect his disappointment at the time that Eddie wasn't working in Ireland.

'It didn't surprise me. We'd pretty much seized on his frustration with Irish rugby to bring him to America and he became absolutely invaluable to us.

'I watched the Irish coverage of the 2007 World Cup, my goodness. Ireland had had one of their best stretches ever under Eddie....yet the commentary was all just one-eyed. I couldn't believe that.

'You know I watch professional rugby now and a lot of it is just mindless. The idea of crafting an attack, all the stuff I believe Eddie is so good at, isn't being done. There's a lot of sloppy skill and tactics. It's as if these directors of rugby and coaches are just rolling out the ball and saying, "Go give it a lash, guys!"

'Rugby teams need systems. I cannot believe that so many clubs pay the wages that they're paying and, essentially, allow a poor mechanic to tinker with their car. It's like buying a Ferrrari and having the lawnmower guy work on it. That's just insane to me.'

BRIAN O'BRIEN: 'It was written that Eddie got rid of me. Nonsense. It was written that he had stopped me going on the 2005 tour to Japan. Nonsense again. I had always decided that I was leaving after the Welsh game in the 2005 Six Nations and Eddie was the one who actually asked me to go to Japan.

'There was a lot of stuff bubbling up in the background at the time and then someone came to the decision that I shouldn't be sent. I know for a fact that that someone wasn't Eddie. We developed a friendship through thick and thin. I suspect it takes Eddie a while to have that kind of friendship, because he needs to trust you first.

'People like John Redmond and I had that trust. We wanted Eddie to be successful. Unfortunately, other people – who could have helped him – probably didn't want him to be successful. The cause should have been Irish rugby. The players. But I feel a lot of people lost that central purpose because they didn't like Eddie. And that's an indictment of those people.

'How would I describe Eddie? Imagine you're standing on a

wharf, the tide is coming in and you fall in. There are two people with you and one of them runs off in search of a lifebuoy. The other dives straight in. Well the guy in the water with you is Eddie O'Sullivan.'

NIALL O'DONOVAN: 'It suited some of the press to depict Eddie as dour. I remember being at a Rugby Writers' event, myself, Declan and Briano. A sports editor approached Briano, complaining about the fact that Eddie wouldn't give this paper's rugby correspondent a one-to-one interview. The same correspondent was lambasting Eddie at every opportunity.

"Jasus, do you see what he's writing," said Briano. "Sure Eddie can't win. Your man doesn't want the team to be successful."

"No, you've got that wrong," the sports editor countered. "He wants the team to be successful, just not Eddie."

'Briano looked at him with disbelief. "Do you realise what you're just after saying there?" he said. It was extraordinary.

'I've had massive run-ins with Eddie. We've been above in the stand and Briano's literally had to step in between the two of us. But you'd get it off your chest and five minutes later there wouldn't be an issue with it. It was done, dusted. That's what I loved about working with him. You knew exactly where you stood.

'I know some depicted him as a megalomaniac, but my own experience would have been the complete opposite. From day one, he never watched over what I was doing. He would give me my slot, "Off you go, Niallo, you've half an hour . . ." He'd never really interfere.

'Would a Grand Slam have been enough for the media? Probably not. I suspect some of them wouldn't have accepted that either. Because they were down his throat. They wanted him to go and they were after him for so long, that – eventually – it had a negative effect on the team.'

★

KEITH WOOD: 'Eddie is blunt to an extreme and I would say oversensitive. He would say he's not, but he is. When he became Irish coach, I would have said we had similar goals. At that stage we were still a little bit laissez-faire in our set-up. We needed to make a significant change. And Eddie ticked all the right boxes to do that.

'Warren Gatland gave us consistency of selection and a simple game plan. And suddenly we became this intransigent rugby team. We may not have been flowery or very capable, but we were bloody awkward to play against. We weren't giving up silly games any more.

'But we needed to do more, we needed to expand. Rugby can change very quickly. What was very organised rugby in 1999, wasn't in 2001. So, suddenly, we weren't as advanced as we should have been.

'When Eddie took over, we became very analytical and technical. I think he did an incredible job. I used to fight with him privately all the time, but he trusted me so it was never a problem.

'It's a simple thing. He's a good friend of mine and he did bloody great things with Ireland. People often don't see that now because we didn't win a championship, but he was the most successful Irish coach in terms of win/loss ratio and still is. So, it's a very fine line.

'One massive thing in sport that people don't want to factor in is luck. I would say very little of that fell Eddie's way. But you can't look at it in that fashion, because down that road lies madness.

'We were very close. Still are, in fact. Eddie and I went through a lot of stuff together, some really good stuff and some bad days as well. The thing that some people miss is that he has a lovely sense of humour. He's a very good guy, very personable. I just wish we delivered a little bit more in his time.'

BRIAN O'DRISCOLL: 'I have a lot of time for Eddie. Technically he was very good and he definitely had a big say in the Grand Slam this year even though he got absolutely no plaudits for it. There's something wrong about that for me. So it was great that Declan mentioned him in Cardiff, that he hadn't been forgotten.

'I don't think that was being said just to pass on an image of being humble. Declan genuinely meant it. Like, for me, that Grand Slam was ten years of work. Not one. No way. All the disappointments, all the near misses . . . we should have had a Grand Slam under Eddie. There's no question about that.

'He did fantastically for Ireland. Obviously, I was captain of the team for a large part of Eddie's tenure as coach and, if I had an issue to challenge him on, I would never have been afraid to. Maybe others didn't feel that comfortable. I mean there were aspects to Eddie that made him difficult to approach, sure.

'And I wouldn't have been going around asking people on a continual basis if they were "OK". If I saw or heard of a problem, I'd try to confront it. But, other than that, I wasn't there to babysit people.

'The only thing the coach owes you if he doesn't pick you is an answer to your question. He doesn't owe you anything beyond that. And you certainly can't go bad-mouthing someone if you never even ask the question.

'I was a little shocked when he made me captain, because I'd never really captained any team before. There were other guys who had far more experience than me. But I enjoyed it. I found Eddie good to deal with, good company.

'I know that, when the camera panned to him, he always seemed to have this very serious front to him. But that was just business. You can't blame a guy for having his poker face on when the camera is in his face.

'The World Cup was a nightmare for us all, but the suggestion that we were overtrained was nonsense. It's simple for me. We focused too much on getting bigger and more powerful and didn't get our focus on rugby early enough.

'I remember playing Scotland in the warm-up and they just seemed sharper from a rugby point of view. They had started training with the ball three weeks earlier than us. So we just got that very wrong. But then the rumours kicked out of control.'

PATRICK 'RALA' O'REILLY: 'Eddie sort of reinvented me. He got me out of a rut that I didn't even know I was in. I mean I know I was at the bottom of the food chain, but I was probably on cruise control and he challenged me to get out of it. I've worked under eight Irish coaches now and he probably had the biggest impact on me.

'He was very different to the guy the public seemed to see. I mean he didn't beat around the bush. If Eddie said you were to be somewhere at 6 p.m, he didn't mean five past. I liked that. But he had a sense of humour too.

'I remember in Bordeaux during the 2007 World Cup, I made the mistake of stepping into this big laundry cage in the hotel. Frankie Sheahan and a few others spotted me, sneaked up behind and locked me in the cage. Then they wheeled me down the corridor, knocking on all the doors along the way, shouting, "Rala's in the cage lads!"

'They brought me down to the team room, put the cage on its side and started pushing bananas in through the bars. They strapped a bottle of Powerade to the side, like you would a guinea-pig's water bottle. And I'm lying there in my bare feet, the cage bound up in bandages and insulating tape, pleading with them to let me out.

There was a team meeting due, so they put the cage behind a big curtain and left me there, sweating. I could hear everyone coming in, some of the players giggling. Next thing, Eddie comes in, the door shuts and – just as he begins to speak – the curtain slowly opens.

'Eddie turns around. And there I am, lying on my side in the cage, barefooted and surrounded by bananas. I can still see the look on his face.

"Eddie, I can explain . . ." I began.

'And the whole room, including Eddie, dissolved into laughter.'

COACHING RECORD

		Oppos.	Result	Venue	Score
6 Nat.	1	Wales	W	H	54–10
(2002)	2	England	L	A	11–45
	3	Scotland	W	H	43–22
	4	Italy	W	H	32–17
	5	France	L	A	5–44
Tour	6	N.Z.	L	A	6–15
(2002)	7	N.Z.	L	A	8–40
Friendly	8	Rom.	W	H	39–8
RWC Q.	9	Russia	W	A	35–3
	10	Georgia	W	H	63–14
Autumn	11	Aust.	W	H	19–9
(2002)	12	Fiji	W	H	64–17
	13	Arg.	W	H	16–7
6 Nat.	14	Scotland	W	A	36–6
(2003)	15	Italy	W	A	37–13
	16	France	W	H	15–12
	17	Wales	W	A	25–24

		Oppos.	Result	Venue	Score
	18	England	L	H	6–42
Tour	19	Aust.	L	A	16–45
2003	20	Tonga	W	A	40–19
	21	Samoa	W	A	40–14
Pre-WC	22	Wales	W	H	35–12
	23	Italy	W	H	61–6
	24	Scotland	W	A	29–10
RWC	25	Rom.	W	A	45–17
2003	26	Namibia	W	A	64–7
	27	Arg.	W	A	16–15
	28	Aust.	L	A	16–17
	29	France	L	A	21–43
6 Nat.	30	France	L	A	17–35
2004	31	Wales	W	H	36–15
	32	England	W	A	19–13
	33	Italy	W	H	19–3
	34	Scotland	W	H	37–16
Tour	35	S. Af.	L	A	17–31
2004	36	S. Af.	L	A	17–26
Autumn	37	S. Af.	W	H	17–12
2004	38	USA	W	H	55–6
	39	Arg.	W	H	21–19
6 Nat.	40	Italy	W	A	28–17
2005	41	Scotland	W	A	40–13
	42	England	W	H	19–13

		Oppos.	Result	Venue	Score
	43	France	L	H	19–26
	44	Wales	L	A	20–32
Tour	45	★Japan	W	A	44–12
2005	46	★Japan	W	A	47–18
Autumn	47	N.Z.	L	H	7–45
2005	48	Aust.	L	H	14–30
	49	Rom.	W	H	43–12
6 Nat.	50	Italy	W	H	26–16
2006	51	France	L	A	31–43
	52	Wales	W	H	31–5
	53	Scotland	W	H	15–9
	54	England	W	A	28–24
Tour	55	N.Z.	L	A	23–34
2006	56	N.Z.	L	A	17–27
	57	Aust.	L	A	15–37
Autumn	58	S. Af.	W	H	32–15
2006	59	Aust.	W	H	21–6
	60	Pac. Is.	W	H	61–17
6 Nat.	61	Wales	W	A	19–9
2007	62	France	L	H	17–20
	63	England	W	H	43–13
	64	Scotland	W	A	19–18
	65	Italy	W	A	51–24
Tour	66	Arg.	L	A	20–22
2007	67	Arg.	L	A	0–16

Eddie O'Sullivan

		Oppos.	Result	Venue	Score
Pre WC	68	Scotland	L	A	21–31
	69	Italy	W	H	23–20
RWC	70	Namibia	W	A	32–17
2007	71	Georgia	W	A	14–10
	72	France	L	A	3–25
	73	Arg.	L	A	15–30
6 Nat.	74	Italy	W	H	16–11
2008	75	France	L	A	21–26
	76	Scotland	W	H	34–13
	77	Wales	L	H	12–16
	78	England	L	A	10–33

★ =   Niall O'Donovan was coach

Total Game Record: Played – 78

Won: 50   Lost: 28   % Success: 64%

6 Nations Record: Played – 35

Won: 24   Lost: 11   % Success: 69%

Autumn Series Record: Played – 12

Won: 10   Lost: 2   % Success: 83%

Home Record: Played – 35

Won: 29   Lost: 6   % Success: 83%

Away Record: Played – 43

Won: 21   Lost: 23   % Success: 48%